U.S. History

Volume 2
1865-Present

Other Titles in This Series

Economics: A Resource Book for Secondary Schools, James E. Davis and Regina McCormick

Geography: A Resource Book for Secondary Schools, A. David Hill and Regina McCormick

U.S. Government: A Resource Book for Secondary Schools, Mary Jane Turner and Sara Lake

U.S. History, Volume 1—1450–1865: A Resource Book for Secondary Schools, James R. Giese and Laurel R. Singleton

Global/International Issues and Problems: A Resource Book for Secondary Schools, Lynn S. Parisi and Robert D. LaRue, Jr.

U.S. History

**Volume 2
1865-Present**

A Resource Book for Secondary Schools

James R. Giese and
Laurel R. Singleton

Social Studies Resources for
Secondary School Librarians, Teachers, and Students
James E. Davis, Series Editor

ABC-CLIO

Santa Barbara, California
Oxford, England

Library of Congress Cataloging-in-Publication Data

Giese, James R.
   U.S. history : a resource book for secondary schools.

   (Secondary school librarians, teachers, and students)
   Includes indexes.
   Bibliography: v. 1, p.   ; v. 2, p.
   Contents: v. 1, 1450–1865—v. 2, 1865 to present.
   1. United States—History—Study and teaching

(Secondary)   I. Singleton, Laurel R., 1950-   .
II. Title.
E175.8.G54   1989   973'.071'273   88-38952

ISBN 0-87436-505-8 (v. 1)
ISBN 0-87436-506-6 (v. 2)

96 95 94 93 92 91 90 89   10 9 8 7 6 5 4 3 2 1

ABC-CLIO, Inc.
130 Cremona Drive, P.O. Box 1911
Santa Barbara, California 93116-1911

Clio Press Ltd.
55 St. Thomas' Street
Oxford, OX1 1JG, England

This book is Smyth-sewn and printed on acid-free paper ∞.
Manufactured in the United States of America

Contents

7. *Classroom Materials,* 197

How To Use
This Reference Work

This resource book has been written for the secondary school librarian, social studies teacher, and student. The narrative information is presented in a nontechnical manner and is intended to provide introductory information helpful to the study of U.S. history from the end of the Civil War to the present. The resources cited, although not exhaustive, encompass many useful current materials available for teaching and researching history at the secondary school level. The annotated bibliographic information regarding reference and classroom materials can assist teachers in selecting course content and can be used by students to gather information for class assignments or special projects. In addition, this work can serve as a supplementary text in the classroom.

The following are descriptions of how each section of this work might be used:

Chapter 1, "Introduction to the Study of History," provides an overview of the subject for secondary school social studies teachers and students. It highlights the value of thinking historically, examines how historians approach the past, and summarizes some of the recent changes in historians' views of U.S. history. For the student who has not been exposed to history as a disciplined way of thinking, this chapter is a good introduction to the subject matter.

Chapter 2 presents "Chronology of U.S. History After 1865." This chapter includes not only some of the significant events in U.S. history that are often highlighted in traditional history courses, it also presents important developments in art, music, literature, science, technology, and sports—events not often covered in traditional textbooks. Students and teachers of U.S. history will find the chronology a useful reference. The events highlighted are selective. The user is therefore invited and encouraged to examine other events and add them to this chronology. Of course, the mere chronicling of events in this fashion is not enough; the reader should further investigate the events.

Chapter 3, "Historians of the United States," is arranged in alphabetical order by the last name of each historian. Thus, the reader needs to keep in mind the time period in which each historian lived. Each biography provides an introduction to the historian as a person, followed by a discussion of the area of his or her intellectual interest and an assessment of the impact each historian had on history as a discipline. The biographies provide the reader some insight into how the discipline of history has changed during the twentieth century.

Chapter 4, "Historical Data," presents thirteen different types of primary sources that have been extensively used by historians. In this chapter, we have avoided the "great documents approach" on the assumption that the Declaration of Independence, the U.S. Constitution, and similar great documents are included in textbooks or are readily available elsewhere. Furthermore, we believe that students usually do not grapple with primary sources—an essential ingredient in understanding the nature of history. The introduction to each source provides an understanding of how to use and interpret that kind of source. The user is encouraged to go beyond the introduction for a more sophisticated understanding of each document.

Many organizations and groups provide information, resources, and services in history education. Chapter 5, "Directory of Organizations, Associations, and Government Agencies," describes such organizations. These organizations are categorized into three groups: those with general interests in U.S. history (i.e., covering the entire span of U.S. history), state associations, and organizations or agencies with an interest in U.S. history in the time period since 1865. Students and teachers can use the directory to find the following information for each group: address, telephone number, name of president or director, and descriptions of the organization's activities and publications.

Chapter 6, "Reference Works," is an annotated bibliography of reference materials that can be used by students and teachers as they conduct historical research and participate in class and library projects. Complete bibliographic information and costs are provided for each entry. The reference materials are categorized according to type; they include:

Atlases. Atlases can be excellent sources of historical information. Some of the atlases cited include modern maps showing information about the past; others present maps drawn in earlier periods of history. Both students and teachers will find the atlases cited very helpful.

Bibliographies and Printed Indexes. Teachers and students looking for information on various topics for research projects or lectures will find a starting point for their research in these bibliographies and indexes.

Only a few printed indexes are listed. Teachers and librarians should note that students may need assistance in learning to use these indexes.

Biographical Dictionaries. Dictionaries listed in this section contain biographical information about historians and prominent Americans throughout history. Students and teachers can use these sources to locate information about individuals they are researching.

Dictionaries. Only those dictionaries dealing specifically with history or the study of history are listed in this section. Excluded are popular general dictionaries to which students can refer for definitions of many historical terms.

Encyclopedias, Almanacs, and Chronologies. This section lists a potpourri of general reference materials on U.S. history. All of these reference materials are suitable for gathering basic information as students begin library research projects. None are likely to provide adequate material to complete such a project.

Handbooks for Conducting Historical Research. The items listed in this section provide guidance on how to go about conducting historical research. As such, they contain extensive bibliographic listings—much more extensive than we could include in this book—and are excellent starting places for research projects. These handbooks also discuss how the results of historical research can be presented.

Online Databases. In this section, we describe online databases that provide information about U.S. history. The databases cited are available through one or both of the following services:

BRS Information Technologies
1200 Route 7
Latham, NY 12110
(800) 468-0908

Dialog Information Services, Inc.
3460 Hillview Avenue
Palo Alto, CA 94304
(800) 3-DIALOG

For each database, we include computer connect hour costs (this does not include telecommunication costs, usually around $9.00 per connect hour using UNINET, TELENET, or TYMNET) and citation costs. Citation costs given are for the full record. Citation costs for BRS, which has various pricing options, are for maximum citation charges.

Periodicals. The listing of periodicals is a very selective one. Cited are outstanding historical periodicals that might be of interest to students doing fairly sophisticated research projects (e.g., projects for the National History Day competition) or teachers pursuing an advanced degree, as well as periodicals specifically addressing history education. Additional information regarding journals and newsletters can be found in the "Publications" section of listings in Chapter 5.

Resources on Teaching History. Included in this section are materials that provide teaching models, background readings, curriculum plans, rationales, or analyses of history education.

Chapter 7 contains annotated listings of classroom materials. Again, complete bibliographic information, plus grade levels, prices, and a brief description, are provided for every item. Entries are organized according to the type of material. Sections include:

Computer Software. In this section are microcomputer software packages in history. The types of software programs are indicated in the heading for each entry. These include drill and practice, tutorials (lessons conducted in the form of a dialogue), games, simulations, and databases. The systems on which the software programs can be used are also indicated in the heading.

Filmstrips, Slide Programs, and Media Kits. This section lists an array of audiovisual materials from which teachers can select appropriate supplements. Programs on various events in the early period of U.S. history are included.

Games, Simulations, and Dramatizations. Another excellent way to supplement a history course is through the use of games and simulations. A great variety, including role plays, simulations, card games, and board games, are described in this section.

Posters, Study Prints, and Other Visual Aids. Described in this section are posters, study prints of various kinds (including historical photographs), wall maps, transparencies, and other visuals. Teachers and librarians can use these materials for instructional purposes or to motivate student interest in historical topics.

Supplementary Print Materials. This section contains a range of materials on various topics and groups in U.S. history, arranged alphabetically by author. Many of the products included here are priced so modestly that they are within the budget of virtually every school. This section is a must for teachers.

Textbooks. Teachers looking for new basal U.S. history texts will find this section helpful. Both texts covering only the later period of U.S. history and survey texts covering the entire span of our nation's development are included. They are arranged alphabetically by author.

Videocassettes and Films. Teachers looking for videocassettes and 16mm films to supplement history units will find this section of interest. These two media are excellent ways to enliven a classroom and stimulate discussion. Video formats are indicated, as are both rental and purchase prices.

Note: Given the volatility of our economy, prices rarely remain the same for more than a year. Thus, despite efforts to have price information as current as possible, one may find in speaking with the publisher of a particular item that the price is not exactly as listed here. Despite the fact that prices will be dated quickly, we have included this information to give teachers and librarians a general, comparative notion of the costs of various resources.

The Glossary provides definitions for terms selected to cover important ideas and events in U.S. history since 1865, as well as terms related to the study of history and historical research.

An index has been provided to further enhance the reader's use of this work. Teachers and students can consult the index for specific subjects or items of particular interest, as well as refer to it as a source of potential research topics or project ideas. By using the index in conjunction with the Contents, readers will have easy access to the information in this volume that is most pertinent to their needs.

Introduction to
the Study of History

THE PROBLEM WITH HISTORY

If you were born in the United States and attended schools here, you have studied history at several grade levels. If your experience was typical, likely you took at least three courses in United States history and probably an additional course or two in world history and world geography. In these courses, you were probably buffeted by hundreds of "objective" historical facts—about colonial America, the Revolutionary War, the Founding Fathers and the writing of the Constitution, the frontier, the industrial revolution, the Progressive movement, the New Deal, and World Wars I and II. Again, if your experience was typical, these facts and thousands like them probably had little significance to you; it is likely you forgot them at least as fast as you memorized them for the test.

According to recent survey data, high school students see the typical history classroom as "one in which they listen to the teacher explain the day's lesson, use the textbook, and take tests. Occasionally they watch a movie. Sometimes they memorize information or read stories about events and people. They seldom work with other students, use original documents, write term papers, or discuss the significance of what they are studying" (Ravitch and Finn, 1987, p. 194). If this description is true (or even partly so), it may explain why high school students dislike their history courses to the extent they do. Students rate their history courses lower than virtually any other course. They do not see the relevance of history, they say those classes are boring, and consequently, they do not enjoy this formal study of history. You may share this attitude, or you may be among the fortunate few who have had teachers who make history come alive for their students.

If you are one of these critics of history, you are certainly not alone. Many people besides students have questioned the value of history. Industrialist Henry Ford said, for example, that "history is more or less bunk." Others have said that history is "a pack of lies agreed upon," and that history is "simply one darned thing after another." Andrew Jackson, seventh president of the United States, saw no connection between history and the present; he said, "the past we cannot recall . . . but the future we can provide for" (in Commager, 1942, p. 260).

It is one thing to see history as irrelevant, but quite another to view it as horribly misleading. "Be it remembered," wrote novelist John Barth (1964, p. 793), "that we all invent our pasts, more or less, as we go along, at the dictates of Whim and Interest." "History is the most dangerous product which the chemistry of the mind has concocted. . . . It produces dreams and drunkenness," Paul Valery (in Fischer, 1970, pp. 307–308) accused, "it fills people with false memories, exaggerates their reactions, exacerbates old grievances, torments them in their repose" (among other evils). Such commentaries on the dangers and inadequacies of history are legion. So if history is really dead or even misleading, why are we writing this book?

EVERYONE HIS OR HER OWN HISTORIAN

It is our belief that the study of history is a characteristically human and humane enterprise for all people, regardless of who they are, what their occupations are, or what their special interests may be. We agree with Carl Becker (1935), who argued that "everyman [is] his own historian," although we would update the language and say that "every person is his or her own historian." This phrase means simply that every person engages in some form of historical inquiry some of the time.

Some of the common forms of historical inquiry consist of specific investigations into small events. They take hundreds, even thousands, of humble forms:

> a renter tries to remember if she paid the rent
>
> a student wants to know if a teacher is "easy" or "tough"
>
> a doctor develops a patient's case history
>
> a jury weighs a fact in dispute in a trial
>
> a dress designer studies market trends
>
> a coach analyzes a team's tendencies
>
> a judge seeks a legal precedent
>
> a businessman wants to know whether to increase his inventory
>
> a homeowner seeks to build an addition onto her house

a child wants to know when his grandfather came to the United
States

a voter compares a political candidate's speeches with her
voting record in Congress

a citizen wants to clarify his views about United States
intervention in Central American affairs

Each of these inquiries is in some respects historical. Some are little
more than exercises of personal memory. Others are attempts to discover a story in collective memory. Yet others seek a more organized
sequence of events; several pursue some explanation of a series of
"facts." Each of the items on the list calls for some exercise of memory,
whether individual, collective, or systematic collective memory. As one
moves down the list, the inquiries call for increasingly sophisticated
procedures and the manipulation of larger bodies of information.

Most of these operations do not involve inquiry on the scale
conducted by professional historians. Few are concerned with the kinds
of issues with which professional historians are commonly engaged.
The history of World War II, the Spanish-American War, the industrial
revolution in the United States, New Deal programs, or the feminist
movement, for example, have little apparent relevance to the more or
less historical questions in the list above. On the other hand, if the
individuals seeking answers to the questions on the list are to achieve the
best possible answers, their method of inquiry, of explanation, and of
argument, should be much like that of working professional historians.

The point of all this is that seeking answers to historical questions
seems to be a characteristic of human beings, at least some of the time.
And if everyone is already involved in historical inquiry (to a greater or
lesser degree) and uses the product, history, then it follows that they
should become better practitioners of that craft. Untrained and left to
one's own devices, the individual may produce rather poor history. If
such history had no effect on anyone, one could ignore the problem and
chalk it all up to "human frailty." History has great influence in our daily
affairs, just as the past does. Now you may ask what this last sentence
means; aren't history and the past the same thing?

THE PAST, THE HISTORICAL RECORD,
AND HISTORY

It is conventional to distinguish among the concepts of "the past," "the
historical record," and "history." For our purposes, the past is everything

that has occurred at all places at all times up to the present moment. This conception makes the past rather imposing. Historians consequently limit their study of the past by inquiring into those things in which human beings were in some way involved. So conceived, geological formations have a past, as do many organisms (found in the fossil record). But these pasts (and areas of inquiry) have little relevance for the historian unless human beings are a part of the story. Historians leave nonhuman pasts to geologists and vertebrate paleontologists, among other scientists.

If the past that interests historians deals with all human activity in all places at all times up to the present (the meeting of past and future), then what is "the historical record"? Simply put, the historical record is the evidence of human activity in the past. The record is therefore composed of the traces of actual human activity—the evidence, artifacts, books, papers, other documents, sometimes oral accounts, etc., that occurred as a result of humans' actions at some point (or points) in the past. The evidence contained in the historical record is, on the one hand, intimidating in its volume. Archives containing huge collections of documents, museums full of artifacts, libraries housing millions of books, papers, and other evidence can be found all over the world. Indeed, the number of accumulated facts about the human past is staggering. On the other hand, the historical record is never complete. Although the historical record is essential, it is not sufficient for producing history.

History, then, is the reconstruction of the past, as best it can be done, based on the historical record—the evidence of past activities that is left to us. We have asserted that the past can never be reconstructed in its entirety and that the historical record is never complete. Working in the context of these constraints, historians attempt to produce the best possible representation of the past, based on the available evidence. History is, however, not just a chronological arrangement of the record. History can be produced only when a person brings some questions and some reasonable order to the record of the past.

An example may serve to clarify these distinctions. While poking around in your storage closet at home, say, you discover a trunk full of family memorabilia, including photographs, letters, newspaper clippings, and assorted artifacts. You find literally hundreds of items, including your report cards from elementary school, papers you wrote, letters from your grandmothers and grandfathers and aunts and uncles, newspaper snippets concerning your sister's volleyball team, your Little League team, your parents' marriage announcement, and much more.

At first glance it looks as though you have uncovered your family's entire past. But a moment's reflection will tell you that what you have discovered is only a portion of your family's historical record—some of the evidence of your family's past.

Think, for example, about any memorable occasion in your life. Say you find a photograph taken at your ninth birthday party. It shows your brother and sister, mother and father, Aunt Tilly, and six friends eating birthday cake and ice cream. The photo does not show Uncle Fred—he was taking the picture. As you look more closely at the photo, you see some of the presents you received on the table. You got several of the things that you really wanted. Aunt Tilly (because you were her favorite) gave you a new watch. Your brother gave you a basketball and your sister gave you four back issues of a comic book series you still collect. Your parents gave you a nifty AM/FM radio-cassette player as well as several pairs of jeans and three shirts (items not high on your wish list). But you just can't recall what your friends gave you, and no other gifts can be seen in the photo.

You dig deeper in the trunk of stuff and discover that twelve birthday cards have also been preserved. Three of the cards contain one-page letters; short notes were written in the others. Several of the cards indicate that some of your relatives sent you money instead of other gifts. One showed that Uncle Gary sent you two dollars—"just like him; he's always pinched a dime," or so your father always said. You also remember the generosity of your mother's cousin Lucille, who always sends birthday presents to everyone in your family.

Because the event was memorable—basically because it was the first "real" birthday party your parents let you have—you have some fairly solid evidence about that occasion even if much of it derives from your own memory of it. (But you also know that your memory has failed you in that you can't remember what presents your friends gave you.) In addition, you shared this experience with others who may also vividly recall the occasion. On the other hand, because it was your birthday, not theirs, they may not remember it well, or at all! You recall that every now and then, you and your family chuckle about your friend Jimmy getting sick after eating five pieces of cake and what seemed like a gallon of ice cream. Jimmy was always doing stuff like that. You recall in passing that Jimmy moved away when you were eleven. You wonder where he is now.

Even though the trunk provides some very good evidence about your ninth birthday party and your memory brings back many warm and enjoyable thoughts about this occasion, a moment of reflection tells you that the whole experience—even as you experienced it and remembered it—cannot be recaptured or reconstructed entirely. You were nine years old only once (even if for a whole year). What's more, you can truly experience that specific day only one time—the combination of people, weather, atmosphere, mood, and all the other things (and their specific interaction at that time) that may have influenced that occasion can never be completely recaptured.

All of this is simply to say that while there is often a pile of evidence, and sometimes vivid memories, about any given historical event, the past can never be relived and its evidence is never complete. What is true with respect to this hypothetical example is equally (and maybe more) true of all historical inquiries.

Think about the difficulty someone who was not at your birthday party might have in reconstructing this episode in your life. Because this person would have no memory of the events of that day, the primary evidence would be your artifact trunk. But without the contents of your memory, or the memories of others who were there that day, this evidence is pretty slim pickings. Many of the things you recalled to put flesh on the evidence in the trunk would have to be discovered or uncovered in some different way. For example, knowing that Uncle Fred took the photograph (which may or may not be important to the story of your ninth birthday party) or that you were Aunt Tilly's favorite nephew and that the watch she gave you was on your wrist as shown in the photograph would not necessarily be known by any persons other than those there that day. Now, our hypothetical investigator may be able to turn this information up. If anyone who was present at your birthday party is still alive, then they could be interviewed about that day. And the more information from these people, the better. If virtually everyone who was there is still alive and accessible, then all could be interviewed and their memories of that event could be cross-checked. In this manner, our hypothetical historian might be able to reconstruct the day of your ninth birthday party and perhaps do it more completely and objectively than you could do it yourself.

So far, you have sorted through the evidence at hand and have laid it all out, as best you can, in chronological order. Would you have thereby produced a history of this episode? No, not yet. You have pieced together some random memories and some stories about your past, and although both memory and stories are important for producing history, they are not by themselves sufficient. Why not? Don't genealogists and others who dig around in family history do this kind of thing?

Certainly, and this kind of activity can be both interesting and rewarding. But these folks aren't really doing history. What distinguishes

history from such encounters with the past as genealogy and antiquari-
anism is that history must be an *integrative* narrative, description, or
analysis of past events or facts *written in a spirit of critical inquiry for the
whole truth.*

Stringing together some, or even all, of the available evidence from
your family's past does not constitute history, although doing so may be
the beginning of producing such a history. The evidence you have
discovered in your attic must be processed by an inquiring mind, which
gives order and meaning to the data. In our example, piecing together
the shards of your family's past would serve little useful purpose because
it does not attempt to explain the meaning of the evidence. Historians
tell not only what happened, but how, when, and to what end.

History is a special mode of inquiry—it is the study of the past, and
study implies a method—a set of procedures, a way of searching for the
truth, no matter how tentative the truth may be when you have finished.
The historian (whether professional or "everyperson") must eschew
common beliefs and standard assumptions and must cultivate a healthy
attitude of uncertainty about the nature of accepted truth. Historians
must also cultivate disciplined thought about the past and the evidence
of that past. History may be seen as a mental construct of the past based
on evidence that has been carefully scrutinized, put to tests of validity,
and then systematically ordered and interpreted to present a story about
mankind's past.

Continuing with the example we used above may also shed some
light on this aspect of our problem. So far, you have rummaged around in
an old trunk of memorabilia and in your own memory of a historical
event. You have found some interesting things there. Most of the
documents you have found in the trunk seem to confirm your own
recollection about what occurred that day. But you have also discovered
several things that lack confirmation or corroboration.

Your brother Frank, as you recall, was being a jerk at your birthday
party. As you recall that day, several things had happened to Frank which
you thought caused his sour mood. He was having continuous spats with
his girlfriend (what was her name?—you can't recall). Your parents
complained to him about his grades. He was thinking about quitting the
basketball team. Frank's behavior at your party wasn't out of line, but it
was also clear he didn't want to be there. You wonder if his mood
affected your mother, father, or friends in some way. This part of the
occasion was noteworthy because Frank was generally a great brother
who was hardly ever moody or out of sorts.

You decide to talk with Frank and the rest of your family about that day. You discover his recollection was almost entirely different from yours. He barely remembered your ninth birthday party, and didn't recall being moody. He had already broken up with that girlfriend, and had just begun dating someone else. If he was out of sorts at all, it was probably because he couldn't stand your friend Jimmy—it certainly had nothing to do with any of the things you thought.

HOW HISTORIANS WORK

Just like everyone else, historians are fascinated by the complexity of the world around them. But perhaps more than most folks they seek to put their study and training to work in exploring what they take to be significant problems or questions about the past. Historians, just like other people, are quite different in their experiences, interests, and values. As a consequence, the number of questions that historians (and others) think are significant are almost infinite. However, not all questions have equal significance (or potential significance). Historians must therefore choose wisely among the available questions. How do they choose?

First, there are some questions that cannot be resolved empirically. "Is there a God?" "What is the nature of the universe?" "Why does evil lurk in the world?" These are examples of metaphysical questions—questions that cannot be resolved by historical (or other empirical) inquiry. Questions of this type are better attended to by philosophers and theologians.

Second, some questions can be resolved by historical inquiry, but one must ask "so what?" The history of your ninth birthday party in our example above would be one of those. The first person to wear a shirt with a button-down collar might be another such example. The lack of utility of these types of questions should be obvious. The problem for historians is usually not in choosing among trivial questions, but choosing wisely among the important questions that can be answered through empirical research.

In the real professional world of historians, a variety of influences help determine the questions on which they will focus their attention for several years. A historian's choice is influenced—perhaps only semi-consciously—by such things as the time in which he or she is living, background and training, funding sources, personal values, or what is most likely to be published by the best journal or the best academic press.

When the historian has chosen a question to research, another set of questions immediately appears. First, the historian must ask what evidence is essential for resolving his/her research question. Does such evidence exist? If it exists, where can it be found? Is it accessible? Are the sources in a language that can be read by the historian? Are they deposited in a country that allows access to them? Are they in a library (or other archive) that has cataloged the sources? These and other questions must be resolved before the historian sets out on the research.

Once these questions have been resolved, yet another set of questions arises. Is the evidence authentic, genuine? Does it relate to the subject as the historian defined the topic? Is the evidence reliable (who produced the evidence, and in what manner)? How accurate does the evidence seem to be; how does it check out against other sources of known reliability? What biases do the records contain? Do these sources conflict with others? How are the conflicts resolved? Finally, is this body of evidence the most relevant for the question at hand?

Determining the reliability of evidence is a very difficult problem. For a variety of reasons, evidence may be inaccurate, biased, or even fraudulent. As E. H. Carr put it in his book *What Is History?* "no document can tell us more than what the author of the document thought—what he thought had happened, what he thought ought to happen, or perhaps only what he wanted others to think he thought, or even only what he himself thought he thought" (1961, p. 16). Eyewitness accounts, although they may be very close to the event, are notoriously unreliable. Conflicting courtroom testimony about traffic accidents and other mishaps attests to the fact that although persons may have no intention of misinforming, their accounts are often inaccurate.

Historians tend to seek the best evidence available about a specific question and usually assume the doctrine of immediacy (i.e., the closer in time and place to the event, the better the evidence). Often, however, the historical actors closest to the event are the most embroiled in its net—and therefore their testimony can be the least accurate. This principle is really quite commonsensical: The closer you are to an event, the more you are involved in it, the less likely you will be an objective, impartial observer of the event. Consequently, historians can never rely on a single participant to tell "the truth, the whole truth, and nothing but the truth." What they must do in such cases is to collect all the evidence possible—all the available accounts produced by all the witnesses—and very carefully compare the accounts.

Yet the weight of evidence is not necessarily the best guide to "truth." There are certainly situations in which ten observers witnessed an event and nine of them were less accurate than the one. The historian is able to sort this out only after intimate familiarity with all the available sources and a good deal of critical thinking about what is read or otherwise assimilated.

As we all should know, even official statements about events can often be misleading. Sometimes such statements are made in the interests of pure propaganda. At times official statements are made to conceal more than they reveal. Occasionally government, interest groups, and individuals make "official" statements they wish other people to believe; sometimes they hope people will act on such "information." The sad truth is that often their intent becomes actuality.

Sometimes misleading statements are made by the government or other groups inadvertently. For example, occasionally the federal government is required to publish statistical information about the economy (for example, unemployment statistics or figures concerning general economic activity) before the best available information can be collected. Occasionally, reports sponsored by foundations or other non-government groups become public in draft form, before all the results are verified. Such information can be quite misleading.

Bias in sources is yet another matter that vitiates their "pureness." In general, people's attitudes toward the world influence the way they perceive and report their experiences. Certainly young people and their parents do not see eye to eye on all things. While the parents may have grown up listening to the Supremes, the Rolling Stones, or the Shirelles, their children's tastes may run more toward Los Lobos, Dokken, Ziggy Marley, or Lisa Lisa. And obviously, there are many other parents whose tastes run more toward Marvin Gaye, Julio Iglesias, and Carly Simon. Indeed, some folks greatly appreciate Beethoven, Leonard Bernstein, and Leontyne Price. There is no accounting for such tastes—in music, or in other areas of interest as well. The point is that people differ as to their values, their attitudes, and their tastes, and these differences influence the way they interpret and report the world they experience.

Once the evidence is amassed, the historian is ready to organize it into some meaningful whole. This is certainly not to say that the sources speak for themselves. Quite the contrary. The ultimate task of the historian is to organize the collected material toward a particular end or conclusion. After all, the historian became engaged with this material to answer a specific and meaningful question. Little wonder, then, that the historian adduces an answer to the question. If the question is meaningful and the evidence accumulated in legitimate ways, the answer to the question must be meaningful and important.

Once the historian is satisfied that the evidence supports some conclusion, he/she is obliged to report the evidence and how the evidence points to the conclusion. Quite often, however, the evidence found through exhaustive research will point to hypotheses (and possible conclusions) different from those with which the historian began. In addition, the historian is responsible for reporting all contrary data—those items that do not support his/her conclusion—as well as all the evidence that does support it. In doing so, the historian must persuasively demonstrate that the evidence supporting his/her conclusion is stronger than the contrary information.

All of the foregoing may indicate that the work of historians is somewhat more interesting than you had previously thought; that their work consists of more problem solving and question answering than you might have imagined (did you think they simply memorized a bunch of facts and then played "twenty questions" with everyone else?). In actuality, history is not even close to a bunch of facts that everyone must memorize. Not only is history about change through time, but history and the manner in which its practitioners pursue their tasks also change through time. In short, historians do not typically ask the same questions from one generation to the next. What is important for one generation of humans is not necessarily of equal importance for subsequent generations. Public issues change. The conventional wisdom changes. The collective body of knowledge changes. As a consequence, one generation's questions of the present and of the past are not the same as those of preceding or subsequent generations.

This situation has led some commentators to believe that history is totally subjective or relative, and therefore meaningless. If history can be written by every generation in its own way, these people argue, then it is not (and cannot be) objectively true. If history cannot be objectively true, then what's the point? Although a case may be made for that position, we think it is essentially a false concern, a distraction. There are historical facts that are true for all time, as, for example, the fact that George Washington was the first president of the United States. There are millions of such facts of history. However, when the historian gets to the most important question of "so what?" the meaning of that fact and all others tends to be different from time to time, generation to generation, historian to historian.

This situation should not concern us greatly. Even in the "hard sciences"—physics, chemistry, and biology, for example—the facts of research deemed to be important depend to a very great extent on the questions the researcher brings to the experiment. Indeed, one of the most profound findings of quantum physics in the twentieth century is the "uncertainty principle" (so called by German physicist Werner Heisenberg), which essentially means that if you ask certain questions you are likely to get certain (predictable) answers.

In *What Is History?* E. H. Carr (1961) deals with this issue as it relates to history. The commonsense view, Carr argues, holds that "history consists of a corpus of ascertained facts. The facts are available to the historian in documents, inscriptions, and so on, like fish on a fishmonger's slab. The historian collects them, takes them home, and cooks and serves them in whatever style appeals to him." Such a conceptualization, he argues, "presupposes a complete separation between subject and object. Facts, like sense impressions, impinge on the observer from outside. . . . The process of reception is passive: having received data, he then acts on them" (p. 6).

Carr, however, does not subscribe to this view. The facts are not at all like fish on a fishmonger's slab. "They [the facts of history] are like fish swimming about in a vast and sometimes inaccessible ocean; and what the historian catches will depend partly on chance, but mainly on what part of the ocean he chooses to fish in and what tackle he chooses to use . . . depending on the kind of fish he wants to catch" (p. 26). To write history is in some sense to create it. "The facts of history never come to us 'pure,' since they do not and cannot exist in a pure form: they are always refracted through the mind of the recorder" (p. 24).

HISTORIOGRAPHY: THE HISTORY OF HISTORY IN THE UNITED STATES

Students often have difficulty understanding that history is not only about change through time, but that history—as produced by historians through what they write—is also ever-changing. First, students are most often exposed to history as a body of agreed-upon facts that have to be mastered, if not for "cultural literacy" and "good citizenship," then for good grades on the weekly tests in their history classes. Second, students are not often exposed to historiography, which we may define as the history of history. When students study historiography, however, they can see at a glance that history has changed markedly since it first became a self-conscious, professional discipline in the nineteenth century. Indeed, history is vastly different today than it was even twenty years ago.

"History," writes Michael Kammen (1980, p. 19), "has been written in what is now the United States ever since the early seventeenth century, when Captain John Smith and Governor William Bradford first began to record the circumstances of exploration and colonization in North America." When the American Historical Association was founded in 1884, however, history came of age as a professional discipline. Since that time, following the general growth of higher education in the United States, the historical profession has expanded greatly. Not only has the profession grown in the sense of numbers of practitioners, but the discipline itself has changed from time to time. Although the changes have not been systematic or even predictable, the characteristic style of historians—in terms of both substance and methods—has changed periodically through the twentieth century.

When history as a discipline came of age in the late nineteenth century, historians emphasized what they called "scientific history." By that they meant the accumulation and cataloging of the sources or the facts from which history was derived. However, changes were soon in the wind, and this school of historians soon gave way to a new "progressive" generation which emphasized looking at history in new ways.

The progressives were concerned about making history relevant, creating an instrumental knowledge that could serve mankind's need for useful, practical knowledge. It was not enough for such historians as James Harvey Robinson and Charles Beard to collect facts as though for a museum. They wanted to know about the processes that pushed "history" forward. Accordingly, the progressives emphasized conflict in the American past. They saw "good guys" and "bad guys" lined up on either side of the major issues that comprised American history. Writing during a time of great social and political ferment, they saw conflict between social and political groups as the primary dynamic in American history. Conflict, for them, was not a problem, for they were certain that the "good guys" would win in the end.

The progressive view of the past in turn gave way to yet another school of historical thought—what historians call the "consensus" approach to American history. The optimism of the progressives and their characteristic reform-mindedness soured during the 1930s and 1940s. The rise of totalitarian dictatorships, the barbarity of World War II, and a seemingly intractable "cold war" between the United States and the Soviet Union pricked the bubble of optimism that was so much a part of the progressives' mindset. Also seeking a usable past, the consensus historians looked to the past not for the history of conflict but for the things upon which, they argued, Americans had by and large agreed throughout the nation's history. Americans, they argued, had reached a consensus on certain fundamentals—free-enterprise capitalism, liberal democracy, and equal opportunity, among others—that set them apart from the rest of the world. In an environment torn by war, racism, death camps, and the like, the American consensus could continue to guide the nation in times of peril.

During the past two decades, the consensus school of historians has been succeeded by yet another period of ferment. At no time since the beginning of the twentieth century has the change of historical style and approach been more apparent than in the 1970s. This shift encompassed many things, some of which are described next.

The "New Social History"

Social history has involved the reorientation of historians from the public sector and politics to social structure, social mobility, and such social institutions as hospitals, asylums, prisons, and churches. In addition, historians have rediscovered the history of women, children, families, blacks and other minority groups, ethnic groups, and the laboring and "dangerous" classes. "The out-pouring of new work in the history of women and of the family," Carl Degler (1980, p. 308) has said about two topics of social history, "has been the most recent example of the way in which the content of the remembered past is constantly being reshaped. . . . As new concerns arise in the present, we ask fresh questions of the past, thereby bringing novel subjects into the purview of the historian." The social concerns of the 1960s and 1970s produced a new set of relevant questions about the past.

"Social history," according to Peter Stearns (1983, pp. 4-5), "involves two broad subject areas that conventional history has largely ignored. First, it deals with ordinary people, rather than the elite . . . [and second] the history of ordinary activities, institutions, and modes of thought." The early slogan of these practitioners, "doing history from the bottom up," suggested that common folk had a vibrant past and contributed greatly to larger historical processes. The perception is that traditional historians had largely ignored such people in the past.

More Explicit Historical Methods

Related to the expansion in the number of topics with which historians now deal was the near revolution in historical methods. With respect to social history, "the people studied were relatively inarticulate, in that few of them spoke or wrote as a matter of public record, but social historians working imaginatively with new sources have found that few if any groups are really inarticulate" (Stearns, 1983, pp. 4–5). Stearns continues:

> Related to topical expansion is the explosion of source materials, as inarticulate people and private activities literally speak volumes. Census data, police records, wills, a surprising array of heretofore neglected worker autobiographies, diaries of unheralded middle-class women, and some limited re-entry into the evidence provided by material artifacts, these records as well as some re-use of more conventional sources have easily supported the range of socio-historical interests. (p. 11)

One consequence of trying to use new types of sources was the increasing use of computers to manipulate large quantities of data gleaned from such sources as the manuscript census pages, wills and other legal documents, town records, and business records, to name a few.

A second result has been that more traditional literary (written) sources are being handled much more self-consciously and circumspectly. "Although it might be exaggerating the case to speak of a methodological revolution in the 1970s," argues Michael Kammen (1980, p. 31), "a revolution in methodological *awareness* surely has occurred" (emphasis in original). Historians now feel an obligation to explain their frames of references, their choices of method, and their borrowings from other social science disciplines.

The Complexity of History

"If there is a single way of characterizing what happened in our historical writing since the 1950s, it must be," according to Richard Hofstadter (1968, p. 442), "the rediscovery of complexity in American history: an engaging and moving simplicity, accessible to the casual reader of history, has given way to a new awareness of the multiplicity of forces." "If those words seemed true more than a decade ago," writes Michael Kammen (1980, p. 20), "how much more compelling they are today!" "Social historians undeniably complicate our sense of what the past was," says Peter Stearns (1983, p. 6).

This complexity may be more the concern of historians than any other users of history. Despite the great accomplishments in women's and family history, Carl Degler (1980, p. 324) has said, "we must still admit that neither women's nor family history has made much headway in being integrated into general history, or, to put the matter more precisely if more mundanely, into college or high school history survey courses or general textbooks." The same thing may be said of other social history topics. Part of the problem is still the absence of apparent linkages among the materials of the social historian and those of other historians and general readers. Bernard Bailyn (1980, p. 38) may have put it best when he wrote:

> The amount of quantitative information available has become so great that *latent* events—events of which contemporaries were largely unaware and which became discernible only in quantitative terms (shifts in birth rate, changes in family size or structure)—have become centers of attention; and they have become important independent of any framework of interpretation that can bring them together with the course of *manifest* events—that is, events that were matters of conscious concern. [Emphasis in original.]

Linking these two types of historical "events" is the central concern of historians in the 1980s, "for the essence and drama of history," Bailyn (1980, p. 38) argues, "lie precisely in the relationship between latent conditions, which set the boundaries of human existence, and the manifest problems with which people consciously struggle" (see also Bailyn, 1982).

The People of History

History "from the bottom up" was motivated by a concern for the common folk of history. Ironically, social historians have tended to drop people out of their writing. "Compared to conventional historians," argues Peter Stearns (1983, p. 6), "social historians are uncomfortable with events. They deal instead with processes, with distinctive trends within the period they mark out. Single events like battles or individual cases of epidemic diseases rarely cause major or durable changes in the way ordinary people behave or in the ordinary activities of life." "An emphasis on events tends to put people into the foreground," observes Kammen (1980, p. 39), "whereas an emphasis on structures and series calls our attention to large socio-economic forces." As real people have fallen out of history, nonhistorians have fallen away from history as well.

A Reorientation of Historians' Values

Traditionally, historians in the United States have strongly held two values in their work: nationalism and detachment. According to Michael Kammen (1980, p. 22), "there has been a stunning inversion with respect to these two traditional values." Nationalism and chauvinism have given way to national self-criticism. The liberal tradition has been severely challenged. National self-congratulation in foreign affairs has been challenged by those who see U.S. foreign policy to be less motivated by altruism than cynical self-interest. National leaders have been shown to have warts as well as virtues. Social reformers have been shown to be motivated by fear of the masses as well as by humane concern about the insane, the infirm, and the diseased.

At the same time, historians have taken a different approach with respect to moral criticism of the society in which they live and have studied. "One thing that has been forced on university teachers by their students in recent years," wrote Henry F. May (1976, p. xvii), "is that they abandon the comforting pose of academic impartiality and declare their allegiances, even—contrary to all their training—admit their emotions." In his presidential address to the American Historical Association in 1976, Gordon Wright (1976, pp. 1-11) asserted that "our search for truth ought to be quite consciously suffused by a commitment to some deeply held humane values." It is in part due to such commitment that historians rediscovered the inarticulate masses who have peopled U.S. history.

THE VALUE OF HISTORY

In *Historians' Fallacies,* David Hackett Fischer (1970) summarized five of the common justifications for historical study professed by historians themselves. According to Fischer, at least some historians have justified history by saying

"It is such fun!"

"It is there."

"Every educated person needs to know certain facts."

"It is an outlet for the creative impulse."

"It promises future usefulness."

Fischer finds each of these justifications for doing history wanting.

First, he argues, to say that history is fun is "scarcely sufficient to satisfy a student who is struggling to master strange masses of facts and interpretations which are suddenly dumped on him in History I" (p. 309).

Second, if historical study can be justified only "because it is there" (to paraphrase Sir Edmund Hillary's reason for climbing Mount

Everest), then there is little reason for requiring masses of students to study history. If history can be justified only in this manner, then historical study, just like climbing high mountains, should be left to those strange few who are fulfilled by doing it.

Third, although there is good evidence to show that the more a person knows the better that person is able to read a newspaper or book or to decipher the arguments of a political candidate, "there are," according to Fischer (1970, p. 311), "*no* facts which *everyone* needs to know—not even facts of the first historiographical magnitude" (emphasis in original). There are simply too many facts—even professional historians don't know all the facts—and how do you decide which facts everyone needs to know? Furthermore, the danger of this rationale for history study is that such factual knowledge is often merely an empty emblem of learnedness.

Fourth, although history may be a creative outlet, there are many outlets to the creative urge of human beings, and such a rationale presents no unique reason for studying history instead of, for example, tombstone rubbing.

Finally, historians cannot, willy-nilly, proceed to investigate just any historical problem in the hopes that someday, someone else will come along and find something worth doing with the results of such study. If historical research is to be relevant, the historian must seek to ask and answer relevant questions from the very beginning.

We believe, with Fischer, that history is a valuable form of inquiry and knowledge, a fact sometimes unappreciated even by historians themselves. Over the years, there have been many definitions of history put forth by its practitioners, but June Goodfield (1980, p. 38) penned one as good as any:

> History is the study of the human past as a form of collective self-understanding of human beings and their world. It is the story of human activities, what men did, what they thought, what they suffered, what they aimed at, what they accepted, what they rejected or conceived or imagined. It tells us about their motives, their purpose, their ambitions, their ways of acting and their ways of creating.

Some people allegedly have argued that history is too important to be left to historians. Yet we would make a counterclaim: History is too important—too much is at stake—to leave history in the hands of ahistorical, present-minded investigators. As William A. Dunning wrote in 1913 (in Kammen, 1982, p. 19), "influence on the sequence of human affairs has been exercised, not by what really happened, but by what men erroneously believed to have happened."

Michael Kammen (1982, p. 19) said it best: "I am utterly persuaded by E. P. Thompson's argument that 'the discipline of history is, above all, the discipline of context; each fact can be given meaning only within an ensemble of other meanings.'" Furthermore, he continues, "to fulfill these imperatives with absolute respect for the particularity of people and the specific integrity of varied social institutions and modes of thought requires the patience of a plodding historian."

REFERENCES

Bailyn, Bernard. 1980. "The Peopling of British North America: Thoughts on a Central Theme in Early American History," quoted in Michael Kammen, ed., *The Past Before Us: Contemporary Historical Writing in the United States.* Ithaca, N.Y.: Cornell University Press.

_____ . 1982. "The Challenge of Modern Historiography," *American Historical Review,* 87, pp. 1–24.

Barth, John. 1964. *The Sot-Weed Factor.* New York: Grossett and Dunlap.

Becker, Carl. 1935. "Everyman His Own Historian," in Carl Becker, *Everyman His Own Historian.* New York, pp. 233–255.

Carr, E. H. 1961. *What Is History?* New York: Vintage.

Commager, Henry Steele, ed. 1942. *Documents of American History.* New York: F. S. Crofts.

Degler, Carl N. 1980. "Women and the Family," in Michael Kammen, ed., *The Past Before Us.* Ithaca, N.Y.: Cornell University Press, pp. 308–326.

Fischer, David Hackett. 1970. *Historians' Fallacies: Toward a Logic of Historical Thought.* New York: Harper.

Goodfield, June. 1980. "Humanity in Science: A Perspective and a Plea," quoted in Michael Kammen, ed., *The Past Before Us: Contemporary Historical Writing in the United States.* Ithaca, N.Y.: Cornell University Press.

Hofstadter, Richard. 1968. *The Progressive Historians: Turner, Beard, Parrington.* New York: Vintage.

Kammen, Michael. 1980. "The Historian's Vocation and the State of the Discipline in the United States," in Michael Kammen, ed., *The Past Before Us: Contemporary Historical Writing in the United States.* Ithaca, N.Y.: Cornell University Press.

————. 1982. "Vanitas and the Historian's Vocation," *Reviews in American History: The Promise of American History,* 10, pp. 1–27.

May, Henry F. 1976. *The Enlightenment in America.* New York: Oxford University Press.

Ravitch, Diane, and Chester E. Finn, Jr. 1987. *What Do Our 17-Year-Olds Know? A Report of the First National Assessment of History and Literature.* New York: Harper.

Stearns, Peter N. 1983. "The New Social History: An Overview," in James B. Gardner and George Rollie Adams, eds., *Ordinary People and Everyday Life.* Nashville: American Association for State and Local History.

Wright, Gordon. 1976. "History as a Moral Science," *American Historical Review,* 81, pp. 1–11.

Chronology of U.S. History After 1865

A N IMPORTANT ASSUMPTION guided the construction of the
timeline that follows. We have assumed that the textbooks you use
contain substantial amounts of political history, including accounts of
wars, treaties, elections, and similar events. We have therefore decided
to include only some of these things in the timeline. Consequently, we
have emphasized items your textbook may not contain—social and
economic history, information concerning leisure time and other amuse-
ments, the history of artworks and buildings, and some of the great
books that have been influential in the history of the United States. In
addition, we have included as much of the history of science and
technology as possible in the space available.

In all these categories, we have barely scratched the surface of the
items that could have been listed. We hope our work will inspire you to
dig more deeply into the study of the nation's past.

Date	Event
1866	Congress enacts Freedman's Bureau bill over President Andrew Johnson's veto.
	Nation's first refrigerated railroad car built in Detroit, Michigan.
	Second Atlantic cable between United States and England laid.
	Severe cholera epidemic strikes many cities—in St. Louis, Missouri, 200 people die each day during height of epidemic.
1867	United States buys Alaska from Russia for $7.2 million.
	Ragged Dick; or, Street Life in New York, first of a long series of "rags to riches" stories by Horatio Alger, published.
	Ku Klux Klan organized in Nashville, Tennessee.
	First elevated railroad line begins in New York City.
	First volume of *Das Kapital* by Karl Marx published.
1868	Fourteenth Amendment to U.S. Constitution ratified by required number of states.
	Printer Christopher Sholes patents first typewriter.
	A new sport, cycling, becomes popular.
	Congress enacts a law that provides eight-hour day for federal employees.
1869	Prohibition party, which promotes the prohibition of making and selling alcoholic beverages, founded.
	John Wesley Powell explores Grand Canyon.
	Little Women by Louisa May Alcott published.
	Cincinnati forms first all-professional baseball team, the Red Stockings.
	First intercollegiate football game, between Rutgers and Princeton, played.
1870	Fifteenth Amendment to U.S. Constitution ratified by required number of states.
	Congress creates Department of Justice in executive branch of federal government.
	Census Bureau shows that of the nation's population of 39.8 million people, nearly 5 million are freed blacks and 2.3 million are immigrants who arrived since 1860.

Date	Event
1871	Congress enacts Indian Appropriation Act, which nullifies all former treaties and makes Indians wards of federal government.
	P. T. Barnum produces "The Greatest Show on Earth" circus in Brooklyn, New York.
	Huge fire engulfs Chicago, Illinois.
1872	Congress passes Amnesty Act, which restores civil rights to virtually all citizens in the South.
	First mail-order house, Montgomery Ward and Company, opens in Chicago.
1873	Mark Twain and Charles Dudley Warner publish *The Gilded Age.*
	Bellevue Hospital in New York City opens first school of nursing.
	Epidemics of cholera, smallpox, and yellow fever sweep the South.
1874	Joseph Glidden invents barbed wire.
	First electric-powered streetcar begins operation in New York City.
1875	Congress enacts Civil Rights Act, which is designed to give blacks equal rights in public places.
	Andrew Carnegie builds first Bessemer process steel factory in United States.
1876	*The Adventures of Tom Sawyer* by Mark Twain published.
	Alexander Graham Bell patents the telephone.
	Thomas Edison establishes industrial research park in Menlo Park, New Jersey.
	First major baseball league, the National League, formed.
1877	*Munn v. Illinois* establishes principle of public regulation of businesses that serve the public interest.
	Last federal troops leave the South, thus ending Reconstruction.
	Copper wire invented.
	Charles Brush invents arc lamp and storage battery.
1878	First regularly operated telephone exchange opens in New Haven, Connecticut.
	Edison patents the phonograph.

Date	Event
1879	Congress passes act that allows women to argue cases before Supreme Court.
	Artificial sweetener saccharin discovered by Constantine Fahlberg.
	Edison invents first practical incandescent light bulb.
	George Selden develops three-cylinder internal combustion engine, using it to power a "horseless carriage."
	Frank Woolworth opens his first "5-and-10-cent" store, in Lancaster, Pennsylvania.
1880	United States and China sign an immigration treaty that gives the former the right to regulate and limit the immigration of Chinese laborers.
	Supreme Court holds exclusion of blacks from jury duty unconstitutional.
1881	In *Springer v. U.S.,* the Supreme Court upholds constitutionality of federal income tax instituted in 1862.
	A Century of Dishonor by Helen Hunt Jackson, about mistreatment of Native Americans, published.
	Former slave Booker T. Washington founds Tuskegee Institute.
	Clara Barton founds National Society of the Red Cross and serves as its president until 1904.
	Frederick Ives produces first color photographs.
1882	Chinese Exclusion Act passed by Congress, prohibiting for ten years the entry of Chinese laborers.
	Nikola Tesla discovers rotating electric field, the basis for using alternating electric current.
	First hydroelectric plant opens in Appleton, Wisconsin.
1883	Supreme Court declares 1875 Civil Rights Act unconstitutional, arguing that black social rights are not among those protected by federal government.
	Ladies' Home Journal and *Life* begin publication.
	U.S. and Canadian railroads adopt four standard time zones to rationalize their operations schedules.
	Brooklyn Bridge, largest suspension bridge to date, completed.

Date	Event
1884	*The Adventures of Huckleberry Finn* by Mark Twain published.
	Ottmar Mergenthaler patents Linotype typesetting machine.
	Dorr Felt invents first accurate adding machine.
1885	*The Rise of Silas Lapham* by William Dean Howells published.
	William Stanley invents electric transformer.
1886	American Federation of Labor founded, Samuel Gompers first president.
	First settlement house in United States established in New York City.
	George Westinghouse builds first commercially successful power plant based on alternating current.
1887	Hatch Act provides federal aid for study of agriculture at state land grant colleges.
	Bauxite, source of aluminum, discovered in Georgia.
	Golf brought from Scotland and introduced in Pennsylvania.
1888	*Looking Backward: 2000–1887* by Edward Bellamy, a critical portrait of the United States, published.
	George Eastman perfects Kodak hand camera.
1889	*The Wall Street Journal* begins publication.
	Charles Hall patents process for making aluminum.
	First electric elevator installed in New York City.
	Reporter Nellie Bly travels around the world in just over 72 days.
1890	U.S. troops massacre 200 Indians at Wounded Knee, South Dakota.
	How the Other Half Lives by Jacob Riis, a grim portrayal of slum life among immigrants, published.
	Principle of Psychology by William James published.
1891	James Naismith invents basketball.
	Main-Travelled Roads by Hamlin Garland, a collection of stories about life in Midwest, published.

Date	Event
1892	Chinese Exclusion Act extended for another ten years.
	First electric automobile driven in Chicago.
	Duryea brothers construct first gasoline-powered automobile.
1893	Katherine Lee Bates writes "America the Beautiful."
	Chlorine used to treat sewage for first time.
	The Cliff Dwellers by Henry Blake Fuller, often considered first American "urban novel," published.
1894	Coxey's army, led by former Civil War general Jacob Coxey, marches on Washington, D.C. to petition for help for the unemployed.
	Congress passes graduated income tax law as part of Wilson-Gorman Tariff Act.
1895	Supreme Court declares income tax law unconstitutional in *Pollack v. Farmers Loan and Trust Company.*
	The Red Badge of Courage by Stephen Crane, a story about the U.S. Civil War, published.
	Homer Martin introduces "Impressionism" into the United States with his painting "The Harp of the Winds."
	First U.S. Open Golf Championship played.
1896	Supreme Court rules in *Plessy v. Ferguson* that "separate but equal" facilities for blacks and whites is constitutional.
	Free rural mail delivery begins.
	Edison introduces fluoroscope (used later to view X-ray images) and fluorescent lamp.
1897	First subway opens in Boston.
1898	John Holland launches *The Holland,* forerunner of modern submarine.
	Food and Drug Act passes because of poor quality of food supplied to U.S. troops in Spanish-American War.
1899	Scott Joplin writes "Maple Leaf Rag," a popular ragtime tune.
	The School and Society by John Dewey argues learning must be based on students' needs and experiences.
1900	*The Son of the Wolf,* a short story collection by Jack London, published.

Date	Event
1900 *(cont.)*	Theodore Dreiser's *Sister Carrie,* a realistic novel about a country girl who moves to the city, published.
	Elmer Sperry sets up laboratory for research in electronics and chemistry.
	Over one million miles of telephone lines in operation.
	Survey shows evangelical religious groups have large numbers of members, with Methodists and Baptists first and second in number.
1901	U.S. citizenship granted to members of "Five Civilized Tribes" (Cherokees, Creeks, Choctaws, Chickasaws, and Seminoles).
	The Octopus by Frank Norris, a realistic novel about the abuses of big business, published.
	Walter Reed discovers cause and spread of yellow fever.
	United States Steel Corporation founded, becoming nation's first billion dollar company.
1902	Maryland passes nation's first workman's compensation law.
	Spooner Act authorizes building and financing of Panama Canal.
	Charles Stiles discovers hookworm, a parasite widespread in the South.
	First Rose Bowl game, between Stanford and Michigan, played.
1903	*The Call of the Wild* by Jack London published.
	Wright brothers make first successful manned flight.
	First Pacific cable opens—message can be sent around the world in 12 minutes.
1904	G. Stanley Hall's two-volume psychology text, *Adolescence,* published.
	Diesel engines introduced into United States.
	Baseball pitcher Cy Young throws the sport's first "perfect game."
1905	Industrial Workers of the World, a radical labor organization, founded.
	New Orleans experiences severe yellow fever epidemic in which 400 persons die.

Date	Event
1905 *(cont.)*	Number of registered automobiles rises to nearly 78,000, up from 300 ten years before.
1906	Upton Sinclair's *The Jungle*, a radical novel about immigrant life in Chicago, published.
	Congress passes Meat Inspection Act and Pure Food and Drug Act, partly as a result of *The Jungle*.
	Fessenden broadcasts first radio program of both voice and music.
1907	"The Gentleman's Agreement" between the United States and Japan establishes right of the former to refuse entry into the United States of Japanese laborers.
	Geneticist Thomas Morgan discovers that chromosomes influence heredity.
	Albert Michelson receives Nobel Prize in physics for his work in measuring the speed of light and invention of optical instruments.
1908	Henry Ford introduces Model T at a cost of only $850, which by 1926 is reduced to $310.
	Singer Building in New York City, first U.S. skyscraper, measures 47 stories.
1909	National Association for the Advancement of Colored People (NAACP) founded to fight for the rights of black Americans.
	Explorers led by Robert Peary reach North Pole for first time.
1910	Boy Scouts and Camp Fire Girls organizations founded.
	The iron, the toaster, and the washing machine introduced.
1911	F. W. Taylor's influential *Principles of Scientific Management* published.
	W. C. Handy composes "The Memphis Blues."
1912	New Mexico and Arizona become 47th and 48th states, completing the continental United States.
	Riders of the Purple Sage by Zane Grey published.
	United States Public Health Service established.
	Attendance at movie theaters rises to over 5 million per day.
	Craze for ragtime produces fox trot, turkey trot, and bunny hug dances.

Date	Event
1913	Sixty-story Woolworth Building in New York City finished.
	Ford Motor Company produces 1000 cars per day, pays workers $5 per day for 40-hour workweek.
	Hollywood, California replaces New York City as center of motion picture industry.
1914	Panama Canal completed.
	Federal Trade Commission and Clayton Anti-trust Act, each representing quite different approaches to problem of business concentration, enacted.
	W. C. Handy composes "The St. Louis Blues."
1915	D. W. Griffith produces *The Birth of a Nation*, a film based on Thomas Dixon's 1905 pro-Klan novel, *The Clansman*.
	Ford's Detroit plant celebrates production of its one-millionth car.
	Margaret Sanger's *Family Limitation* published; author jailed for advocating birth control.
1916	Norman Rockwell begins illustrating covers for *Saturday Evening Post* (continues until 1964).
	National Park Service established.
1917	Immigration Act, requiring literacy test for alien admission, enacted.
	Jeannette Rankin, a California Republican, becomes first woman member of U.S. House of Representatives.
	United States enters World War I.
1918	Supreme Court upholds constitutionality of conscription.
	Flu epidemic breaks out, eventually kills a half million Americans.
	My Antonia by Willa Cather published.
1919	Eighteenth Amendment, prohibiting manufacture and sale of alcoholic beverages, ratified.
	Volstead Act, enforcing Eighteenth Amendment, enacted.
	U.S. House of Representatives refuses to seat Victor Berger (from Wisconsin) because he is a Socialist and opposed Americans participating in World War I.
1920	"Red Scare" following World War I produces fear of Communists, anarchists, and labor agitators; government

Date	Event
1920 *(cont.)*	agents raid offices of suspected radicals; many persons deported.
	This Side of Paradise by F. Scott Fitzgerald published.
	Sinclair Lewis's *Main Street,* a portrait of small town America, published.
	First commercial radio station, KDKA in Pittsburgh, begins operation.
	So-called "black sox scandal": members of Chicago White Sox accused of fixing World Series.
1921	Congress further limits immigration with National Emergency Quota Act.
	Ku Klux Klan emerges as important political force in many communities in both the North and the South, advocating 100 percent Americanism.
	Movie star Rudolph Valentino appears in his first successful film, *The Four Horsemen of the Apocalypse.*
1923	*Time* magazine begins publication.
	President Calvin Coolidge pardons 31 persons convicted under Espionage Act for speaking out against U.S. involvement in World War I.
1924	Congress enacts law making native-born Indians full U.S. citizens.
	George Gershwin composes "Rhapsody in Blue," an example of symphonic jazz.
	2.5 million radios in use (up from 5,000 in 1920).
1925	Colonel Billy Mitchell found guilty of insubordination for criticizing military policy toward air power.
	Teacher John Scopes on trial for teaching theory of evolution in Dayton, Tennessee.
	Bell Laboratories established to conduct research in physics.
1926	Ernest Hemingway's *The Sun Also Rises* published.
	Robert Goddard launches first liquid-fueled rocket.
	Gertrude Ederly becomes first woman to swim English Channel.
1927	*The Art of Dance* by Isadora Duncan published.
	Charles Lindbergh flies solo across Atlantic.

Date	Event
1927 *(cont.)*	Babe Ruth sets home run record: 60 in one season.
1928	*Home to Harlem* by Claude McKay published.
	First U.S. station begins television broadcasts.
	Margaret Mead's *Coming of Age in Samoa*, a classic cultural anthropology study, published.
	Walt Disney produces *Steamboat Willie*, first animated film to use sound.
1929	Ernest Hemingway's *A Farewell to Arms* published.
	Look Homeward Angel by Thomas Wolfe published.
	Clarence Birdseye introduces frozen foods.
	"St. Valentine's Day Massacre," in Chicago, one example of warfare between rival gangs of bootleggers.
	Stock market crashes.
1930	Supreme Court rules that buying liquor does not violate Eighteenth Amendment.
	Sinclair Lewis becomes first American to receive Nobel Prize in literature.
	Grant Wood exhibits "American Gothic."
	Karl Landsteiner receives Nobel Prize in medicine for discovering human blood types.
	Marx brothers star in *Animal Crackers*.
1931	Wickersham Commission reports enforcement of prohibition has almost completely failed.
	102-story Empire State Building completed.
	Duke Ellington composes "Mood Indigo."
	Ernest Lawrence invents the cyclotron, a particle accelerator (atom-smasher).
	Al Capone, notorious Chicago gang leader, sentenced to prison for income tax evasion.
1932	Veterans of World War I demonstrate in Washington, D.C., to lobby Congress for payment of their annuities, and are dispersed by army troops.
	Arkansas Democrat Hattie Caraway becomes first woman elected to U.S. Senate.
	William Faulkner's *Light in August* published.
	Dashiell Hammett's *The Thin Man* published.

Date	Event
1933	Twenty-first Amendment, repealing prohibition, ratified.
	President Franklin D. Roosevelt begins practice of speaking directly to the American people via radio in his "fireside chats."
1934	Wallace Carothers produces synthetic nylon.
	Catholic Legion of Decency begins censorship of movies.
	Charles Beebe descends over 3,000 feet into the ocean in a bathysphere.
1935	Rural Electrification Administration enacted to provide electrical power to areas not served by private power companies.
	George and Ira Gershwin collaborate on their jazz-opera *Porgy and Bess*.
	John Steinbeck's *Tortilla Flat*, a sympathetic novel about Mexican-Americans, published.
	U-235, an isotope of uranium, discovered (later used in producing nuclear weapons).
	First night game in major league baseball played in Cincinnati.
1936	*Gone With the Wind*, Margaret Mitchell's romantic novel of the U.S. Civil War, published.
	The Higher Learning in America by Robert M. Hutchins published; criticizes progressive education and college elective courses.
	Anastasio Somoza seizes power in Nicaragua.
	Hitler and Mussolini sign agreement known as Rome-Berlin Axis.
1937	Count Basie composes "One O'Clock Jump."
	Golden Boy by Clifford Odets published.
	Walt Disney produces first feature-length cartoon, *Snow White and the Seven Dwarfs*.
	Theodosius Dobzhansky's *Genetics and the Origin of Species* published, establishes evolutionary genetics as a science.
	Optics scientist Edwin Land establishes Polaroid Corporation.
1938	*Our Town* by Thornton Wilder published.

Date	Event
1938 *(cont.)*	Congress establishes House Committee on Un-American Activities to investigate Communist, Fascist, Nazi and other un-American organizations.
	Orson Welles's radio play, "Invasion From Mars," causes public panic as people think it is an actual news broadcast.
	Neville Chamberlain accedes to Hitler's demands in western Czechoslovakia at Munich.
1939	*Gone With the Wind* produced as a movie.
	Igor Sikorsky develops first practical U.S. helicopter.
	Hatch Act prohibits political activities by federal employees.
	The Grapes of Wrath by John Steinbeck published.
	Nylon stockings are sold for first time.
	Albert Einstein urges President Franklin Roosevelt to develop atomic bomb.
	World War II begins with German invasion of Poland.
1940	Smith Act (also known as the Alien Registration Act) makes advocating the overthrow of U.S. government illegal. Congress creates Selective Service System, the first peacetime conscription in U.S. history.
	The Heart Is a Lonely Hunter by Carson McCullers published.
	For Whom the Bell Tolls by Ernest Hemingway published.
	Richard Wright's *Native Son,* a novel about a Southern black who migrates to the North, published.
	World War II continues to expand; Germans bomb London and blockade England with submarines.
1941	World War II continues in Europe and Africa; the United States prepares for war.
	Electron microscope photographs a virus magnified 65,000 times.
	Manhattan Project (for building an atomic bomb) begins.
	Vannevar Bush selected to direct newly formed Office of Scientific Research and Development.
	New York Yankee Joe DiMaggio hits safely in 56 games (still a major league record).
	Japan attacks U.S. fleet at Pearl Harbor, bringing the United States into World War II.

Date	Event
1942	Federal wartime agencies take control of housing, shipping, transportation, censorship, and scientific research.
	Carrier-based aircraft fight battles of Coral Sea and Midway, important turning points in Pacific war.
	Aaron Copland composes *Rodeo,* a western ballet.
	Leo Szilard and Enrico Fermi split the atom, producing first nuclear reaction.
	Domestic rationing of materials necessary for war effort begins.
	Americans of Japanese descent sent to internment camps.
1943	The United States and its allies take the initiative on all war fronts.
	Antibiotic penicillin, used to treat various infectious diseases, produced on large scale.
	Industrialist Henry Kaiser develops mass-production techniques for building ships.
	China is a wartime ally, thus Chinese Exclusion acts are repealed.
1944	U.S. planes bomb Berlin and southern Japan for first time.
	Largest amphibious assault in history occurs when Allies invade France.
	Serviceman's Readjustment Act (G.I. Bill of Rights) enacted.
	Dangling Man, Saul Bellow's story of an army inductee, published.
1945	First atomic bombs dropped on Japan end war in the Pacific.
	United Nations begins operations in San Francisco.
	President Harry Truman asks Congress to admit persons displaced by the war.
	Black Boy by Richard Wright published.
	Cannery Row by John Steinbeck published.
1946	Trials of German and Japanese war criminals by an international tribunal result in death sentences for 19 and lengthy prison sentences for many others.
	Bernard Baruch proposes plan for international control of atomic energy.

Date	Event
1946 *(cont.)*	U.S. Atomic Energy Commission established.
	Winston Churchill makes his "Iron Curtain" speech in Fulton, Missouri, warning of Soviet aggression.
	Irving Berlin composes score for *Annie Get Your Gun.*
	Relations among wartime Allies begin to deteriorate.
1947	National Security Act unifies armed services into Department of Defense; creates Central Intelligence Agency for gathering intelligence information.
	A Streetcar Named Desire by Tennessee Williams published.
	James Michener's *Tales of the South Pacific* published.
	Heparin, a blood coagulant, synthesized.
	Jackie Robinson becomes first black to play major league baseball.
1948	Trumpeter Miles Davis pioneers "cool" jazz.
	Norman Mailer's *The Naked and the Dead* published.
	William Faulkner's *Intruder in the Dust* published.
	Guard of Honor, a novel by James Gould Cozzens about racial discrimination on an air force base, published.
	Berlin blockade by Soviet troops creates severe war scare; the United States airlifts supplies, breaking blockade.
1949	First computer with built-in accuracy checking devices produced.
	Atomic Energy Commission designs breeder reactor that produces more fuel than it consumes.
	Arthur Miller's *Death of a Salesman* published.
	Architect Philip Johnson designs "Glass House."
	Rogers and Hammerstein collaborate on musical, *South Pacific.*
1950	Senator Joseph McCarthy charges State Department infiltrated by Communists.
	Over Truman's veto, Congress passes McCarran Act, providing for internal security.
	Truman approves work on hydrogen bomb although some scientists are fearful of atomic weapons.
	Congress establishes National Science Foundation to promote scientific research.

Date	Event
1950 *(cont.)*	Abstract expressionist Jackson Pollock creates "Lavender Mist."
	United States stops trading with Communist China.
1951	Julius and Ethel Rosenberg sentenced to death for passing military secrets to Soviet Union.
	Abstract expressionist Willem de Kooning creates "Night Square."
	J. D. Salinger's *Catcher in the Rye* published.
	UNIVAC I becomes first mass-produced computer.
	Rachel Carson's *The Sea Around Us* published, raising Americans' consciousness of ecological issues.
1952	Congress enacts "G.I. Bill of Rights" for veterans of Korean War.
	John Steinbeck's *East of Eden* published.
	The Invisible Man, Ralph Ellison's novel about blacks searching for a place in U.S. society, published.
	UFOs (unidentified flying objects) reported in numerous locations.
1953	Refugee Relief Act allows victims of Communist persecution admittance to the United States.
	James Baldwin's *Go Tell It On the Mountain* published.
	Battle Cry by Leon Uris published, one of many novels about U.S. soldiers during World War II.
	Alfred Kinsey's controversial *Sexual Behavior in the Human Female* published.
	Maureen Connolly becomes first woman to win "grand slam" in tennis.
1954	Senate censures Senator Joseph McCarthy for his tactics and behavior after his hearings on subversion in the army.
	Communist Control Act strips professed Communists of their civil rights.
	Nautilus, first atomic-powered submarine, launched.
	Jonas Salk produces polio vaccine.
	In *Brown v. Topeka Board of Education,* Supreme Court rules segregation of school children violates Fourteenth Amendment.
	Concern about atmospheric testing of atomic weapons grows when scientists discover radioactive traces in food.

Date	Event
1955	Blacks boycott segregated bus lines in Montgomery, Alabama.
	Marian Anderson becomes first black singer to perform at Metropolitan Opera.
	United States begins economic aid to South Vietnam.
	Warsaw Pact formed by Russia's eastern European allies to counter NATO.
	Albert Sabin develops oral polio vaccine.
	Biologist Gregory Pincus develops effective oral contraceptive for birth control.
	Rock 'n' roll music denounced as immoral and a cause of juvenile delinquency.
1956	Federal Highway Act, largest peacetime expenditure to date, authorizes interstate highway system.
	Elvis Presley sings "Heartbreak Hotel"; becomes a national phenomenon.
	First transatlantic telephone cable begins operation.
	Three Americans receive Nobel Prize in physics for inventing transistor.
	Singer Billie Holiday's *Lady Sings the Blues* published.
1957	Distant Early Warning system, a U.S.-Canadian project, begins operation.
	Civil Rights Act, first since Reconstruction, enacted to end discrimination against blacks in public places.
	On the Road by "beat" author Jack Kerouac published.
	The Wapshot Chronicle, John Cheever's novel about life in the suburbs, published.
	Nation's first large nuclear power plant opens in Pennsylvania.
	Federation of American Scientists urges complete ban on nuclear weapons testing.
	Office of Education reports scientific and technical education in Soviet Union far ahead of that in the United States.
	Soviets launch first artificial satellite, *Sputnik,* creating great concern in the United States.
1958	National Aeronautics and Space Administration (NASA) established.

Date	Event
1958 *(cont.)*	United States launches its first earth satellites, producing important scientific information.
	Project Mercury formed to put American in orbit around the earth.
	Xerox Corporation produces its first commercial copier.
	Ultraconservative Robert Welch's *The Blue Book of the John Birch Society* published, the basic beliefs of the newly formed organization.
	U.S. churches report large gains in membership.
1959	Fidel Castro seizes power in Cuba.
	Raisin in the Sun becomes first play by a black person (Lorraine Hansberry) produced on Broadway.
	U.S.S. George Washington becomes first nuclear-powered submarine able to launch missiles.
	D. H. Lawrence's *Lady Chatterley's Lover* published after a thirty-year ban for obscenity.
	Numerous space probes and orbiting satellites rapidly increase scientific knowledge.
	St. Lawrence Seaway, largest inland waterway, opens.
1960	Fidel Castro confiscates property of U.S. citizens in Cuba.
	U-2 spy plane, piloted by Gary Powers, shot down over Soviet Union.
	Nonviolent demonstrations ("sit-ins") begin in the South to force desegregation of public facilities.
	Alfred Hitchcock's film *Psycho* released.
	Birth control pills widely available for consumption.
	Willard Libby receives Nobel Prize in chemistry for inventing carbon-14 dating.
1961	"Freedom Rides," sponsored by Congress of Racial Equality (CORE), attempt to end segregation in public facilities in the South.
	Newton Minow calls television "a vast wasteland" and urges various educational programs.
	Roger Maris breaks Babe Ruth's record for home runs by hitting 61.
	Soviet cosmonaut Yuri Gagarin becomes first man in space.

Date	Event
1962	Rachel Carson's *Silent Spring* published, shows effects of chemicals on environment.
	Supreme Court rules public schools cannot require saying prayers because of the First Amendment.
	Folk singer Bob Dylan emerges with his song "Blowin' in the Wind."
	Astronauts John Glenn, Scott Carpenter, and Walter Schirra each get space rides in earth orbit.
1963	Civil Rights demonstrations occur throughout the United States; March on Washington D.C. the largest.
	Supreme Court rules all defendants in criminal cases must be represented by counsel.
	Astronaut Gordon Cooper orbits earth 22 times and manually controls his spacecraft.
	Color TV signals relayed by satellite for first time.
	Lasers used for first time in eye surgery.
1964	U.S. Surgeon General's *Smoking and Health* reports strong connection between cigarette smoking and lung cancer.
	Stanley Kubrick's film *Dr. Strangelove* released.
	U.S. Navy begins *Sealab* project, an experiment designed to test human capacity to work on the ocean floor.
	Warren Commission reports no conspiracy connected with President John F. Kennedy's assassination.
	Incident in Tonkin Gulf, off North Vietnam, leads Congress to pass Tonkin Gulf Resolution.
1965	Blacks riot in Watts (in Los Angeles) for six days.
	New immigration law abolishes national origins quota system.
	Manchild in the Promised Land, Claude Brown's autobiographical account of growing up in Harlem, published.
	Malcolm X, black nationalist leader, assassinated.
	Viet Cong soldiers attack U.S. base in South Vietnam; United States responds by bombing North Vietnam.
	Five million color TV sets in use; virtually all prime-time programs broadcast in color.

Date	Event
1966	Supreme Court affirms accused criminals must be informed of their constitutional rights *(Miranda)*.
	Race riots occur in many U.S. cities.
	U.S. involvement in Vietnam steadily increases: more ground troops and bombings of North Vietnam escalate.
	Space probe *Surveyor 1* achieves soft landing on the Moon; and *Lunar Orbiter 1* studies potential landing sites on the surface.
1967	Thurgood Marshall becomes first black Justice on Supreme Court.
	Riots continue in black sections of U.S. cities.
	William Styron's *The Confessions of Nat Turner* published.
	Numerous space probes continue to explore the Moon; *Mariner 5* studies Venus.
	Three astronauts trapped and killed by a fire in their capsule while waiting to be launched.
1968	Tet offensive by Viet Cong and North Vietnamese troops engulfs South Vietnam, causes devastating setback for U.S. policy there.
	Martin Luther King, Jr. assassinated in Memphis, Tennessee; more riots break out.
	Kerner Commission reports white racism primary cause of black rioting in U.S. cities.
	Stanley Kubrick's film *2001: A Space Odyssey* released.
	The Double Helix, James Watson's book describing DNA, published.
	Apollo 8 becomes first manned space vehicle to orbit the Moon.
1969	Warren Burger succeeds Earl Warren as Chief Justice of Supreme Court.
	Anti-Vietnam War protests increase.
	Neil Armstrong becomes first person to walk on the Moon.
	Rock concert in Woodstock, New York, draws almost a half million persons.
	Oil spill in Santa Barbara Channel causes widespread ecological concern.
1970	After U.S. troops invade Cambodia, antiwar protests occur throughout country; four students killed by National Guardsmen at Kent State University.

Date	Event
1970 *(cont.)*	Congress creates Environmental Protection Agency (EPA) to centralize federal programs for pollution control.
	Beatles disband.
1971	*Pentagon Papers,* a secret Defense Department study, published by *The New York Times.*
	Twenty-sixth Amendment, lowering voting age to 18, ratified.
	In the *Swann* case, Supreme Court rules busing of school children to achieve integration is permissible.
	TV comedy program "All in the Family," which deals with many controversial social issues, begins.
	Mariner 9 orbits Mars, sending back thousands of photographs.
	Laundry detergents containing phosphates shown to cause water pollution.
	Cigarette advertising banned from TV.
1972	In bold foreign policy moves, President Richard Nixon visits the People's Republic of China and the Soviet Union.
	Equal Rights Amendment sent to states for ratification.
	Feminist Gloria Steinem's *Ms.* magazine begins publication.
	Use of pesticide DDT banned in United States.
	Apollo 17 becomes last manned vehicle to land on the Moon.
1973	Senate committee investigates the Watergate scandal; its hearings carried live on TV.
	Members of American Indian Movement (AIM) publicize their grievances during lengthy occupation of Wounded Knee.
	Numerous manned and unmanned space probes launched, including Skylab project and fly-bys of various planets.
	Endangered Species Act prohibits federal support of any project possibly harmful to such animals.
	United States experiences energy crisis as Organization of Petroleum Exporting Countries (OPEC) embargoes oil to the United States and Western Europe.
1974	Richard Nixon becomes first president to resign from office—because of Watergate scandal.

Date	Event
1974 *(cont.)*	Central Intelligence Agency (CIA) accused of improper conduct in both foreign and domestic spheres.
	Frank Robinson becomes first black manager in major league baseball (Cleveland Indians).
	OPEC ends embargo on oil shipments to the United States; gasoline, however, in short supply.
1975	South Vietnam falls under Communist control.
	Bruce Springsteen's album *Born to Run* released.
	Soviet and U.S. space vehicles dock in space.
	National Cancer Institute announces link between cancer and pollution.
1976	*Roots* by Alex Haley published; popular novel about black history and the basis of an even more popular TV movie series.
	Movie *Rocky* enjoys immense popularity.
	North and South Vietnam reunited after more than 20 years of civil war.
	Space probes *Viking 1* and *Viking 2* land on the surface of Mars, send back scientific data.
	Supersonic *Concorde* begins regularly scheduled flights between Europe and Washington D.C., cutting flight time in half.
1977	Trans-Alaska oil pipeline begins operation.
	Congress creates Department of Energy, reflecting Americans' increasing concern about energy issues.
	Panama Canal Treaties signed.
	George Lucas's film *Star Wars* released, becomes very popular science fiction movie.
	Fluorocarbons banned from aerosol spray cans because evidence shows they damage earth's ozone layer.
	Space shuttle *Enterprise* completes successful test flights.
1978	Smallpox declared eradicated; 120 million cases of malaria reported.
	First "test-tube baby" born, in England.
	Interferon, potentially valuable antivirus against cancer, tested.

Date	Event
1978 *(cont.)*	Congress extends ratification time for Equal Rights Amendment to 1982.
	In *Bakke* decision, Supreme Court rules affirmative action to help disadvantaged groups legal; holds reverse discrimination could be a problem.
1979	Americans stationed in U.S. embassy in Teheran, Iran, taken hostage, beginning ordeal lasting more than a year.
	President Jimmy Carter helps Egypt and Israel negotiate a peace treaty, a significant breakthrough in the Middle East.
	Historian Christopher Lasch's *The Culture of Narcissism* published; about "me" orientation of U.S. society.
	Writer Tom Wolfe's *The Right Stuff* published; about Mercury astronauts.
	Government researchers urge Americans to change their diet to prevent cancer and other diseases.
	Nuclear power plant at Three Mile Island, Pennsylvania, suffers damage (and a near-meltdown) following an accident.
1980	Supreme Court rules new forms of life resulting from scientific experiments can be patented.
	Lung cancer found increasing among women, linked to their increased amount of cigarette smoking.
	Mount Saint Helens, Washington, a long-dormant volcano, erupts several times, ruining surrounding countryside and spreading ash over very great distances.
	United States boycotts Moscow Summer Olympics to protest Soviet invasion of Afghanistan.
1981	U.S. hostages held by Iran released after 444 days of captivity.
	Swiss scientists announce first successful cloning of mammals (mice).
	Space probe *Voyager II* sends back dramatic photos of Saturn's rings.
	Space shuttle *Columbia* has its first successful flight.
	Scientists warn of "greenhouse effect," predicting a general warming of the environment because of too much carbon dioxide in the atmosphere.
1982	U.S. Department of Justice, in one of the largest antitrust cases in U.S. history, breaks up American Telephone and Telegraph Company (AT&T).

Date	Event
1982 *(cont.)*	Political problems intensify in Central American countries of El Salvador, Guatemala, and Nicaragua.
	Equal Rights Amendment (ERA) fails ratification by the necessary 38 states (only 35 did so).
	Law of the Sea Convention, covering arrangements for exploiting natural resources in the oceans, signed by 119 nations; the U.S. and other industrialized countries did not sign.
	First artificial heart (Jarvik I) transplant accomplished.
	Public becomes aware of Acquired Immune Deficiency Syndrome (AIDS).
	Space shuttle *Columbia* makes two more successful flights; two Soviet cosmonauts set record, remaining in space for 211 days.
1983	United States and Soviet Union resume negotiations on treaty to limit intermediate-range nuclear missiles.
	Congress amends near-bankrupt Social Security system.
	Space probe *Pioneer 10* launched on March 2, 1972; leaves solar system, but continues to send back data.
	In three separate trips, space shuttle *Challenger* takes first woman, first black American, and first foreign national into space.
	President Ronald Reagan announces Strategic Defense Initiative (SDI or "Star Wars"), a space-based antiballistic missile defense system.
1984	Geraldine Ferraro becomes first woman vice-presidential candidate.
	Protests of blacks continue to rock South Africa; Desmond Tutu, a black Anglican bishop in that country, receives Nobel Peace Prize.
	Problems continue in Middle East, especially in Lebanon; President Reagan orders U.S. Marines home from Lebanon.
	Congress stops all aid to Contra rebels in Nicaragua.
1985	Federal deficit reaches $200 billion mark.
	Mikhail Gorbachev, seen to be a moderate, becomes leader of Soviet Union.
	President Reagan and General Secretary Gorbachev hold summit meeting in Geneva.

Date	Event
1985 *(cont.)*	Rock concert, "Live Aid," held to raise money (nearly $70 million) for African famine relief.
	Congress passes major tax reform act.
1986	Gramm-Rudman Act (1985) takes effect, sets limits on the level of government spending and deficits.
	U.S. space program experiences devastating blow when space shuttle *Challenger* explodes after launch—all aboard are killed.
	Tower Commission formed to investigate "Iran-Contra" (also called "Irangate") scandal.
	President Reagan and General Secretary Gorbachev meet in Iceland to discuss nuclear arms reductions.
	Congress enacts new immigration law, meant to better control U.S. borders and solve problem of illegal immigrants in the country.
	Nuclear reactor at Chernobyl (in Soviet Union) explodes, sends massive amounts of radioactive gases into the atmosphere.

Historians of
the United States

3

THIS CHAPTER PRESENTS brief biographies of 15 historians of the United States. We have included only a select few, choosing historians who have had great influence on how we think about the past or how we go about researching and writing about that past. Some have exerted this influence through their own scholarship and writing. Others have not only written widely, but have trained and guided younger scholars who, in turn, have exerted substantial influence on the profession. Some have even had great social influence by force of their personality, their personal courage in taking unpopular stands on current issues of their day, and their work in or around government, the military, or the diplomatic corps.

We have tried to include representatives from the major fields of historical scholarship (economic, social, intellectual, and political history) as well as subfields within those broad areas of scholarly interest (e.g., such topics as family, women, cities, immigrants, blacks). To a certain extent, the individual intellectual biographies of these historians may serve to gauge the state of the art of United States history when the individual was (or is) doing his or her major scholarly work. While their ideas and influence on how we think about history are the most significant aspects of these historians' lives for our purposes here, the biographies also sketch the personal dimension insofar as possible.

You will probably notice several things about the historians we have included. First, there are few young people. Even though a young historian may have influenced the way we think about history or practice historical research, judging the significance of a young scholar's work is difficult because so much of that work, presumably, is yet to be done. Second, biographical information about younger historians is much more difficult to gather.

One consequence of the foregoing is that the historians included here tend to be (1) older—many were even born in the nineteenth century; (2) male—women in prior generations had great difficulty becoming professional historians; and (3) white—blacks and other minorities also faced difficulties in securing professional training and employment opportunities in the historical profession. To say this is to say that the history of the historical profession in this century reflects many of the characteristics of the larger society. Until fairly recently (some would say this watershed is still to be crossed), the historical profession was dominated by white males trained largely at northeastern universities. The historical profession now reflects much greater pluralism within its ranks than was once the case, and the discipline's creativity and substance has begun to reflect this change.

Charles A. Beard (1874–1948)

Few scholars have been as influential in the intellectual and cultural life of the United States as Charles Beard. He was an expert on municipal government, a proponent of public administration as a field of academic study, an educational reformer who believed that schools should be more relevant to current problems and needs, and a political scientist who helped orient that discipline toward realistic analysis of current problems and issues. In addition, Beard was a towering figure as a historian. As such, Beard is most commonly associated with (1) the economic interpretation of American history, particularly *An Economic Interpretation of the Constitution of the United States* (1913), (2) "the new history," which urged that historical study should encompass the full range of human experience as well as politics, and (3) the idea that history should be an instrument for improving the present and reshaping the future.

In the period between World War I and World War II, as historian John Higham wrote, Beard "came close to dominating the study of American history." But Beard was not simply an ivory tower scholar. Indeed, after he resigned from Columbia University in 1917 to protest the dismissal of several other faculty members who were opposed to U.S. entry into World War I, he held no full-time university post until 1940. Although he himself firmly supported U.S. entry, he resigned to defend its opponents. Historian Richard Hofstadter says of this: "It is on such courageous moments of self-assertion that the American tradition of academic freedom has been built."

During much of his life Beard was a controversial figure, often taking unpopular stands on the issues of the day as well as staking out innovative and sometimes unpopular scholarly positions. "When I come to an end," Beard wrote, "my mind will still be beating its wings against the bars of thought's prison." His passion was "new facts . . . [which were] constantly challenging old mental patterns and imagery." The words *skeptical, pragmatic, realistic, hard-bitten, irreverent, iconoclastic* were often used by both devotees and critics to characterize the man. But in addition to hard analysis, dispelling myths, challenging conventional wisdom (even his own), and provoking his audiences, he was very much concerned with social uplift, with helping the society's disadvantaged persons, with generally "doing good."

Beard's background helps, in part, explain his behavior and beliefs. Charles was born in Indiana in 1874 to a successful and well-to-do family. His father, William, was a successful farmer, contractor, and land speculator as well as a loyal Republican who strongly believed in the United States as the land of opportunity. Beard's parents encouraged him to expand his horizons through extensive reading and other intellectual pursuits. Perhaps most important was his exposure to local Quakers, whose beliefs had a deep and lasting impact on him. Throughout his life, Charles believed in the dignity of all human beings, in helping the needy and oppressed, and in the courage of one's own convictions.

After Charles graduated high school, his father bought him and his brother Clarence the local weekly newspaper, *The Knightstown Sun,* which they successfully operated for four years. But Charles was persuaded to go to college. He enrolled at DePauw University, where he was very active in campus social and political affairs. Beard graduated in only three years, but his experience there was formative. In one social science course, for example, Beard and his fellow students were required to supplement their academic reading with actual field experiences. Beard spent part of the summer of 1896 in Chicago, where he was shocked by the slums and poverty he saw. At the same time, he visited Jane Addams's Hull House, a settlement house for immigrants, and was exposed to the reform ferment (intellectual and political) at work there.

From Depauw, Beard went on to Oxford and Columbia universities for graduate studies. Receiving his Ph.D. degree in 1904, Beard stayed at Columbia until he resigned in 1917. He was nevertheless a prolific writer who wrote, by our count, at least 35 books not counting those he edited. In addition, he wrote hundreds of articles for academic journals and other periodicals and hundreds of book reviews. It is impossible to summarize this volume of work. But Hofstadter may help us judge this prolific scholar: "He had never been content with the role of the historian or academic alone; he always hoped to be politically relevant, had always aspired to become a public force . . . he relished the part of the public moralist, the gadfly, the pamphleteer." "He had made himself foremost among the American historians . . . in the search for a usable past."

Thomas Cochran (1902–   )

Thomas Cochran was born in the house of his paternal grandparents in Brooklyn, New York. He spent most of his youth and early adult life in the New York City area. His father was a failed businessman who eventually turned to teaching to support his family. It may have been this experience in downward social mobility that turned the younger Cochran's attention to the history of business in the United States.

Cochran was less than a serious student during most of his school life. His father apparently believed elementary schools to be ineffective, so he kept Thomas out of school until he was eight years old. He then attended school for two years and was out of school the next two. Nevertheless, his father saw to it that young Thomas learned. When he was ready for college, he enrolled at New York University to study engineering. Tiring of engineering in his sophomore year in college, Thomas decided to pursue history. He graduated with a double degree— in chemistry and history.

From 1923 to 1937, when he married his third wife, Cochran attended graduate school, wrote his Ph.D. dissertation, and earned his doctorate. His attention was never, in this period, solely riveted on his profession. He was often more interested in socializing with friends, and playing bridge, tennis, and golf. In addition, his first marriage ended in divorce, his second in the death of his wife. His third marriage, however, seemed to add the stability and direction that had been missing before. Almost immediately upon marrying Rosamond Beebe, Cochran's work began to take on greater importance for him, and he began to pursue it with much greater vigor.

Cochran's most enduring contribution to United States history was his advocacy of business history as an important dimension of the discipline. He urged, first, that business history be separated from economic history and, second, that business history was an important ally of social history because it has been business that has most influenced social change throughout the nation's history. Perhaps his next most important contribution was his emphasis on the use of the social sciences—particularly their methods and some of their concepts—to make history speak to the problems of the day.

Cochran's work includes *The Age of Enterprise: A Social History of Industrial America* (1942), a book that is still quite valuable for its treatment of the late nineteenth century; *Railroad Leaders, 1845-1890: The Business Mind in Action* (1953), a pioneering use of quantitative methods that looked at such issues as innovation, competition, and government regulation through the collective eyes of railroad executives; *The American Business System: A Historical Perspective, 1900-1955* (1957), a cogent combination of business and economic history; *The Inner Revolution: Essays on the Social Sciences in History* (1964) and *The Uses of History* (1973), in which he argued that history had to be useful—which meant using the social sciences—or it would be ignored; and *Frontiers of Change: Early Industrialism in America* (1981), an extended essay about the roots of industrialization in the United States. Finally, among the articles Cochran wrote during his career, none has received more notice than "The 'Presidential Synthesis' in American History," *American Historical Review* (July 1948), in which he took to task the traditional manner of organizing U.S. history. History teaching and research traditionally focused on politics and presidential administrations—most high school textbooks still reflect what Cochran was criticizing—while ignoring virtually everything else.

Henry Steele Commager (1902–   )

Henry Steele Commager was born in Pittsburgh, Pennsylvania, but spent his childhood in Chicago, Illinois. He received all three of his degrees from the University of Chicago, undertaking further study in several European universities. His teaching career began at New York University in 1926, but from 1939 to 1956—with an interruption during World War II to serve as a historian with the United States Army and the Office of War Information—he taught at Columbia; from 1956 to 1972, he was a professor at Amherst College. Even though he retired from his teaching duties, he has remained quite active in the profession.

From the beginning of his career in history, Commager has been concerned about reaching the widest possible audience with history.

In 1930, Commager collaborated with Samuel Eliot Morison on the widely used textbook, *The Growth of the American Republic.* He followed this text for college students with similar books for high school students *(Our Nation)* and for the general reader *(America: The Story of a Free People).*

Much of Commager's career has been given over to making history more accessible to historians and nonhistorians alike. One of his finest contributions was the collection of primary source documents, *Documents of American History* (1934, with frequent revisions), which gave readers access to important sources for understanding the American historical experience. This collection remains the best single collection of documents in American history. Commager followed this book with several similar volumes, including *The Heritage of America* (1939, with Allan Nevins); *The Blue and the Gray: The Story of the Civil War as Told by Participants* (two volumes, 1950); *Living Ideas in America* (1951); and *The Spirit of 'Seventy-Six* (1958, with Richard Morris). These collections were all based on the same idea—making historical sources available to a wide audience.

Commager has also produced many interpretive historical works. In 1950, for example, he published *The American Mind: An Interpretation of American Thought and Character Since the 1880s.* In this book, Commager explored whether or not a nation possessed a "mind" or "character," and grappled with the problem of how to deal with ideas in history—asking whether it was more fruitful to look at the thinking of intellectuals or at the popular expressions of intellectuals' ideas. This problem has continued to be debated among intellectual historians and historians of popular culture.

The American Mind was a wide-ranging and provocative book, one which exhibited many, sometimes inconsistent, themes. First, Commager explored the development of the American character. He argued that it had been forged in the conflict between two world views. One was a brutal Social Darwinism, which preached the sanctity of unregulated economic enterprise and survival of the fittest. The other was based on a socially minded pragmatism, which held that unbridled economic exploitation ravaged many powerless individuals and which embraced government as an agent of social welfare. The dialogue between these two sets of ideas had been the basic framework of American thinking. Second, even as one set of ideas won out over the other—the decade of the 1890s was a watershed with respect to these ideas—the American character had not really changed much over time. The basic traits of

Americans—optimism, materialism, experimentalism, pragmatism, individualism—were just as real and just as powerful in 1950 as in 1890.

Third, Commager explored the changes in American character—which were quantitative, not fundamental—in the period between the 1890s and 1950s. Finally, Commager was concerned about the homogenizing tendencies of an increasingly centralized political and economic system, fearing that creative ideas and pluralistic values of Americans—fundamentals of American character—would be suffocated. The latter was a theme to which Commager would return time and again in his later work.

During the 1950s, Commager constantly advocated open, rational discussion of ideas. In *Civil Liberties Under Attack* (1951) and *Freedom, Loyalty, Dissent* (1954), he argued that efforts to restrict how people thought tended to stifle any thought and led eventually to the death of society. He further argued that while Americans paid lip service to the legal and philosophical bases of freedom of speech, they actually ignored both. In the latter book, Commager despaired that "uncertain of principles, we fall back on emotion, unfamiliar with the past we guess at the future." As an advocate of freedom of inquiry (and terribly concerned about the effects of forced conformity in the 1950s through such assaults as those by such people as Senator Joseph McCarthy), Commager argued that "the great danger that threatens us is neither heterodox thought nor orthodox thought, but the absence of thought."

In his later books, Commager continued to hammer home his beliefs in free inquiry and expression. In *Freedom and Order: A Commentary on the Political Scene* (1966), he asserted, among other things, that the government should explain its policy course in Vietnam and make available accurate information. Only with freedom of inquiry could citizens of the United States discuss the goals and policy options and perhaps avoid being pulled further into the Vietnam quagmire. He noted that the government tended to equate hostility to United States Vietnam policy with disloyalty or stupidity—certainly not a hospitable environment for open inquiry.

Commager continually asserted the importance of history as the collective memory of humankind. Only by studying the past could humankind either use its heritage or, if necessary, transcend it. But grappling with the past was not solely the task of a trained elite (i.e., historians): it was the task of every citizen to come to terms with the nation's past and heritage. All people were capable of measuring up to this task if only they operated in an intellectual environment that fostered free inquiry and if only they had sufficient information.

Merle Curti (1897–   )

Merle Curti was born and raised in Nebraska, but received all his academic degrees from Harvard University. In 1942, he was appointed to the history faculty at the University of Wisconsin, where he remained for the rest of his professional career. Curti became an elder statesman (and sometimes an embattled defender) of U.S. intellectual history. His book, *The Growth of American Thought* (1943), received the Pulitzer Prize in history and was selected in a poll of historians as the "most preferred" book written between 1936 and 1950. For many years this book served as a major synthesis of the history of ideas in the United States. Its standing declined in the 1970s, when intellectual history as a subfield of U.S. history fell into disfavor among professional historians.

Curti's social views were very close to the "progressive" views of Beard. The nature of his specific social views can be seen in the scholarship he pursued. His earliest work, in the 1920s and 1930s, was concerned with pacifist ideas and peace movements in U.S. history. *The American Peace Crusade, 1815–1860* (1929) and *Peace or War: The American Struggle, 1636–1936* (1936), to name two, were sympathetic to pacifist ideas. Moreover, these ideas were presented as possible instruments to change the world. To be sure, arguments against war, he contended, had failed in the past, not as a result of defeat by other "rational" ideas, but because of turbulence in the social, economic, and political environment. But Curti believed that this "body of brilliant arguments against war" might serve as a reservoir of resources that could influence people's future behavior. Indeed, Curti wrote in another context, "that the historian should select and emphasize those memories of the past that will impel men consciously to seek and build a more desirable future."

In *The Social Ideas of American Educators* (1935), Curti stressed the connection between ideas and the social and economic system. In this book, he championed those educators whose ideas promoted democratization of the schools and criticized those whose ideas retarded "educational reform." In both cases, however, Curti criticized those who failed to understand the connection between the schools and their environment. As he said, "education cannot rise above the existent social system and the virtues sponsored by that system."

In *The Growth of American Thought,* Curti extended his earlier views to all of U.S. intellectual history. The book was organized around the conflict between reform ideas (which, not surprisingly, looked forward) and antireform ideas (which tended to look backward). Like other "progressive" historians, Curti was more likely to emphasize the environmental origins of ideas for which he had little sympathy than for those ideas he admired. Despite Curti's basic historical relativism, his book seemed to celebrate the achievements of American ideas and institutions. Some of these seemed to possess virtually "absolute" value.

In a review of *The Growth of American Thought,* Richard Shryock noted that "most striking is the catholicity of interests, the broad conception of what constitutes the cultural life of a people." What Shryock referred to was Curti's treatment of science and education, the arts and architecture, and popular culture and minority thought as well as that of the elite. It is little wonder that many considered Curti's work encyclopedic.

In *The Making of an American Community: A Case Study in a Frontier County* (1959), Curti applied social science methods and concepts to the study of history to a much greater extent than had his mentor Beard. This book was his attempt to write scientific history, in the sense of discovering the connection between environmental factors and the beliefs that sprang from them. But his investigation not only showed what Americans in this Wisconsin county believed and thought but also suggested a good deal about the nature of the community in which those ideas came to life.

David Herbert Donald (1920–   )

David Donald was born on a plantation in rural Mississippi. His father's family had lived in the South for over 300 years. His mother was the daughter of a Union Army officer who had moved to Mississippi during Reconstruction to operate a school for the newly freed slaves. Donald attended high school and a local junior college, graduating with honors from Millsaps College in 1941. He went to the University of Illinois to study with James G. Randall, a leading scholar on the Civil War and Reconstruction. Donald received his master's degree there in 1942 and his Ph.D. four years later.

Growing up in the South shaped Donald's outlook (and eventually some of his historical work), particularly his concern about the conflict between majority rule and minority rights. Donald himself recalled that "I grew up a white Southerner in a state where the dominant white majority gave not the least attention to the rights of the numerous black minority." But this theme cut in yet another way. As an adult living in the North, Donald became quite aware of his Southern origins: "I have been part of the Southern minority in the United States that has, whether willingly or under duress, been obliged to accept drastic social changes decreed by the national majority." These twin experiences influenced Donald's thinking about the Civil War era and the late nineteenth century, to which he has devoted most of his scholarly life.

Donald's early forays into the archives produced several important books. The first was *Lincoln's Herndon* (1948), a biography of Abraham Lincoln's law partner and biographer. Much of the folklore—and many inaccuracies—about Lincoln's public and private lives was the result of Herndon's prose. Donald put many of these to rest with exhaustive research. This book also outlined an agenda for further research on Lincoln and the Civil War era.

In 1956, Donald published *Lincoln Reconsidered,* a set of essays that explored Lincoln and his times from several fresh and provocative perspectives. Perhaps the most controversial of these concerned a revisionist account of the abolitionists in which Donald questioned the motives of antislavery politicians. He argued that the abolitionists basically suffered from status anxiety; they were a displaced elite with little sense of purpose or leadership—that is, until they seized upon antislavery agitation as a way to reestablish their place in American society. His interpretation rankled many, in part, at least, because of the growing momentum of the black civil rights movement.

Despite the criticisms of this work, Donald followed it with a two-volume biography of Charles Sumner, a leading radical antislavery politician. The first volume, *Charles Sumner and the Coming of the Civil War,* appeared in 1960; and ten years later the second, *Charles Sumner and the Rights of Man,* appeared. Donald showed Sumner to be a man of ideas who learned to be quite effective in the world of practical politics. While the first volume was principally concerned with the period before the Civil War, the later volume focused on an area of research that came more and more to dominate Donald's work—Reconstruction.

In 1961, Donald published a major revision of his mentor's—James G. Randall—*The Civil War and Reconstruction,* until recent times the most exhaustive single volume on this period. *The Politics of Reconstruction, 1863-1867* (1965), Donald's next book, demonstrated solid research as well as methodological innovation—common to much of his work—in its analysis of politicians' stands on Reconstruction policies.

Donald suggested that the "safer" a congressman's district was, the firmer his position on controversial Reconstruction policies.

In the early 1970s, Donald undertook two books that, when completed, presented a comprehensive view of the nineteenth century. The first was a textbook—*The Great Republic*—which appeared in 1977. The text was a collaborative project of several eminent historians including Donald, Bernard Bailyn, John L. Thomas, David B. Davis, Robert Wiebe, and Gordon S. Wood. Some have judged it to be the best college textbook ever written for U.S. history courses.

Donald's section of this book was the period 1860–1890. He argued that despite apparent differences and conflicts between North and South, the two sections were essentially similar. Common history, common values, and common goals, Donald held, suggested there was really little difference between the two sections. The notion that the Civil War was caused by the development of two very different civilizations was, therefore, incorrect. Too, the notion that the North was somehow purer in its approach to slavery and race relations during this period was also incorrect.

To show just how similar the two sections were, Donald suggested that during the Civil War itself, the Union and Confederate governments faced similar problems and approached those problems in remarkably similar ways. To further develop these insights, Donald published *Liberty and Union* (1978), which expanded on what appeared in *The Great Republic*.

This book's primary contribution was in helping people reconceptualize the second half of the nineteenth century. This period has traditionally been divided into the era before the war, the war itself, Reconstruction, and the era of economic expansion after Reconstruction. Donald attempted to offer an alternative framework, one that treated the period from 1845 to 1890 as a whole, rather than in pieces. Donald confessed his own conservatism:

> compromise is better than conflict, that pragmatic adjustments are more lasting than programmatic solutions, and that the power of an individual, a group, or even a generation to effect drastic changes in the course of history is minuscule.

Furthermore:

> I have not much faith in those who claim they possess magic formulas that will protect minorities, and I have even less faith in those who assert that the will of the majority is in all cases to prevail.

Whether or not one agrees with Donald, these are words all would do well to think about.

John Hope Franklin (1915-   )

John Hope Franklin is one of the most celebrated current historians in the United States. In part at least, his professional career mirrors an important aspect of twentieth-century U.S. social history—the struggle for equal social, economic, and political rights for black Americans.

In 1832, Franklin's great-grandfather, a slave, was taken from Alabama to Oklahoma by his Chickasaw Indian masters. His son David Burney escaped slavery to join the Union Army during the Civil War. David eventually changed his surname to Franklin, married a half-Indian woman, and settled on a ranch deeded to him by the federal government. Buck Franklin, John Hope's father, attended college in Tennessee, became an attorney, and moved to Rentiesville, Oklahoma (an all-black town of about 2,000 people) to practice law and double as the town's postmaster.

As John Hope grew up, he had intended to follow his father in the practice of law. After graduating high school he enrolled at Fisk University in Nashville, Tennessee (his parents had studied in Nashville; his brother had attended Fisk). John Hope's plans for becoming a lawyer changed abruptly—he met Theodore S. Currier, a young white professor of history. Currier taught Latin American history as well as U.S. history. About the U.S. history course Franklin had taken from Currier he said, "I had never had such an intellectual experience."

Franklin graduated from Fisk with honors when he was twenty years of age even though he had worked the entire time to put himself through school. He had applied to and had been accepted by Harvard University for graduate work. But in 1935, the United States was in the depths of the Great Depression. As Franklin put it, "My father's law business had been crushed by the Depression, so the family could not finance my graduate study." He went home for the summer wondering how he could pay for graduate school. When Professor Currier discovered Franklin's problem, he said, "Money will not keep you from going to Harvard," and proceeded to take out a personal bank loan to pay for Franklin's first year at Harvard. Thereafter, Franklin taught and received several fellowships that defrayed the costs of his education. He was awarded his Ph.D. in 1941.

Between 1943 and 1981, Franklin authored or edited seventeen books (an average of nearly one book every two years) and numerous scholarly articles. Considering this volume, it may not be surprising that he calls his office "the slave quarters." Franklin's primary scholarly concern was the history of black Americans and of the South. His first book, *The Free Negro in North Carolina, 1790–1860,* looked closely at the social and economic dimensions of black degradation in antebellum North Carolina. In *From Slavery to Freedom: A History of American Negroes* (first edition, 1947), Franklin surveyed the black experience in the United States from colonial times to World War II. Since its publication, this book has been revised several times and has sold over a half-million copies. In *The Militant South, 1800–1860* (1956), Franklin moved beyond the history of blacks to a description of the emergence of a unique military spirit in the South before the Civil War. More recently, Franklin published *Southern Odyssey* (1975).

In addition to teaching and substantial scholarly work, Franklin is notable for the many "firsts" he has experienced. He was, for example, the first black president of the American Historical Association, of the Organization of American Historians, and of the Southern History Association. Of these and other firsts, Franklin says, "What business did I have being on the front page of *The New York Times* for becoming a history department chairman, except that it told you something about where we were, or where we were not [in making racial progress in the United States]?" He believes that scholars should have an impact on society as well as pursue academic interests. As one example of his social activism, in 1954 Franklin supplied a historical brief for the lawsuit *Brown v. Topeka Board of Education,* which led to the Supreme Court ruling school segregation illegal. An unpretentious man despite celebrity, Franklin's scholarly and personal lives have served similar ends.

Constance M. Green (1897–1975)

Constance McLaughlin Green was born in Ann Arbor, Michigan. Her father, Andrew C. McLaughlin, was a professor of history at the University of Michigan when she was born. Constance grew up in Chicago after her father was appointed to the faculty of the University of

Chicago. She attended University High School, where she participated in athletics and served on the yearbook staff. After graduating, she spent a year in Europe before enrolling at the University of Chicago.

Green transferred to Smith College, where she received her A.B. degree in 1919. She then returned to Chicago to teach English. In 1921, she married Donald R. Green, a textile manufacturer, and moved to Holyoke, Massachusetts. To keep in touch with the academic community, Green enrolled at Mount Holyoke College, from which she received a master's degree in history in 1925. For the next seven years, Green taught part-time at Mount Holyoke while raising a family (she and her husband had three children) and trying her hand at writing detective fiction. Between 1932 and 1937, Green studied for her doctorate at Yale University, receiving her Ph.D. in 1937. Her dissertation was published by Yale University Press as *Holyoke, Massachusetts: A Case History of the Industrial Revolution in America*. This book demonstrated both of Green's primary research interests: industrialism and urban history.

In 1938, Green returned to Smith College as an instructor in the history department. A year later, she was appointed the head of the Smith College Council on Industrial Relations, a post from which she directed the research of numerous graduate students on industrial history. In 1942, Green left Smith College to become a historian for the United States Army Ordnance Department at the Springfield, Massachusetts Armory, a post she held through World War II. In 1946, Green's husband died, and she moved to Washington, D.C. Two years later, she headed a team of historians that collectively wrote a major volume in a historical series on the United States Army during World War II.

Following a short teaching stint in London, England, Green was appointed a historian for the secretary of defense in 1952. Two years later, she became head of a team of historians that undertook to reconstruct the history of Washington, D.C. The project culminated in the book, *Washington, Village and Capital, 1800–1878,* for which Green received a Pulitzer Prize for history. A second volume, *Washington, Capital City, 1879–1950* was also published.

Green's other books reflect her abiding interest in urban and industrial topics. These include *The Role of Women as Production Workers in the War Plants of the Connecticut Valley* (1946); *History Naugatuck, Connecticut* (1949); *Eli Whitney and the Birth of American Technology* (1956); *American Cities in the Growth of the Nation* (1957); *The Rise of Urban America* (1965); and *The Secret City: A History of Race Relations in the Nation's Capital* (1967). In a period in which few women were able to become professionals, Green became an outstanding professional historian.

Oscar Handlin (1915–   )

O scar Handlin ranks as one of the most prolific and influential historians of the modern era. Handlin was born in New York City to recently arrived Jewish immigrants. Although he was expelled from school on several occasions, Handlin excelled at academics; by age eight he had decided to become a historian. Not surprisingly, Handlin became a voracious reader. After graduating high school in 1931, Handlin attended Brooklyn College, where he earned his bachelor's degree in three years. He was admitted to the graduate program at Harvard University.

There, Handlin had wanted to study medieval history, but Charles Haskins, the professor with whom he wanted to study, had retired. He therefore decided to study with Arthur M. Schlesinger, Sr., because he was reputed to be the next best person on the Harvard faculty. It was Schlesinger who suggested that Handlin write his doctoral dissertation on Boston's Irish immigrants. In 1940, he received his doctoral degree and the next year his dissertation was published as *Boston's Immigrants, 1790–1865: A Study in Acculturation.* The book was a model study of the manner in which poor Irish immigrants adapted to Boston, a rather unpromising city both culturally and economically. For this effort, Handlin received immediate and widespread acclaim. The author was praised for his use of primary historical sources, including census materials and the immigrant press, and his use of social science concepts to explain Irish adaptation.

Handlin soon showed that he would not be a one-book wonder. Since the publication of *Boston's Immigrants,* Handlin has written or edited more than 30 books. These include *This Was America: True Accounts of People, Places, Manners and Customs, As Recorded by European Travelers . . .* (1949); *The Uprooted* (1952), one of the most beautifully written books ever produced about European immigrants to the United States; *The American People in the Twentieth Century* (1954), a history of ethnic groups in the United States; *Race and Nationality in American Life* (1957), a collection of essays on immigration and ethnic history; *Al Smith and His America* (1958), a lively sketch of the governor of New York and 1928 presidential candidate; *Fire Bell in the Night: The Crisis in Civil Rights* (1964), in which Handlin argued against busing, quotas, and other preferential treatment for blacks, while emphasizing vastly expanded educational opportunities; and *Facing Life: Youth and the Family in American History* (1971), a history of adolescence, among many others.

In these books and through his influence with his students, Handlin has made pioneering and profound contributions to U.S. history, especially in the fields of social, ethnic, and urban history. The list of his former graduate students is like a Who's Who of U.S. history and includes Bernard Bailyn, Anne Firor Scott, Moses Rischin, David Rothman, Neil Harris, Nathan Huggins, Stephan Thernstrom, Sam Bass Warner, and many, many more. These scholars, in turn, have been among the most influential in their respective chosen specialties. In 1979, his former students published a festschrift, *Uprooted Americans: Essays to Honor Oscar Handlin.* Although Handlin has made substantial contributions to many areas of U.S. history, he will probably be best remembered for his contributions to social history, the history of immigration, and the history of U.S. cities.

Richard Hofstadter (1916–1970)

R ichard Hofstadter was one of the most influential historians in the United States in the period after World War II. The subjects of his work ranged from the Puritans to the 1960s, but despite such breadth, his work was always penetrating and suggestive. For much of his professional life, he sought to counter the often single-cause explanations of such "progressive" historians as Charles Beard, whose economic explanations of the U.S. past Hofstadter found wanting. Because he often criticized Beard and other progressive historians, Hofstadter is commonly associated with the so-called "consensus" school of U.S. historiography (as are Daniel Boorstin and Louis Hartz) that emerged in the 1950s. Consensus historians minimized the degree of conflict in the American past, asserting that there was little disagreement on fundamental social and political values. But because of the subtlety and complexity of Hofstadter's work, it is difficult to categorize him so simply.

Born in 1916 in Buffalo, New York, Hofstadter attended the university there and moved on for graduate work at Columbia University in New York City. From 1937 to his premature death in 1970, Hofstadter was affiliated with Columbia for all but four years. He received his Ph.D. degree in 1942 after completing the manuscript of what would become his first book, *Social Darwinism in American Thought, 1860–1915.*

This book had less to do with the active role of evolutionary ideas in the late nineteenth century than about contemporary social thinkers whose ideas rationalized the status quo, the existing political, social, and moral order. As Hofstadter said, "There is nothing in Darwinism that inevitably made it an apology for competition or force." This book showed Hofstadter's interest in ideas as powerful historical forces, a central theme in most of his subsequent scholarship.

His next project was *The American Political Tradition and the Men Who Made It* (1948), a book that earned him fame. It consisted of twelve essays about key political figures in U.S. history, including the "Founding Fathers," Thomas Jefferson, Andrew Jackson, John C. Calhoun, and Abraham Lincoln. According to Hofstadter, the U.S. political tradition "overwhelmingly supported exploitative individualism and a rapacious entrepreneurial capitalism." In this, Hofstadter's work ran counter to progressive historians' view that the American past could be explained by the battles between the forces of good and evil, liberal democracy versus conservative interests.

Hofstadter suggested that all Americans (not only conservatives) were in some measure influenced by material forces and perceived self-interest. In addition, the story became even more complicated as political traditions, ideas, and ideologies themselves became so powerful as to impede necessary adjustments in thinking necessitated by changes in the material environment. His point was that ideologies could be dysfunctional as well as functional, but were powerful historical forces in either case. As the United States was transformed by such material forces as industrialization, immigration, and urbanization, the American political tradition of Jeffersonian democracy and equality of opportunity (and the assumptions on which this tradition was based) came to be outdated. Material conditions had changed faster than Americans' ideas, resulting in inappropriate responses to new problems. Only Franklin D. Roosevelt was able to discard such outmoded thinking during the tremendous economic crisis that characterized the 1930s. But Hofstadter was no great fan of FDR because he was unable to provide the nation with what it needed most—a revitalized democratic philosophy appropriate to an industrial age.

The Age of Reform: From Bryan to FDR (1955) was perhaps Hofstadter's best book. It combined his twin interests in political and intellectual history. The book described the impulse to reform as the dynamic political force in the period from 1890 to the New Deal. But it was also much more. It described the tenacity of traditional values and ideas and how these influence persons' actions and self-perceptions. Emerging reform strategies were defined and constrained by such American values as equality of opportunity, free enterprise, and rugged individualism even after these ideas were no longer appropriate or effective. Therefore the liberal ideology of which these ideas and values were a part was also a conservative tradition and reform strategies were steeped in nostalgia for the certainties and superiority of bygone eras. The Populists (farmer-reformers) were inspired by a preindustrial, Jeffersonian worldview that cast farmers as exemplars of virtue; Progressives were inspired by small-town America, a place where God-fearing, Protestant people were respected leaders of the community. The problem was that no one perceived that all this was only nostalgia, not instrumental knowledge for solving current problems.

Hofstadter always worked hard, often with a discipline that astonished his colleagues. Historian C. Vann Woodward commented that "he was not always an easy man to vacation with . . . langorous tropical mornings tended to be disturbed by the clatter of a typewriter. He gave us all an inferiority complex."

In the last two years of his life, Hofstadter published two books: *The Progressive Historians: Turner, Beard, Parrington* (1968) and *The Idea of a Party System: The Rise of Legitimate Opposition in the United States* (1969). In addition, he completed several chapters of what was to have been a massive project which was published, in part, after his death as *America at 1750: A Social Portrait.*

Christopher Lasch (1932–   )

Christopher Lasch was born in Omaha, Nebraska, the son of a journalist father and social worker mother. Little about his early life is commonly known. We do know that he enrolled at Harvard University in 1951, roomed for a short time with novelist John Updike, and graduated with honors in history in 1954. Lasch went on to graduate work at Columbia University, earning his master's degree in 1955 and his Ph.D. in 1961. During this time, Lasch held a number of teaching jobs as well as research fellowships.

Lasch's early research and writing focused on the late nineteenth- and early twentieth-century United States, developing such themes as the radical political tradition, the roles and responsibilities of intellectuals in U.S. society, and the barriers to developing social awareness and concern. But Lasch, particularly in his latest work, has been content with examining nothing less than U.S. culture as a whole.

His first book, *American Liberals and the Russian Revolution* (1962), dealt with the domestic political consequences for Americans (mostly liberals) who viewed favorably the Russian Revolution. His second book, *The New Radicalism in America, 1889–1963: The Intellectual as a Social Type* (1965), examined American intellectuals as an emerging, self-conscious group that advocated reform. This group—educated, middle-class, and Protestant by upbringing—pinned its hopes for personal liberation and a less repressive social environment on "scientific progressivism," including urban planning, public education, and good government politics, among other things.

Lasch argued that by the mid-twentieth century, ironically, these ideas had evolved into a legacy of conservatism and social adjustment— parts of a culture of management. By following the progressive approach to problems, Americans had become confused to the point of despair, while political power still rested in the hands of traditional economic elites.

Lasch's concern with intellectual responsibility and with fashioning an effective radical political tradition continued to animate his research and writing. During the 1960s, a time of great political and cultural turmoil, Lasch wrote *The Agony of the American Left* (1969), a series of essays on such topics as populism, socialism, black power, and the radical "new left" Students for a Democratic Society (SDS). The book described the American left's failure to influence U.S. politics in any significant way since World War II. Lasch scorned the apparent goals of the new left—sexual liberation, personal expression, and the denial of authority—which he thought tended to undermine rational discourse and development of a rational society.

In 1973, Lasch published *The World of Nations*, a series of essays he had written over the preceding 15 years. The book was divided into three sections, each devoted to a theme that has dominated his thought: "The Limits of Liberal Reform"; "Alternatives to Liberalism"; and "The So-Called Post-Industrial Society." Lasch's next important book, *Haven in a Heartless World: The Family Besieged* (1977, 1979), continued these themes. This work appeared at a time when the traditional nuclear family seemed to be in crisis, but Lasch offered not just another study of the family in crisis, but a study *of the study* of the family in crisis. Lasch claimed that the family had been a subject of social concern at least since the turn of the century. He further argued that after nineteenth-century economic changes robbed the family of its control of work, others (including social scientists, medical and mental health professionals, among others) had helped to erode parental authority and responsibility. The result, Lasch contended, was yet another generation of narcissistic adults who possessed broken ideals and a passive approach to a life and culture they could neither understand nor change.

Lasch has continued to explore the implications of this work, first in *The Culture of Narcissism* (1978), and then in its sequel, *The Minimal Self: Psychic Survival in Troubled Times* (1984). In these books, Lasch argues that the narcissistic personality has been a pathological (but adaptive) response to the unremitting grimness of the contemporary world. Even most attempts at improving the individual's life—education, sports, self-awareness, etc.—have become part of the problem. His argument is, essentially, that the contemporary belief in individual "liberation" has played into the hands of the status quo, making significant change impossible.

Arthur S. Link (1920–   )

A rthur S. Link is widely viewed as the foremost historian of President Woodrow Wilson, having devoted nearly four decades to research and writing about Wilson. It is interesting to note that at least some of Link's life has paralleled Wilson's. Link, like Wilson, was born in Virginia and attended school in the South. Link received his bachelor's degree with highest honors in 1941, his master's in 1942, and his Ph.D. in 1945, all from the University of North Carolina (although he also studied at Columbia with Henry S. Commager in 1944-45). Like Wilson, Link taught at Princeton University (from 1945 to 1948). For the next 12 years, Link held various faculty positions at Northwestern University, but returned to Princeton to stay in 1960. In 1954, Link also became director of the project to collect and edit the Woodrow Wilson papers.

Whereas Wilson left college teaching and scholarship for a career in politics, Link has remained a scholar. Yet their views of history appear to be quite similar. Both, for example, viewed history as an important vehicle for teaching moral values. In addition, the men shared a similar devotion to Christian principles. Link wrote of Wilson that he was "a man committed very deeply to fundamental Christian affirmations about moral law, but also enormously flexible about details and methods, so long as they did not violate what he thought was right." Link himself was the vice president of the National Council of Churches and a lay leader within the Presbyterian Church.

Much of Link's early scholarship focused on the South. His doctoral dissertation was titled *The South and the Democratic Campaign of 1910-1912*. In 1966, Link coedited a collection of essays to honor his mentor at the University of North Carolina: *Writing Southern History: Essays in Historiography in Honor of Fletcher M. Green*. Through these and other studies of the South, Link was able to understand the regional influences that shaped Woodrow Wilson. Although both men lived outside the South for much of their adult lives, they were able to maintain their attachments to their families and their sense of place.

Link began his work on Wilson in the late 1940s. In his first books and journal articles, Link was critical of Wilson, describing him as "so contradictory, so baffling, so enigmatic." Link found it difficult to explain the many apparent contradictions that comprised Wilson—while possessing many admirable qualities, the man craved affection, could not give friendship on equal terms, and was occasionally petty in his feelings and prejudices. As he began to explore Wilson more deeply, Link began to reevaluate his earlier conclusions.

In *Wilson: The Road to the White House* (1947), Link detailed the years in which Wilson became governor of New Jersey to his election as president of the United States. In his second major book, *Woodrow Wilson and the Progressive Era, 1910-1917* (1954), Link basically outlined the research he had only begun on Wilson. In *Wilson: The New Freedom* (1956), Link remained critical of Wilson's moralistic diplomacy—views he would subsequently alter—but he also broke new ground with his treatment of Wilson's domestic program and his adoption of much of Theodore Roosevelt's "new nationalism" platform. In 1960, Link published *Wilson: The Struggle for Neutrality, 1914-1915,* in which he began to reevaluate his earlier interpretations of Wilson's idealistic diplomacy. Link produced a number of other books on Wilson, each seeming to temper somewhat his earlier critical interpretations of Wilson. The most recent, *Woodrow Wilson: Revolution, War, and Peace*

(1979), is short and quite accessible for both college and high school students.

Whatever disagreements other scholars may have with Link's interpretations of Wilson, probably none can rival him in his grasp of the documentary record. By virtue of the Wilson Papers project, Link has been instrumental in locating, copying, selecting, and editing hundreds of thousands of documents relating to Wilson. The projected 60 volumes of these papers (41 volumes had appeared as of 1983) may be Link's most important contribution to historical scholarship and to understanding Wilson as well.

Arthur M. Schlesinger, Jr. (1917–   )

Arthur M. Schlesinger, Jr., may be the most visible and well-known historian in the United States. Perhaps it is small wonder. His father was a widely respected and innovative social and cultural historian, Harvard faculty member, and president of the American Historical Association. His mother was a descendant of nineteenth-century historian George Bancroft and was herself a pioneer in women's history. Schlesinger has received two Pulitzer Prizes and two National Book Awards for his work. Yet he may be better known for his political activities and advocacy, his contributions to numerous periodicals, and his "scholarly partisanship" than for his work as a historian.

Arthur was born in Columbus, Ohio, while his father was on the faculty at Ohio State University. In 1919, the family moved to Iowa City, Iowa, where Arthur, Sr., took a post at the University of Iowa. Five years later, the family moved to Cambridge, Massachusetts, after the father received his appointment at Harvard. Arthur and his brother, it was finally agreed, would receive their schooling in private schools—much in keeping with the tradition of Harvard faculty; the decision was made only after great anguish on the part of Arthur's parents, who firmly believed in the idea of the public schools, but not in their quality. Arthur graduated from Phillips Exeter Academy in 1934, just before his sixteenth birthday. He enrolled at Harvard that fall.

Schlesinger graduated from Harvard with honors in 1938. His first book, a revision of his senior thesis, was published the next year as

Orestes A. Brownson: A Pilgrim's Progress. This work was quite favorably reviewed and paved the way for Schlesinger's acceptance to Harvard's Society of Fellows, whose mission was to nurture young scholars with demonstrated aptitude for creative thought. Schlesinger viewed this appointment as a way to continue studying history without being put through the "Ph.D. mill." He eventually gravitated toward the study of the age of President Andrew Jackson; this work became the basis of his first major historical work, *The Age of Jackson* (1945).

This book was immediately seen, by at least some reviewers, to be a major contribution to American historical writing. Others argued that *The Age of Jackson* was less a work of history than a justification of Franklin D. Roosevelt's New Deal. Whatever the merits of either position, there is little question that Schlesinger's book sparked an historiographical debate that has continued to the present. There is also little doubt that this debate established Schlesinger's reputation as a major U.S. historian—he received the 1946 Pulitzer Prize in history and an appointment as associate professor at Harvard.

At the same time, Schlesinger began contributing to numerous periodicals and newspapers and became deeply involved in liberal Democratic politics. He helped found the liberal organization Americans for Democratic Action (ADA) in 1947 to promote New Deal domestic policies and anti-Communist foreign policies. These views— what Schlesinger would call non-doctrinaire, pragmatic liberalism— were put forth in *The Vital Center: The Politics of Freedom* (1949). Schlesinger said he had undertaken this book to get private views out of his system so they would not cloud his scholarly work on the New Deal.

Schlesinger moved in and out of academic life. In the late 1940s, for example, he served briefly in the State Department during the implementation of the Marshall Plan in Europe. In 1952 and again in 1956, he took leaves of absence from Harvard to write speeches for Democratic presidential candidate Adlai Stevenson. Extremely disappointed when Stevenson failed to win, Schlesinger turned back to historical scholarship. In a three-year period, Schlesinger published the first three volumes of *The Age of Roosevelt* series: *The Crisis of the Old Order, 1919–1933* (1957); *The Coming of the New Deal* (1959); and *The Politics of Upheaval* (1960). Many believe these books to be his most important contribution to historical scholarship.

After this brief interlude, Schlesinger became deeply involved in the presidential campaign of John F. Kennedy and, after Kennedy's victory, was appointed to the White House staff. There he served as a policy adviser for Latin American affairs and the U.S. mission to the United Nations and, more informally, as a liaison between the administration and the scholarly/intellectual community. After Kennedy was assassinated, Schlesinger soon resigned from the White House staff to begin working on a memoir of the Kennedy years.

The next four books Schlesinger wrote involved his experience close to the center of power in the Kennedy White House. In *A Thousand Days: John F. Kennedy in the White House* (1965), Schlesinger detailed Kennedy's presidency, including several observations that became highly controversial. He was accused of being a "peephole historian" and castigated for writing a history so close to the time of the events it described. Whatever the ultimate judgment of the book—it did receive a Pulitzer Prize—it is still a valuable source on the Kennedy years.

In 1967, Schlesinger published *The Bitter Heritage: Vietnam and American Democracy, 1941-1966,* a series of previously published essays. In this book, he argued that U.S. intervention in Vietnam had occurred incrementally—almost inadvertently—certainly not by conscious policy decision. He implied that had Kennedy lived, the United States would not have become so deeply involved, a contention impossible to prove or refute. Schlesinger was also concerned about the impact of the Vietnam War on the United States, particularly as it seemed to engender an atmosphere that would stifle discussion and dissent.

In 1969, Schlesinger published a collection of essays titled *The Crisis of Confidence: Ideas, Power, and Violence in America,* to some degree the result of his reaction to Robert F. Kennedy's assassination. In this book Schlesinger observed that "we are a good deal less buoyant today about ourselves and our future. Events seem to have slipped beyond our control; we have lost our immunity to history." The 1960s had demonstrated to him that centrist liberalism could be as aggressively challenged by the political left—especially the youthful new left—as by the traditional conservative right.

Schlesinger's *The Imperial Presidency* appeared in 1973. This bestseller outlined the history of the aggrandizement of the presidency. That expanded role, Schlesinger contended, was largely an artifact of the expanded international role of the United States after World War II. He further argued that this pattern of accumulating power in the White House reached its apogee during the Nixon administration and was a culmination, not an aberration. The Watergate scandal, therefore, served a useful purpose—it stopped the revolutionary presidency in its tracks.

Frederick Jackson Turner (1861-1932)

Frederick Turner was born in Portage, Wisconsin, in 1861, and grew up in the midst of small-town, Midwestern life. His father worked on the local newspaper, first as a typesetter, eventually as owner/publisher. Exposed to his father's library of over 400 books, Freddie (as he was dubbed as a child and later by students) read widely and did quite well at Portage High School. He also became interested in local history and politics and in such outdoor pastimes as hunting and fishing. Indeed, it appears that Turner would drop virtually anything in favor of a fishing adventure.

Although Freddie did well in high school, when he enrolled at the University of Wisconsin (then having fewer than 500 students) in 1878, his academic training was found to be inadequate. He therefore had to enroll in a remedial program in which he studied the classics, mathematics, botany, and oratory. Turner did quite well in improving his academic skills, but he became ill and his sophomore year in college had to be postponed. In 1881, Turner returned to classes intent upon becoming a journalist. In 1884, Turner finally graduated with distinction and with an abiding interest, not only in journalism, but in history as well.

At that time, professional historians were virtually unknown in the United States. There had been no professorships in history at any U.S. university until 1881; even three years later, there were fewer than twenty such positions. Until the 1880s, people wrote history as a hobby or after retirement from other, "real" professions. But professional training was becoming more common in the United States, and more teaching and research positions were being created in the growing number of colleges and universities just as Turner was finishing college. To choose to become a professional historian at this time was not an especially good decision compared to other opportunities. Nevertheless, Turner decided to pursue history as a profession, first earning a master's degree at Wisconsin (1888) and finally his Ph.D. at Johns Hopkins University (1890).

Turner then returned to teach history at the University of Wisconsin. His friend and mentor, Professor William F. Allen, died the year Turner returned, leaving the latter as the sole historian on the university faculty. Turner's professional life rapidly advanced as he taught numerous courses, served as inspector of high schools in Wisconsin (in which capacity he tried to improve high school history teaching), and served as curator of the Wisconsin State Historical Society, where he engaged in an unremitting schedule of historical research.

Although he published little in this period (as was true for his entire academic career, at least compared to other "great" historians), a very important idea was germinating in his mind. That idea concerned the influence of the frontier on U.S. history. Through his research, Turner became convinced that the single most important feature of American experience was the frontier. In 1893, he put forth these ideas at a meeting in Chicago, where he read a paper entitled "The Significance of the Frontier in American History." Though his paper received little notice at the time, it proved to be one of the most influential scholarly essays in American history.

Turner argued that the frontier had molded the American nation and the personal traits seen to be distinctively American in nature. The characteristics of the frontier—an area of sparse settlement, a fault line that separated savagery from civilization, and an area of expansive opportunities—produced a distinctive experience. Consequently, the frontier fostered the values that came to dominate U.S. history: individualism, freedom, ingenuity, self-reliance, materialism, and democracy, among others.

Turner further argued that individuals who moved to the frontier found themselves in similar economic circumstances which, in turn, fostered notions of equality and political programs for the good of "the common man." Moreover, the frontier had long served as a "safety valve" for individuals discontented with their present situation; these equally available opportunities not only fostered democracy but also the dislike of authority, belief in individual initiative, natural resource exploitation, and the American penchant for tangible works and products.

It is interesting, though not surprising, that Turner's paper (and his idea) received virtually no notice at first. His audience—a rather august lot of other professional historians and graduate students—appeared to be unreceptive. Few others noticed Turner's work. But his ideas eventually caught on, at least in part because other Americans noticed (as the Bureau of the Census had reported in 1890) that there was no longer a discernible frontier line—there was no longer free land in the west to which young people could stake a claim and get a new start in life. The growing popularity of Turner's "frontier thesis" was also the result of a growing American nationalism. The frontier thesis gave intellectual grounds for an American exceptionalism—an explanation for how

Americans differed from (and, implicitly, were superior to) other peoples.

Whatever the reasons for receptivity, Turner himself had little to do with the growing avalanche of work on the frontier. His graduate students and converts spread Turner's ideas and variations of those ideas far and wide until the 1930s when a reaction among historians emerged. Nevertheless, the debate about Turner's frontier thesis—one that has animated hundreds of scholars—has persisted, largely, one suspects, because that debate is essentially about who we are and what we as a people value.

William Appleman Williams (1921-)

William Williams was born and reared on a farm in rural Iowa, where he was imbued with such values as hard work and a sense of community and family. He attended college at a small military academy in Missouri, where he played basketball on scholarship. In 1941, he received an appointment to the United States Naval Academy at Annapolis, studying science and engineering. During World War II, he served in the South Pacific theater, but was transferred in the last months of the war to Texas to train as a Navy pilot. There he became involved with a National Association for the Advancement of Colored People (NAACP) effort to secure voting rights for area blacks and to integrate local naval operations. After being beaten up several times, he offered the Navy his resignation, which it refused to accept.

After the war, Williams thought briefly about working for General Electric or Lockheed as an engineer. He decided instead to attend graduate school at the University of Wisconsin. He chose history because he thought that discipline was the best way to find out what was going on in the world. He received a master's degree in Russian history in 1948, but switched to the history of U.S. foreign policy because of a lack of access to source materials for studying Russian history. He received his doctorate in 1950 and published his expanded dissertation two years later—*American-Russian Relations, 1781–1947.*

Williams's next book, *The Shaping of American Diplomacy: Readings and Documents in American Foreign Relations, 1750–1955* (1956), is a collection of documents suggesting that U.S. foreign relations were driven, not just by political and military considerations, but by economic and ideological ones as well. Various interest groups in the United States had exerted great influence on the course of the nation's foreign policy although these groups often disagreed and therefore created contradictory pressures. While public opinion was important in U.S. foreign policies, the public was seldom in a position to actually initiate policy, largely because of a lack of information.

In 1959, Williams published his best-known work, *The Tragedy of American Diplomacy*. This book was published at a time when the conventional wisdom regarding U.S. foreign relations tended to emphasize public opinion and formal diplomatic negotiations and to disregard economic factors. Convention also held that while the United States had flirted with imperialism at the end of the nineteenth century (the Spanish-American War), such expansion was seen as "a great aberration," in Samuel Flagg Bemis's memorable phrase. In fact, the exercise of U.S. power in world affairs was seen as a virtually unavoidable response to external forces.

Williams challenged these central tenets. He argued that Americans' humanitarian ideals and their belief in self-determination for all peoples ran head-on into another set of beliefs—their desire for domestic economic prosperity, their perceived need to constantly expand U.S. markets overseas to assure such prosperity, and their fear of social changes in other countries that did not conform to the U.S. pattern.

Williams argued that the economic crisis of the 1890s was a critical experience in the development of the policy of "open door imperialism." What emerged in that period was a firm arrangement between business interests and government to encourage overseas expansion and to protect U.S. interests throughout the world. That arrangement continued unabated through the years and, for Williams, helped to explain the problems U.S. foreign policy had experienced—particularly the onset of the cold war with Russia following World War II.

The Tragedy of American Diplomacy raised other scholars' hackles from the outset. One reviewer termed the book "an argument rather than diplomatic history"; another said that "it cannot be taken seriously as history." In 1973, Robert James Maddox in *The New Left and the Origins of the Cold War* took Williams to task for what Maddox termed sloppy methodology, particularly with respect to the manner in which Williams had used quotations from his source materials. But the final jury is still out on the veracity of Williams's interpretations. What cannot be doubted is the influence Williams has had on discussions of U.S. diplomatic relations.

C. Vann Woodward (1908–   )

C Vann Woodward was born in Vanndale, Arkansas, a small town named for his great-grandfather. He spent much of his youth in central Arkansas, where his father was superintendent of public schools. His childhood was steeped in Southern history as well as in a liberal tradition he got from both parents and an uncle, Comer M. Woodward, a professor of sociology at Southern Methodist University in Texas.

Woodward became a historian almost by accident. He attended a small college in Arkansas before transferring to Emory University in Atlanta, Georgia (where his uncle was then teaching sociology). He graduated from Emory in 1930 with a degree in philosophy. The next year he taught English at Georgia Tech. In 1932, Woodward received a master's degree in political science from Columbia. He then spent a summer traveling in Europe, viewing firsthand the Soviet Union, Germany, and France. In the Soviet Union, in particular, he was impressed by others' views of the United States, particularly their criticism of U.S. race relations in the South. He returned to teach English at Georgia Tech.

During his tenure in Atlanta, Woodward became involved with a committee formed to save a black Communist, Angelo Herndon, accused of inciting an insurrection—a capital crime. Though Woodward chaired this committee for a short time, his involvement was brief because he became disillusioned with the petty squabbles and the manipulation of the Herndon case by the Communists for propaganda purposes. (The Herndon case ended in 1937 when the Supreme Court declared the insurrection law unconstitutional.) In any event, Woodward's involvement, regardless of how brief and high-minded, may have cost him his job at Georgia Tech.

After a brief stint with the WPA farm survey in Georgia, Woodward decided to pursue his doctoral studies at the University of North Carolina. The former experience had interested Woodward in Tom Watson, a leader of the southern Populists in the late 1890s. Receiving permission from the Watson family to work on the Populist's papers, Woodward went to North Carolina because the Watson papers were housed there. He also chose a history degree because the project was logically a history project.

Woodward received his Ph.D. in 1937. His doctoral dissertation on Tom Watson was published the next year as *Tom Watson, Agrarian Rebel.* It was the first of four books that remade post–Civil War Southern history. The others were *Reunion and Reaction: The Compromise of 1877 and the End of Reconstruction* (1951); *The Origins of the New South, 1877-1913* (1951); and *The Strange Career of Jim Crow* (1955). In addition to these works, Woodward has also published *The Burden of Southern History* (1960); *American Counterpoint: Slavery and Racism in the North-South Dialogue* (1971); and *Mary Chesnut's Civil War* (1981), which received the Pulitzer Prize in history in 1982.

Since the publication of *The Origins of the New South*, Woodward has been rightly regarded as the master of Southern history. Though this book has not been widely read outside the ranks of professional historians, Woodward has become widely read and influential through numerous periodical articles and *The Strange Career of Jim Crow*, a widely used textbook in college courses. Perhaps one of the reasons for his influence has been that he believes history has much to teach the present.

In *The Strange Career of Jim Crow*, for example, Woodward argued that the system of legal discrimination that came to characterize the South did not spring up immediately after Reconstruction, a view popularly and widely held. Rather, Jim Crow laws of racial oppression emerged in the 1890s and evolved slowly in the early years of the twentieth century. The book, published in 1955 just as the black civil rights movement was gaining momentum, showed an important historical truth—discriminatory laws in the South were not the necessary fruit of a distant past (and therefore sacred and inviolable). Rather, they were the product of the recent past and of the political expediency of local elites. The upshot was that if those laws were rescinded, race relations in the South could be improved.

Historical Data

4

THIS CHAPTER CONTAINS examples of many different kinds of primary sources. Historians use these and other kinds of primary (and secondary) sources to reconstruct the past. The intent of the chapter is fourfold. First, we want you to be aware of the great variety of materials that comprise the historical record of human activity. Second, we want to introduce you to the uses and limitations of specific kinds of primary sources. Not all sources are equally reliable; each type of source has its strengths and weaknesses; each type of source must be handled by the historian in different ways.

Third, we think that you should know that any one source (or even many of the same types of source) is usually not adequate evidence upon which to base reliable history. Historians use multiple sources in order to achieve as complete an image as possible of the past, to cross-check one source against others, and to verify the truthfulness and possible bias of specific sources, among other things. Fourth, we want you to be aware that primary sources are not simply inert objects; truth just lying around to be discovered. In other words, not only does the historian need his or her facts to produce history, but "the facts" need their historian before they are of any value to anyone. The historian must closely question each source, much like a trial lawyer questions a witness. Only through such open dialogue with the sources is the historian able to discover their usefulness and validity.

Each of the following primary sources is prefaced by a description of the source and some of the questions that a historian should ask about such sources. The sources are quite varied; the topics with which the sources deal are also quite different. Yet we have obviously only scratched the surface. There are many other types of primary historical sources that, because of limitations of space, we have not included in this chapter. For example, we have not included excerpts of sermons, literature, business account books, or foreign policy pronouncements, among many other types of primary sources. In addition, we have not been able to include sources that relate to many of the important topics in U.S. history. There are literally thousands of worthy historical topics, and we have obviously mentioned only a few. Despite these limitations, we hope this excursion into the historical record is both interesting and enjoyable.

One final word is in order. In the following sources, we have retained the original language, punctuation, capitalization, and so forth. This may make the sources somewhat more difficult to read than if we had modernized the language. We thought that you should experience the sources as historians do. Don't be dismayed as you enter the working world of the historian.

Autobiography

Frederick Douglass and Booker T. Washington were both distinguished black men who had once been slaves in the American South. Douglass gained his freedom in the 1830s, moved to the North, and participated in the abolitionist (antislavery) movement. The younger Washington was freed by the Civil War and went on to become a strong, though conservative, voice among blacks. The former's autobiography was published in 1883, Washington's in 1900. As you read these autobiographies, you should ask such questions as, under what conditions were the autobiographies published; who published them and why? Do persons of all social classes and ethnic groups publish their memoirs, recollections, or autobiographies? What might this suggest about such sources? When were the autobiographies written; contemporary with events, or long after the fact; from notes or from memory? Douglass and Washington differed in their descriptions of Reconstruction—what might account for these differences?

Frederick Douglass

Though slavery was abolished, the wrongs of my people were not ended. Though they were not slaves, they were not yet quite free. No man can be truly free whose liberty is dependent upon the thought, feeling, and action of others, and who has himself no means in his own hands for guarding, protecting, defending, and maintaining that liberty. Yet the Negro after his emancipation was precisely in this state of destitution. The law on the side of freedom is of great advantage only where there is power to make that law respected. I know no class of my fellowmen, however just, enlightened, and humane, which can be wisely and safely trusted absolutely with the liberties of any other class. Protestants are excellent people, but it would not be wise for Catholics to depend entirely upon them to look after their rights and interests. Catholics are a pretty good sort of people (though there is a soul-shuddering history behind them), yet no enlightened Protestants would commit their liberty to their care and keeping. And yet the government had left the freedmen in a worse condition than either of these. It felt that it had done enough for him. It had made him free, and henceforth he must make his own way in the world, or, as the slang phrase has it, "root, pig, or die." Yet he had none of the conditions for self-preservation or self-protection. He was free from the individual master, but the slave of society. He had neither money, property, nor friends. He was free from the old plantation, but he had nothing but the dusty road under his feet. He was free from the old quarter that once gave him shelter, but a slave to the rains of summer and the frosts of winter. He was, in a word, literally turned loose, naked, hungry, and destitute, to the open sky. The first feeling toward him by the old master classes was full of bitterness and wrath. They resented his emancipation as an act of hostility toward them, and, since they could not punish the emancipator, they felt like punishing the object which that act had emancipated. Hence they drove him off the old plantation, and told him he was no longer wanted there. They had not only hated him because he had been freed as a punishment to them, but because they felt that they had been robbed of his labor. An element of greater bitterness still came into their hearts; the freedman had been the friend of the government, and many of his class had borne arms against them during the war. The thought of paying cash for labor that they could formerly extort by the lash did not in any wise improve their disposition to the emancipated slave, or improve his own condition. Nor, since poverty has, and can have, no chance against wealth, the landless against the landowner, the ignorant against the intelligent, the freedman was powerless. He had nothing left him but a slavery-distorted and diseased body, and lame and twisted limbs, with which to fight the battle of life. I therefore soon found that the Negro had still a cause, and that he needed my voice and pen with others to plead for it. The American Anti-Slavery Society under the lead of Mr. Garrison had disbanded, its newspapers were discontinued, its agents were withdrawn from the field, and all systematic efforts by abolitionists were abandoned. Many of the society, Mr. Phillips and myself amongst the number, differed from Mr. Garrison as to the wisdom of this course. I felt that the work of the society was not done; that it had not fulfilled its mission, which was not merely to emancipate, but to elevate the enslaved class. But against Mr. Garrison's leadership, and the surprise and joy occasioned by the emancipation, it was impossible to keep the association alive, and the cause of the freedmen was left mainly to individual effort and to hastily-extemporized societies of an ephemeral character; brought together under benevolent impulse, but having no history behind them, and being new to the work, they were not as effective for good as the old society would have been had it followed up its work and kept its old instrumentalities in operation.

From the first I saw no chance of bettering the condition of the freedman until he should cease to be merely a freedman and should become a citizen. I insisted that there was no safety for him or for anybody else in America outside the American government; that to guard, protect, and maintain his liberty the freedman should have the ballot; that the liberties of the American people were dependent upon the ballot-box, the jury-box, and the cartridge-box; that without these no class of people could live and flourish in this country; and this was now the word for the hour with me, and the word to which the people of the North willingly listened when I spoke. Hence, regarding as I did the elective franchise as the one great power by which all civil rights are obtained, enjoyed, and maintained under our form of government, and the one without which freedom to any class is delusive if not impossible, I set myself to work with whatever force and energy I possessed to secure this power for the recently-emancipated millions.

The demand for the ballot was such a vast advance upon the former objects proclaimed by the friends of the colored race, that it startled and struck men as preposterous and wholly inadmissible. Anti-slavery men themselves were not united as to the wisdom of such demand. Mr. Garrison himself, though foremost for the abolition of slavery, was not yet quite ready to join this advanced movement. In this respect he was in the rear of Mr. Phillips, who saw not only the justice, but the wisdom and necessity of the measure. To his credit it may be said, that he gave the full strength of his character and eloquence to its adoption. While Mr. Garrison thought it too much to ask, Mr. Phillips thought it too little. While the one thought it might be postponed to the future, the other thought it ought to be done at once. But Mr. Garrison was not a man to lag far in the rear of truth and right, and he soon came to see with the rest of us that the ballot was essential to the freedom of the freedman. A man's head will not long remain wrong, when his heart is right. The applause awarded to Mr. Garrison by the conservatives, for his moderation both in respect of his views on this question, and the disbandment of the American Anti-Slavery Society must have disturbed him. He was at any rate soon found on the right side of the suffrage question.

The enfranchisement of the freedmen was resisted on many grounds, but mainly these two: first, the tendency of the measure to bring the freedmen into conflict with the old master-class, and the white people of the South generally. Secondly, their unfitness, by reason of their ignorance, servility, and degradation, to exercise so great a power as the ballot, over the destinies of this great nation.

These reasons against the measure which were supposed to be unanswerable, were in some sense the most powerful arguments in its favor. The argument that the possession of suffrage would be likely to bring the negro into conflict with the old master-class at the South, had its main force in the admission that the interests of the two classes antagonized each other and that the maintenance of the one would prove inimical to the other. It resolved itself into this, if the negro had the means of protecting his civil rights, those who had formerly denied him these rights would be offended and make war upon him. Experience has shown in a measure the correctness of this position. The old master was offended to find the negro whom he lately possessed the right to enslave and flog to toil, casting a ballot equal to his own, and resorted to all sorts of meanness, violence, and crime, to dispossess him of the enjoyment of this point of equality. In this respect the exercise of the right of suffrage by the negro has been attended with the evil, which the opponents of the measure predicted, and they could say "I've told you so," but immeasurably and intolerably greater would have been the evil consequences resulting from the denial to one class of this natural means of protection, and granting it to the other, and hostile class. It would have been, to have committed the lamb to the care of the wolf—the arming of one class and disarming the other—protecting one interest, and destroying the other, making the rich strong, and the poor weak—the white man a tyrant, and the black man a slave. The very fact therefore that the old master-classes of the South felt that their interests were opposed to those of the freedmen, instead of being a reason against their enfranchisement, was the most powerful one in its favor. Until it shall be safe to leave the lamb in the hold of the lion, the laborer in the power of the capitalist, the poor in the hands of the rich, it will not be safe to leave a newly emancipated people completely in the power of their former masters, especially when such masters have not ceased to be such from enlightened moral convictions but by irresistible force.

. . .

And now while I am not blind to the evils which have thus far attended the enfranchisement of the colored people, I hold that the evils from which we escaped, and the good we have derived from that act, amply vindicate its wisdom. The evils it brought are in their nature temporary, and the good is permanent. The one is comparatively small, the other absolutely great. . . .

(Source: Frederick Douglass, *Life and Times of Frederick Douglass,* Cleveland, Ohio: Hamilton, Rewell, and Co., 1883, pp. 458–464.)

Booker T. Washington

During the whole of the Reconstruction period our people throughout the South looked to the Federal Government for everything, very much as a child looks to its mother. This was not unnatural. The central government gave them freedom, and the whole Nation had been enriched for more than two centuries by the labour of the Negro. Even as a youth, and later in manhood, I had the feeling that it was cruelly wrong in the central government, at the beginning of our freedom, to fail to make some provision for the general education of our people in addition to what the states might do, so that the people would be the better prepared for the duties of citizenship.

It is easy to find fault, to remark what might have been done, and perhaps, after all, and under all the circumstances, those in charge of the conduct of affairs did the only thing that could be done at the time. Still, as I look back now over the entire period of our freedom, I cannot help feeling that it would have been wiser if some plan could have been put in operation which would have made the possession of a certain amount of education or property, or both, a test for the exercise of the franchise, and a way provided by which this test should be made to apply honestly and squarely to both the white and black races.

Though I was but little more than a youth during the period of Reconstruction, I had the feeling that mistakes were being made, and that things could not remain in the condition that they were in then very long. I felt that the Reconstruction policy, so far as it related to my race, was in a large measure on a false foundation, was artificial and forced. In many cases it seemed to me that the ignorance of my race was being used as a tool with which to help white men into office, and that there was an element in the North which wanted to punish the Southern white men by forcing the Negro into positions over the heads of the Southern whites. I felt that the Negro would be the one to suffer for this in the end. Besides, the general political agitation drew the attention of our people away from the more fundamental matters of perfecting themselves in the industries at their doors and in securing property.

. . .

Of course the coloured people, so largely without education, and wholly without experience in government, made tremendous mistakes, just as any people similarly situated would have done. Many of the Southern whites have a feeling that, if the Negro is permitted to exercise his political rights now to any degree, the mistakes of the Reconstruction period will repeat themselves. I do not think this would be true, because the Negro is a much stronger and wiser man than he was thirty-five years ago, and he is fast learning the lesson that he cannot afford to act in a manner that will alienate his Southern white neighbours from him. More and more I am convinced that the final solution of the political end of our race problem will be for each state that finds it necessary to change the law bearing upon the franchise to make the law apply with absolute honesty, and without opportunity for double dealing or evasion, to both races alike. Any other course my daily observation in the South convinces me, will be unjust to the Negro, unjust to the white man, and unfair to the rest of the states in the Union, and will be, like slavery, a sin that at some time we shall have to pay for.

In the fall of 1878, . . . I decided to spend some months in study at Washington, D.C. I remained there for eight months. I derived a great deal of benefit from the studies which I pursued, and I came into contact with some strong men and women. At the institution I attended there was no industrial training given to the students, and I had an opportunity of comparing the influence of an institution with no industrial training with that of one like the Hampton Institute, that emphasized the industries. At this school I found the students, in most cases, had more money, were better dressed, wore the latest style of all manner of clothing, and in some cases were more brilliant mentally. At Hampton it was a standing rule that, while the institution would be responsible for securing some one to pay the tuition for the students, the men and women themselves must provide for their own board, books, clothing, and room wholly by work, or partly by work and partly in cash. At the institution at which I now was, I found that a large proportion of the students by some means had their personal expenses paid for them. At Hampton the student was constantly making the effort through the industries to help himself, and that very effort was of immense value in character-building. The students at the other school seemed to be less self-dependent. They seemed to give more attention to mere outward appearances. In a word, they did not appear to me to be beginning at the bottom, on a real, solid foundation, to the extent that they were at Hampton. They knew more about Latin and Greek when they left school, but they seemed to know less about life and its conditions as they would meet it at their homes. Having lived for a number of years in the midst of comfortable surroundings, they were not as much inclined as the Hampton students to go into the country districts of the South, where there was little of comfort, to take up work for our people, and they were more inclined to yield to the temptation to become hotel waiters and Pullman-car porters as their life-work.

During the time I was a student in Washington the city was crowded with coloured people, many of whom had recently come from the South. . . . Washington [was] an attractive place for members of the coloured race. Then, too, they knew that at all times they could have the protection of the law in the District of Columbia. The public schools in Washington for coloured people were better then than they were elsewhere. I took great interest in studying the life of our people there closely at that time. I found that while among them there was a large element of substantial, worthy citizens, there was also a superficiality about the life of a large class that greatly alarmed me. I saw young coloured men who were not earning more than four dollars a week spend two dollars or more for a buggy on Sunday to ride up and down Pennsylvania Avenue in, in order that they might try to convince the world that they were worth thousands. I saw other young men who received seventy-five or one hundred dollars per month from the Government, who were in debt at the end of every month. I saw men who but a few months previous were members of Congress, then without employment and in poverty. Among a large class there seemed to be a dependence upon the Government for every conceivable thing. The members of this class had little ambition to create a position for themselves, but wanted the Federal officials to create one for them. How many times I wished then, and have often wished since, that by some power of magic I might remove the great bulk of these people into the country districts and plant them upon the soil, upon the solid and never deceptive foundation of Mother Nature, where all nations and races that have ever succeeded have gotten their start,—a start that at first may be slow and toilsome, but one that nevertheless is real.

In Washington I saw girls whose mothers were earning their living by laundrying. These girls were taught by their mothers, in rather a crude way it is true, the industry of laundrying. Later, these girls entered the public schools and remained there perhaps six or eight years. When the public-school course was finally finished, they wanted more costly dresses, more costly hats and shoes. In a word, while their wants had been increased, their ability to supply their wants had not been increased in the same degree. On the other hand, their six or eight years of book education had weaned them away from the occupation of their mothers. The result of this was in too many cases that the girls went to the bad. I often thought how much wiser it would have been to give these girls the same amount of mental training—and I favour any kind of training, whether in the languages or mathematics, that gives strength and culture to the mind—but at the same time to give them the most thorough training in the latest and best methods of laundrying and other kindred occupations.

(Source: Booker T. Washington, *Up From Slavery,* New York: A. L. Burt Company, 1900, pp. 83-91.)

Testimony in Official Proceedings

Testimony given in official proceedings has been used extensively by historians in their work. Because testimony is often given under oath it is seen as being rather unimpeachable and less biased than other sources. But is it really? The following testimony was given by Conrad Carl to a Senate subcommittee investigating the relations between capital and labor.

A resident of New York City, Carl had been a tailor for over thirty years when he testified. From that vantage point, he personally witnessed a number of changes in his work. This document is interesting because both Carl and the Committee discuss the constraints he felt as he testified. Given what Carl himself says about possible reprisals by his employer, how truthful do you think his testimony was? Do you think the historical information (e.g., changes in tailoring) he mentions is more accurate than that concerning more contemporary working conditions? How accurate do you think Carl's testimony was in general? Are some aspects more likely to be accurate and representative than other aspects (speed of work versus savings)? What information would you want to have to verify his testimony? What information would you want to know about Carl himself? Do you think testimony in a Court or legislative body is better information than that obtained elsewhere? Do you think the things he mentions were typical of workers in the late nineteenth century? If this was the only document with which you had to work, what could you say about the impact of machinery on working conditions?

Testimony of Conrad Carl

Sen. Pugh: Please give us any information that you may have as to the relation existing between the employers and the employees in the tailoring business in this city, as to wages, as to treatment of the one by the other class, as to the feeling that exists between the employers and the employed generally, and all that you know in regard to the subject that we are authorized to inquire into?

A. During the time I have been here the tailoring business is altered in three different ways. Before we had sewing machines we worked piecework with our wives, and very often our children. We had no trouble then with our neighbors, nor with the landlord, because it was a very still business, very quiet; but in 1854 or 1855, and later, the sewing machine was invented and introduced, and it stitched very nicely, nicer than the tailor could do; and the bosses said: "We want you to use the sewing machine; you have to buy one." Many of the tailors had a few dollars in the bank, and they took the money and bought machines. Many others had no money, but must help themselves; so they brought their stitching, the coat or vest, to the other tailors who had sewing machines, and paid them a few cents for the stitching. Later, when the money was given out for the work, we found out that we could earn no more than we could without the machine; but the money for the machine was gone now, and we found that the machine was only for the profit of the bosses; that they got their work quicker, and it was done nicer. . . . The machine makes too much noise in the place, and the neighbors want to sleep, and we have to stop sewing earlier; so we have to work faster. We work now in excitement—in a hurry. It is hunting; it is not work at all; it is a hunt.

Q. You turn out two or three times as much work per day now as you did in prior times before the war?

A. Yes, sir; two or three times as much; and we have to do it, because the wages are two-thirds lower than they were five or ten years back. . . .

Sen. Blair: What proportion of them are women and what proportion men, according to your best judgment?

A. I guess there are many more women than men.

Q. The pay of the women is the same as the pay of the men for the same quantity of work, I suppose?

A. Yes; in cases where a manufacturer—that is, a middleman—gets work from the shop and brings it into his store and employs hands to make it, women get paid by the piece also. If the manufacturer gets $.25 for a piece, he pays for the machine work on that piece so many cents to the machine-worker, he pays so many cents to the presser, so many cents to the finisher, and so many to the button-sewer—so much to each one—and what remains is to pay his rent and to pay for the machinery.

Q. What is your knowledge as to the amount that workers of that class are able to save from their wages?

A. I don't know any one that does save except those manufacturers.

Q. As a class, then, the workers save nothing?

A. No.

Q. What sort of house-room do they have? . . .

A. They live in tenement houses four or five stories high, and have two or three rooms.

Q. What is the state of feeling between the employers and their employees in that business? How do you workingmen feel towards the people who employ you and pay you?

A. Well, I must say the workingmen are discouraged. If I speak with them they go back and don't like to speak much about the business and the pay. They fear that if they say how it is they will get sent out of the shop. They hate the bosses and the foremen more than the bosses, and that feeling is deep. . . .

Q. But can you explain why they hate the foremen, as you say they do, more than the bosses, when the bosses keep the foremen there and could discharge them and get better ones in their places if they desired?

A. Gentlemen, if I say all this here—if it is made public I come out of work.

Sen. Pugh: Then you are testifying here under the apprehension of punishment for what you have stated?

A. Well, I have no fear for anyone, you know, and if you think it is better that I say it, I do so.

Q. What is your feeling of restraint in testifying? What injury would you be subjected to for telling the truth? Would the workingmen in your business testify under a fear of being punished by their employers for telling the truth?

A. Yes, it is nothing but a fear. . . .

Sen. Blair: . . . This committee desires to obtain such information as you can give in regard to the condition of those engaged in your trade, and if there is any attempt to punish you for giving such information I think you can find protection from the country, or from some source. We cannot compel you to give the information, but we desire you to state, if you will, the names of some of these bosses and foremen, so that if they do not think proper to come here and speak for themselves the country will understand that you have told us the truth.

A. Now, sir, if I lose my work who can give me another work? I am an old man now, you know, and the young ones, they get the work and they say, "He is an old man; what can he do?" . . .

(Source: U.S. Congress, Senate Committee on Education and Labor, 1885, *Report of the Committee of the Senate Upon the Relations Between Labor and Capital,* Washington, D.C.: U.S. Government Printing Office, vol. 1, pp. 413–421.)

Diary

People's diaries and personal journals have long been used by historians to gain insight into the lives of their writers, often highly visible public figures. Increasingly, historians are finding and using such documents to help them reconstruct the daily lives of more ordinary people. What follows is an excerpt from the diary of George Washington Plunkitt. To be sure, Plunkitt was not an ordinary person; he was a district leader for Tammany Hall, a Democratic party political machine that dominated New York City government in the late nineteenth and early twentieth centuries. Tammany and other urban political machines were often criticized by contemporary government reformers because of corruption and inefficiency. While political machines were often both, they also performed positive functions. Plunkitt's diary provides insight into these functions. What does this document tell us about the Tammany political machine?

George Washington Plunkitt

The life of the Tammany district leader is strenuous. To his work is due the wonderful recuperative power of the organization.

One year it goes down in defeat and the prediction is made that it will never again raise its head. The district leader, undaunted by defeat, collects his scattered forces, organizes them as only Tammany knows how to organize, and in a little while the organization is as strong as ever.

No other politician in New York or elsewhere is exactly like the Tammany district leader or works as he does. As a rule, he has no business or occupation other than politics. He plays politics every day and night in the year, and his headquarters bears the inscription, "Never closed."

Everybody in the district knows him. Everybody knows where to find him, and nearly everybody goes to him for assistance of one sort or another, especially the poor of the tenements.

He is always obliging. He will go to the police courts to put in a good word for the "drunks and disorderlies" or pay their fines, if a good word is not effective. He will attend christenings, weddings, and funerals. He will feed the hungry and help bury the dead.

A philanthropist? Not at all. He is playing politics all the time.

Brought up in Tammany Hall, he has learned how to reach the hearts of the great mass of voters. He does not bother about reaching their heads. It is his belief that arguments and campaign literature have never gained votes.

He seeks direct contact with the people, does them good turns when he can, and relies on their not forgetting him on election day. His heart is always in his work, too, for his subsistence depends on its results.

. . .

This is a record of a day's work by Plunkitt:

2 a.m.: Aroused from sleep by the ringing of his door bell; went to the door and found a bartender, who asked him to go to the police station and bail out a saloon-keeper who had been arrested for violating the excise law. Furnished bail and returned to bed at three o'clock.

6 a.m.: Awakened by fire engines passing his house. Hastened to the scene of the fire, according to the custom of the Tammany district leaders, to give assistance to the fire sufferers, if needed. Met several of his election district captains who are always under orders to look out for fires, which are considered great vote-getters. Found several tenants who had been burned out, took them to a hotel, supplied them with clothes, fed them, and arranged temporary quarters for them until they could rent and furnish new apartments.

8:30 a.m.: Went to the police court to look after his constituents. Found six "drunks." Secured the discharge of four by a timely word with the judge, and paid the fines of two.

9 a.m.: Appeared in the Municipal District Court. Directed one of his district captains to act as counsel for a widow against whom dispossess proceedings had been instituted and obtained an extension of time. Paid the rent of a poor family about to be dispossessed and gave them a dollar for food.

11 a.m.: At home again. Found four men waiting for him. One had been discharged by the Metropolitan Railway Company for neglect of duty, and wanted the district leader to fix things. Another wanted

a job on the road. The third sought a place on the Subway and the fourth, a plumber, was looking for work with the Consolidated Gas Company. The district leader spent nearly three hours fixing things for the four men, and succeeded in each case.

3 p.m.: Attended the funeral of an Italian as far as the ferry. Hurried back to make his appearance at the funeral of a Hebrew constituent. Went conspicuously to the front both in the Catholic church and the synagogue, and later attended the Hebrew confirmation ceremonies in the synagogue.

7 p.m.: Went to district headquarters and presided over a meeting of election district captains. Each captain submitted a list of all the voters in his district, reported on their attitude toward Tammany, suggested who might be won over and how they could be won, told who were in need, and who were in trouble of any kind and the best way to reach them. District leader took notes and gave orders.

8 p.m.: Went to a church fair. Took chances on everything, bought ice-cream for the young girls and the children. Kissed the little ones, flattered their mothers and took their fathers out for something down at the corner.

9 p.m.: At the club-house again. Spent $10 on tickets for a church excursion and promised a subscription for a new church-bell. Bought tickets for a base-ball game to be played by two nines from his district. Listened to the complaints of a dozen push-cart peddlers who said they were persecuted by the police and assured them he would go to Police Headquarters in the morning and see about it.

10:30 p.m.: Attended a Hebrew wedding reception and dance. Had previously sent a handsome wedding present to the bride.

12 p.m.: In bed.

That is the actual record of one day in the life of Plunkitt. He does some of the same things every day, but his life is not so monotonous as to be wearisome.

Sometimes the work of a district leader is exciting, especially if he happens to have a rival who intends to make a contest for the leadership at the primaries. In that case, he is even more alert, tries to reach the fires before his rival, sends out runners to look for "drunks and disorderlies" at the police stations, and keeps a very close watch on the obituary columns of the newspapers. . . .

(Source: William Riordon, *Plunkitt of Tammany Hall,* New York: Knopf, 1948, pp. 121-127; nondiary commentary by Riordon.)

Oral History

W hile the following excerpt is not strictly a result of oral history—in the sense that someone interviewed and recorded a structured conversation with Sadie Frowne—it has many similar characteristics of oral history. As you read "The Story of a Sweatshop Girl," think about how historians might use this kind of primary source for understanding the working class. What were her hopes and desires? What was the quality of her life? What was her work experience; how much did she earn; was it sufficient for living comfortably? What was her diet like; other aspects of her life? How typical do you think her experience was? What are the potential strengths and weaknesses of this type of source? Do better sources exist for this type of information?

My mother was a tall, handsome, dark complexioned woman with red cheeks, large brown eyes and a great quantity of jet black, wavy hair. She was well educated, being able to talk in Russian, German, Polish and French, and even to read English print, tho[ugh], of course, she did not know what it meant. She kept a little grocer's shop in the little village where we lived at first. That was in Poland, somewhere on the frontier, and mother had charge of a gate between the countries, so that everybody who came through the gate had to show her a pass. She was much looked up to by the people, who used to come and ask her for advice. Her word was like law among them.

She had a wagon in which she used to drive around the country, selling her groceries, and sometimes she worked in the fields with my father.

The grocer's shop was only one story high, and had one window, with very small panes of glass. We had two rooms behind it, and were happy while my father lived, altho[ugh] we had to work very hard. By the time I was six years of age I was able to wash dishes and scrub floors, and by the time I was eight I attended to the shop while my mother was away driving her wagon or working in the fields with my father. She was strong and could work like a man.

When I was a little more than ten years of age my father died. He was a good man and a steady worker, and we never knew what it was to be hungry while he lived. After he died troubles began, for the rent of our shop was about $6 a month and then there were food and clothes to provide. We needed little, it is true, but even soup, black bread and onions we could not always get.

We struggled along till I was nearly thirteen years of age and quite handy at housework and shop keeping, so far as I could learn them there. But we fell behind in the rent and mother kept thinking more and more that we should have to leave Poland and go across the sea to America where we heard it was much easier to make money. Mother wrote to Aunt Fanny, who lived in New York, and told her how hard it was to live in Poland, and Aunt Fanny advised her to come and bring me. I was out at service at this time and mother thought she would leave me—as I had a good place—and come to this country alone, sending for me afterward. But Aunt Fanny would not hear of this. She said we should both come at once, and she went around among our relatives in New York and took up a subscription for our passage.

We came by steerage on a steamship in a very dark place that smelt dreadfully. There were hundreds of other people packed in with us, men, women and children, and almost all of them were sick. It took us twelve days to cross the sea, and we thought we should die, but at last the voyage was over, and we came up and saw the beautiful bay and the big woman with the spikes on her head and the lamp that is lighted at night in her hand . . . [Statue of Liberty].

Aunt Fanny and her husband met us at the gate of this country and were very good to us, and soon I had a place to live out (domestic servant), while my mother got work in a factory making white goods.

I was only a little over thirteen years of age and a greenhorn, so I received $9 a month and board and lodging, which I thought was doing well. Mother, who, as I have said, was very clever, made $9 a week on white goods, which means all sorts of underclothing, and is high class work.

But mother had a very gay disposition. She liked to go around and see everything, and friends took her about New York at night and she caught a bad cold and coughed and coughed. . . . [A]t last she died and I was left alone. I had saved money while out at service, but mother's sickness and funeral swept it all away and now I had to begin all over again.

Aunt Fanny had always been anxious for me to get an education, as I did not know how to read or write, and she thought that was wrong. Schools are different in Poland from what they are in this country, and I was always too busy to learn to read and write. So when mother died I thought I would try to learn a trade and then I could go to school at night and learn to speak the English language well.

So I went to work in Allen street (Manhattan) in what they call a sweatshop, making skirts by machine. I was new at the work and the foreman scolded me a great deal.

"Now, then," he would say, "this place is not for you to be looking around in. Attend to your work. That is what you have to do."

I did not know at first that you must not look around and talk, and I made many mistakes with the sewing, so that I was often called a "stupid animal." But I made $4 a week by working six days in the week. For there are two Sabbaths here—our own Sabbath, that comes on a Saturday, and the Christian Sabbath that comes on a Sunday. It is against our law to work on our own Sabbath, so we work on their Sabbath.

In Poland I and my father and mother used to go to the synagogue on the Sabbath, but here the women don't go to the synagogue much, tho[ugh] the men do. They are shut up working hard all the week long and when the Sabbath comes they like to sleep long in bed and afterward they must go out where they can breathe the air. The rabbis are strict here, but not so strict as in the old country.

I lived at this time with a girl named Ella, who worked in the same factory and made $5 a week. We had the room all to ourselves, paying $1.50 a week for it, and doing light housekeeping. It was in Allen street, and the window looked out of the back, which was good, because there was an elevated railroad in front, and in summer time a great deal of dust and dirt came in at the front windows. We were on the fourth story and could see all that was going on in the back rooms of the houses behind us, and early in the morning the sun used to come in our window.

We did our cooking on an oil stove, and lived well, as this list of our expenses for one week will show:

Ella and Sadie for Food (One Week).

Tea	$0.06
Cocoa	.10
Bread and rolls	.40
Canned vegetables	.20
Potatoes	.10
Milk	.21
Fruit	.20
Butter	.15
Meat	.60
Fish	.15
Laundry	.25
Total	$2.42
Add rent	1.50
Grand total	$3.92

Of course, we could have lived cheaper, but we are both fond of good things and felt that we could afford them.

We paid 18 cents for a half pound of tea so as to get it good, and it lasted us three weeks, because we had cocoa for breakfast. We paid 5 cents for six rolls and 5 cents a loaf for bread, which was the best quality. Oatmeal cost us 10 cents for three and one-half pounds, and we often had it in the morning, or Indian meal porridge in the place of it, costing about the same. Half a dozen eggs cost about 13 cents on an average, and we could get all the meat we wanted for a good hearty meal for 20 cents—two pounds of chops, or a steak, or a bit of veal, or a neck of lamb—something like that. Fish included butter fish, porgies, codfish and smelts, averaging about 8 cents a pound. . . .

It cost me $2 a week to live, and I had a dollar a week to spend on clothing and pleasure, and saved the other dollar. I went to night school, but it was hard work learning at first as I did not know much English.

Two years ago I came to this place, Brownsville, where so many of my people are, and where I have friends. I got work in a factory making underskirts—all sorts of cheap underskirts, like cotton and calico for the summer and woolen for the winter, but never the silk, satin or velvet underskirts. I earned $4.50 a week and lived on $2 a week, the same as before. . . .

It isn't piecework in our factory, but one is paid by the amount of work done just the same. So it is like piecework. All the hands get different amounts, some as low as $3.50 and some of the men as high as $16 a week. The factory is in the third story of a brick building. It is in a room twenty feet long and fourteen broad. There are fourteen machines in it. I and the daughter of the people with whom I live work two of these machines. The other operators are all men, some young and some old.

At first a few of the young men were rude. When they passed me they would touch my hair and talk about my eyes and my red cheeks, and make jokes. I cried and said that if they did not stop I would leave the place. The boss said that that should not be, that no one must annoy me. Some of the other men stood up for me, too, especially Henry, who said two or three times that he wanted to fight. Now the men all treated me very nicely. It was just that some of them did not know better, not being educated.

. . .

I get up at half-past five o'clock every morning and make myself a cup of coffee on the oil stove. I eat a bit of bread and perhaps some fruit and then go to work. Often I get there soon after six o'clock so as to be in good time, tho[ugh] the factory does not open till seven. I have heard that there is a sort of clock that calls you at the very time you want to get up, but I can't believe that because I don't see how the clock would know.

At seven o'clock we all sit down to our machines and the boss brings to each one the pile of work that he or she is to finish during the day, what they call in English their "stint." This pile is put down beside the machine and as soon as a skirt is done it is laid on the other side of the machine. Sometimes the work is not all finished by six o'clock and then the one who is behind must work overtime. Sometimes one is finished ahead of time and gets away at four or five o'clock, but generally we are not done till six o'clock.

The machines go like mad all day, because the faster you work the more money you get. Sometimes in my haste I get my finger caught and the needle goes right through it. It goes so quick, tho[ugh], that it does not hurt much. I bind the finger up with a piece of cotton and go on working. We all have accidents like that. Where the needle goes through the nail it makes a sore finger, or where it splinters a bone it does much harm. Sometimes a finger has to come off. Generally, tho[ugh], one can be cured by a salve.

All the time we are working the boss walks about examining the finished garments and making us do them over again if they are not just right. So we have to be careful as well as swift. But I am getting so good at the work that within a year I will be making $7 a week, and then I can save at least $3.50 a week. I have over $200 saved now.

The machines are all run by foot power, and at the end of the day one feels so weak that there is a great temptation to lie right down and sleep. But you must go out and get air, and have some pleasure. So instead of lying down I go out, generally with Henry. Sometimes we go to Coney Island, where there are good dancing places, and sometimes we go to Ulmer Park to picnics. I am very fond of dancing, and, in fact, all sorts of pleasure. I go to the theater quite often, and like those plays that make you cry a great deal. "The Two Orphans" is good. Last time I saw it I cried all night because of the hard times that the children had in the play. I am going to see it again when it comes here.

For the last two winters I have been going to night school at Public School 84 on Glenmore avenue. I have learned reading, writing and arithmetic. I can read quite well in English now and I look at the newspapers every day. I read English books, too, sometimes. The last one that I read was "A Mad Marriage," by Charlotte Braeme. She's a grand writer and makes things just like real to you. You feel as if you were the poor girl yourself going to get married to a rich duke.

I am going back to night school again this winter. Plenty of my friends go there. Some of the women in my class are more than forty years of age. Like me, they did not have a chance to learn anything in the old country. It is good to have an education; it makes you feel higher. Ignorant people are all low. People say now that I am clever and fine in conversation.

We have just finished a strike in our business. It spread all over and the United Brotherhood of Garment Workers was in it. That takes in the cloakmakers, coatmakers, and all the others. We struck for shorter hours, and after being out four weeks won the fight. We only have to work nine and a half hours a day and we get the same pay as before. So the union does good after all in spite of what some people say against it—that it just takes our money and does nothing.

I pay 25 cents a month to the union, but I do not begrudge that because it is for our benefit. The next strike is going to be for a raise of wages, which we all ought to have. But tho[ugh] I belong to the Union I am not a Socialist or an Anarchist. I don't know exactly what those things mean. There is a little expense for charity, too. If any worker is injured or sick we all give money to help.

Some of the women blame me very much because I spend so much money on clothes. They say that instead of a dollar a week I ought not to spend more than twenty-five cents a week on clothes, and that I should save the rest. But a girl must have clothes if she is to go into high society at Ulmer Park or Coney Island or the theater. Those who blame me are the old country people who have old-fashioned notions, but the people who have been here a long time know better. A girl who does not dress well is stuck in a corner, even if she is pretty, and Aunt Fanny says that I do just right to put on plenty of style.

I have many friends and we often have jolly parties. Many of the young men look to talk to me, but I don't go out with any except Henry.

Lately he has been urging me more and more to get married— but I think I'll wait.

(Source: "The Story of a Sweatshop Girl," *The Independent*, 54, no. 2808, September 25, 1902: 2279–2282.)

Fiction

The use of fiction as a historical source is a very slippery matter. Writers of fiction are artists engaged in producing an artform. They can give full vent to their imaginations; they are quite free to create their own worlds, unfettered (as are historians) by any canons of objectivity or method. You might therefore ask, "why bother"; "why not leave fiction to literature courses or pleasure reading?"

Historians interested in ideas, intellectuals, and culture (both high and popular) analyze fiction to discover common themes, the breadth of impact of particular ideas, and reflections of the popular mind. In these ways, fiction has much to tell the historian about times past. In addition, the fiction writer will occasionally produce a book that attempts to make a social statement as well as tell a story. Sometimes these books make a tremendous impact on their contemporaries.

Such is the case with Upton Sinclair's *The Jungle*, published in 1906. Sinclair was a socialist who wanted to call attention to the miserable lives of new immigrants in industrial America. What happened instead was that the public read his descriptions of the meat packing industry and were enraged: filthy conditions, putrid meat, careless food preparation sickened Americans who consumed these products. The controversy Sinclair contributed to helped promote the passage of new federal legislation regulating the food industry. As you read the following excerpt, ask how this result might have occurred.

Promptly at seven the next morning Jurgis reported for work. He came to the door that had been pointed out to him, and there he waited for nearly two hours. The boss had meant for him to enter, but had not said this, and so it was only when on his way out to hire another man that he came upon Jurgis. He gave him a good cursing, but as Jurgis did not understand a word of it he did not object. He followed the boss, who showed him where to put his street clothes, and waited while he donned the working clothes he had bought in a second-hand shop and brought with him in a bundle; then he led him to the "killing-beds." The work which Jurgis was to do here was very simple, and it took him but a few minutes to learn it. He was provided with a stiff besom, such as is used by street sweepers, and it was his place to follow down the line the man who drew out the smoking entrails from the carcass of the steer; this mass was to be swept into a trap, which was then closed, so that no one might slip into it. As Jurgis came in, the first cattle of the morning were just making their appearance; and so, with scarcely time to look about him, and none to speak to any one, he fell to work. It was a sweltering day in July, and the place ran with steaming hot blood—one waded in it on the floor. The stench was almost overpowering, but to Jurgis it was nothing. His whole soul was dancing with joy—he was at work at last! He was at work and earning money! All day long he was figuring to himself. He was paid the fabulous sum of seventeen and a half cents an hour; and as it proved a rush day and he worked until nearly seven o'clock in the evening, he went home to the family with the tidings that he had earned more than a dollar and a half in a single day!

. . .

That was Thursday; and all the rest of the week the killing-gang at Brown's worked at full pressure, and Jurgis cleared a dollar seventy-five every day. That was at the rate of ten and one-half dollars a week, or forty-five a month; Jurgis was not able to figure, except it was a very simple sum, but Ona was like lightning at such things, and she worked out the problem for the family.

. . .

This was the first time in his life that he had ever really worked, it seemed to Jurgis; it was the first time that he had ever had anything to do which took all he had in him. Jurgis had stood with the rest up in the gallery and watched the men on the killing-beds, marvelling at their speed and power as if they had been wonderful machines; it somehow never occurred to one to think of the flesh-and-blood side of it—that is, not until he actually got down into the pit and took off his coat. Then he saw things in a different light, he got at the inside of them. The pace they set here, it was one that called for every faculty of a man—from the instant the first steer fell till the sounding of the noon whistle, and again from half-past twelve till heaven only knew what hour in the late afternoon or evening, there was never one instant's rest for a man, for his hand or his eye or his brain. Jurgis saw how they managed it; there were portions of the work which determined the pace of the rest, and for these they had picked men whom they paid high wages, and whom they changed frequently. You might easily pick out these pace-makers, for they worked under the eye of the bosses, and they worked like men possessed. This was called "speeding up the gang," and if any man could not keep up with the pace, there were hundreds outside begging to try.

Yet Jurgis did not mind it; he rather enjoyed it. It saved him the necessity of flinging his arms about and fidgeting as he did in most work. He would laugh to himself as he ran down the line, darting a glance now and then at the man ahead of him. It was not the pleasantest work one could think of, but it was necessary work; and what more had a man the right to ask than a chance to do something useful, and to get good pay for doing it?

So Jurgis thought, and so he spoke, in his bold, free way; very much to his surprise, he found that it had a tendency to get him into trouble. For most of the men here took a fearfully different view of the thing. He was quite dismayed when he first began to find it out—that most of the men *hated* their work. It seemed strange, it was even terrible, when you came to find out the universality of the sentiment; but it was certainly the fact—they hated their work. They hated the bosses and they hated the owners; they hated the whole place, the whole neighborhood—even the whole city, with an all-inclusive hatred, bitter and fierce. Women and little children would fall to cursing about it; it was rotten, rotten as hell—everything was rotten. When Jurgis would ask them what they meant, they would begin to get suspicious, and content themselves with saying, "Never mind, you stay here and see for yourself."

One of the first problems that Jurgis ran upon was that of the unions. He had had no experience with unions, and he had to have it explained to him that the men were banded together for the purpose of fighting for their rights. Jurgis asked them what they meant by their rights, a question in which he was quite sincere, for he had not any idea of any rights that he had, except the right to hunt for a job, and do as he was told when he got it. Generally, however, this harmless question would only make his fellow-workingmen lose their tempers and call him a fool. There was a delegate of the butcher-helpers' union who came to see Jurgis to enroll him; and when Jurgis found that this meant that he would have to part with some of his money, he froze up directly, and the delegate, who was an Irishman and only knew a few words of Lithuanian, lost his temper and began to threaten him. In the end Jurgis got into a fine rage, and made it sufficiently plain that it would take more than one Irishman to scare him into a union. Little by little he gathered that the main thing the men wanted was to put a stop to the habit of "speeding-up"; they were trying their best to force a lessening of the pace, for there were some, they said, who could not keep up with it, whom it was killing. But Jurgis had no sympathy with such ideas as this—he could do the work himself, and so could the rest of them, he declared, if they were good for anything. If they couldn't do it, let them go somewhere else. Jurgis had not studied the books, and he would not have known how to pronounce "laissez-faire"; but he had been round the world enough to know that a man has to shift for himself in it, and that if he gets the worst of it, there is nobody to listen to him holler.

· · ·

Now Antanas Rudkus was the meekest man that God ever put on earth; and so Jurgis found it a striking confirmation of what the men all said, that his father had been at work only two days before he came home as bitter as any of them, and cursing Durham's with all the power of his soul. For they had set him to cleaning out the traps; and the family sat round and listened in wonder while he told them what that meant. It seemed that he was working in the room where the men prepared the beef for canning, and the beef had lain in vats full of chemicals, and men with great forks speared it out and dumped it into trucks, to be taken to the cooking-room. When they had speared out all they could reach, they emptied the vat on the floor, and then with shovels scraped up the balance and dumped it into the truck. This floor was filthy, yet they set Antanas with his mop slopping the "pickle" into a hole that connected with a sink, where it was caught and used over again forever; and if that were not enough, there was a trap in the pipe, where all the scraps of meat and odds and ends of refuse were caught, and every few days it was the old man's task to clean these out, and shovel their contents into one of the trucks with the rest of the meat!

. . .

All of these were sinister incidents; but they were trifles compared to what Jurgis saw with his own eyes before long. One curious thing he had noticed, the very first day, in his profession of shoveller of guts; which was the sharp trick of the floor-bosses whenever there chanced to come a "slunk" calf. Any man who knows anything about butchering knows that the flesh of a cow that is about to calve, or has just calved, is not fit for food. A good many of these came every day to the packing-houses—and, of course, if they had chosen, it would have been an easy matter for the packers to keep them till they were fit for food. But for the saving of time and fodder, it was the law that cows of that sort came along with the others, and whoever noticed it would tell the boss, and the boss would start up a conversation with the government inspector, and the two would stroll away. So in a trice the carcass of the cow would be cleaned out, and the entrails would have vanished; it was Jurgis's task to slide them into the trap, calves and all, and on the floor below they took out these "slunk" calves, and butchered them for meat, and used even the skins of them.

One day a man slipped and hurt his leg; and that afternoon, when the last of the cattle had been disposed of, and the men were leaving, Jurgis was ordered to remain and do some special work which this injured man had usually done. It was late, almost dark, and the government inspectors had all gone, and there were only a dozen or two of men on the floor. That day they had killed about four thousand cattle, and these cattle had come in freight trains from far states, and some of them had got hurt. There were some with broken legs, and some with gored sides; there were some that had died, from what cause no one could say; and they were all to be disposed of, here in darkness and silence. "Downers," the men called them; and the packing-house had a special elevator upon which they were raised to the killing-beds, where the gang proceeded to handle them, with an air of businesslike nonchalance which said plainer than any words that it was a matter of everyday routine. It took a couple of hours to get them out of the way, and in the end Jurgis saw them go into the chilling-rooms with the rest of the meat, being carefully scattered here and there so that they could not be identified. When he came home that night he was in a very somber mood, having begun to see at last how those might be right who had laughed at him for his faith in America.

. . .

And shortly afterward one of these, a physician, made the discovery that the carcasses of steers which had been condemned as tubercular by the government inspectors, and which therefore contained ptomaines, which are deadly poisons, were left upon an open platform and carted away to be sold in the city; and so he insisted that these carcasses be treated with an injection of kerosene—and was ordered to resign the same week! So indignant were the packers that they went farther, and compelled the mayor to abolish the whole bureau of inspection; so that since then there has not been even a pretense of any interference with the graft. There was said to be two thousand dollars a week hush-money from the tubercular steers alone; and as much again from the hobs which had died of cholera on the trains, and which you might see any day being loaded into box-cars and hauled away to a place called Globe, in Indiana, where they made a fancy grade of lard.

Jurgis heard of these things little by little, in the gossip of those who were obliged to perpetrate them. It seemed as if every time you met a person from a new department, you heard of new swindles and new crimes. There was, for instance, a Lithuanian who was a cattle-butcher for the plant where Marija had worked, which killed meat for canning only; and to hear this man describe the animals which came to his place would have been worth while for a Dante or a Zola. It seemed that they must have agencies all over the country, to hunt out old and crippled and diseased cattle to be canned. There were cattle which had been fed on "whiskey-malt," the refuse of the breweries, and had become what the men called "steerly"—which means covered with boils. It was a nasty job killing these, for when you plunged your knife into them they would bust and splash foul-smelling stuff into your face; and when a man's sleeves were smeared with blood, and his hands steeped in it, how was he ever to wipe his face, or to clear his eyes so that he could see? It was stuff such as this that made the "embalmed beef" that had killed several times as many United States soldiers as all the bullets of the Spaniards; only the army beef, besides, was not fresh canned, it was old stuff that had been lying for years in the cellars.

(Source: Upton Sinclair, *The Jungle*, New York: Doubleday, 1906, pp. 49–50; 54–55; 66–68; 71–74; 113–114.)

Nongovernmental Reports

In the excerpt that follows, John Spargo, an advocate of child labor reform, describes young children at work in the mines of West Virginia and Pennsylvania. As you read, keep in mind the following cautions about this type of source.

Reports of all kinds, whether produced by government agencies or by private organizations and individuals have long been a staple source for historians. But just because contemporaries were most often trying to produce objective reports, the results were not always accurate or objective. Producing reports is often done with incomplete information. Collection of statistical data, for example, is a relatively recent phenomenon and, in any event, numbers may be distorted in many ways. On-site observation has numerous pitfalls as well, including limited observations, observer bias, and so forth. In addition, people in the past held values often different from our own; they therefore "saw" different things than we might have had we been present.

The Bitter Cry of the Children

According to the census of 1900, there were 25,000 boys under sixteen years of age employed in and around the mines and quarries of the United States. In the state of Pennsylvania alone,— the state which enslaves more children than any other,—there are thousands of little "breaker boys" employed, many of them not more than nine or ten years old. The law forbids the employment of children under fourteen, and the records of the mines generally show that the law is "obeyed." Yet in May, 1905, an investigation by the National Child Labor Committee showed that in one small

borough of 7000 population . . . over 150 boys [were] illegally
employed in one section of boy labor. . . .

Work in the coal breakers is exceedingly hard and dangerous.
Crouched over the chutes, the boys sit hour after hour, picking out
the pieces of slate and other refuse from the coal as it rushes past
to the washers. From the cramped position they have to assume,
most of them become more or less deformed and bent-backed like
old men. When a boy has been working for some time and begins
to get round-shouldered, his fellows say that "He's got his boy to
carry round whenever he goes." The coal is hard, and accidents to
the hands, such as cut, broken, or crushed fingers are common
among the boys. Sometimes there is a worse accident: a terrified
shriek is heard, and a boy is mangled and torn in the machinery, or
disappears in the chute to be picked out later smothered and dead.
Clouds of dust fill the breakers and are inhaled by the boys, laying
the foundations for asthma and miners' consumption.

I once stood in a breaker for half an hour and tried to do the
work a twelve-year-old boy was doing day after day, for ten hours
at a stretch, for sixty cents a day. The gloom of the breaker appalled
me. Outside the sun shone brightly, the air was pellucid, and the
birds sang in chorus with the trees and the rivers. Within the
breaker there was blackness, clouds of deadly dust enfolded
everything, the harsh, grinding roar of the machinery and the
ceaseless rushing of coal through the chutes filled the ears. I tried
to pick out the pieces of slate from the hurrying stream of coal,
often missing them; my hands were bruised and cut in a few
minutes; I was covered from head to foot with coal dust, and for
many hours afterwards I was expectorating some of the small
particles of anthracite I had swallowed.

I could not do that work and live, but there were boys of ten and
twelve years of age doing it for fifty and sixty cents a day. Some of
them had never been inside of a school; few of them could read a
child's primer. True, some of them attended the night schools, but
after working ten hours in the breaker the educational results from
attending school were practically *nil.* "We goes fer a good time, an'
we keeps de guys wots dere hoppin' all de time," said little Owen
Jones, whose work I have been trying to do. . . . It was hard to
realize amid the danger and din and blackness of that Pennsylvania
breaker that such a thing as belief in a great All-good God existed.

From the breakers the boys graduate to the mine depths, where
they become door tenders, switch boys, or mule-drivers. Here, far
below the surface, work is still more dangerous. At fourteen or
fifteen the boys assume the same risks as the men, and are
surrounded by the same perils. Nor is it in Pennsylvania only that
these conditions exist. In the bituminous mines of West Virginia,

boys of nine or ten are frequently employed. I met one little fellow ten years old in Mt. Carbon, W. Va., last year, who was employed as a "trap boy." Think of what it means to be a trap boy at ten years of age. It means to sit alone in a dark mine passage hour after hour, with no human soul near; to see no living creature except the mules as they pass with their loads, or a rat or two seeking to share one's meal; to stand in water or mud that covers the ankles, chilled to the marrow by the cold draughts that rush in when you open the trap door for the mules to pass through; to work for fourteen hours—waiting—opening and shutting a door—then waiting again—for sixty cents; to reach the surface when all is wrapped in the mantle of night, and to fall to the earth exhausted and have to be carried away to the nearest "shack" to be revived before it is possible to walk to the farther shack called "home."

Boys twelve years of age may be *legally* employed in the mines of West Virginia, by day or by night, and for as many hours as the employers care to make them toil or their bodies will stand the strain. Where the disregard of child life is such that this may be done openly and with legal sanction, it is easy to believe what miners have again and again told me—that there are hundreds of little boys of nine and ten years of age employed in the coal-mines [sic] of this state.

(Source: John Spargo, *The Bitter Cry of the Children,* New York: Macmillan, 1906, pp. 163–167.)

Propaganda

A ccording to *Webster's Ninth New Collegiate Dictionary,* propaganda is defined as "the spreading of ideas, information, or rumor for the purpose of helping or injuring an institution, a cause, or a person"; and as "ideas, facts, or allegations spread deliberately to further one's cause or to damage an opposing cause." The following item was produced by the Committee on Public Information, a U.S. government agency during World War I. The committee was charged with swaying public opinion to support our involvement in the war. As you read this document, note the use of certain images (e.g., "German soldiers were drunkards," "they defile a house," "they are savage and know no rules"). What do you suppose the effect of hundreds of similar stories might be on public opinion? What other sources might you want to draw upon to discover the effect of such propaganda on American public opinion?

Why America Fights Germany

Now let us picture what a sudden invasion of the United States by these Germans would mean; sudden, because their settled way is always to attack suddenly.

First, they set themselves to capture New York City. While their fleet blockades the harbor and shells the city and the forts from far at sea, their troops land somewhere near and advance toward the city in order to cut its rail communications, starve it into surrender, and then plunder it.

One body of from 50,000 to 100,000 men lands, let us suppose, at Barnegat Bay, New Jersey, and advances without meeting resistance, for the brave but small American army is scattered elsewhere. They pass through Lakewood, a station on the Central Railroad of New Jersey. They first demand wine for the officers and beer for the men. Angered to find an American town does not contain large quantities of either, they pillage and burn the post office and most of the hotels and stores. They then demand $1,000,000 from the residents. One feeble old woman tries to conceal $20 which she has been hoarding in her desk drawer; she is taken out and hanged (to save a cartridge). Some of the teachers in two district schools meet a fate which makes them envy her. The Catholic priest and Methodist minister are thrown into a pig-sty, while the German soldiers look on and laugh. Some of the officers quarter themselves in a handsome house on the edge of town, insult the ladies of the family, and destroy and defile the contents of the house.

By this time some of the soldiers have managed to get drunk; one of them discharges his gun accidentally, the cry goes up that the residents are firing on the troops, and then hell breaks loose. Robbery, murder, and outrage run riot. Fifty leading citizens are lined up against the First National Bank Building, and shot. Most of the town and the beautiful pinewoods are burned, and then the troops move on to treat New Brunswick in the same way—if they get there.

This is not just a snappy story. It is not fancy. The general plan of campaign against America has been announced repeatedly by German military men. *And every horrible detail is just what the German troops have done in Belgium and France.*

(Source: J. S. P. Tatlock, *Why America Fights Germany,* War Information Series No. 15, Cantonment Edition, U.S. Committee on Public Information, March 1918, pp. 9-10.)

Personal Correspondence

O f all primary sources, personal letters may be the most perverse. Why perverse? On one hand, they may be documents closest in time and place to an event or to ordinary people's lives. Before the widespread and cheap use of telecommunications, most personal long-distance interaction occurred by letter. Up to current times, then, millions of letters documented people's lives. A level of intimacy and thoughtfulness often attached to letter writing as well—at least as compared to phone conversations.

On the other hand, letters are written for many purposes other than exchanging pleasantries and family or business information. The most obvious case might be a letter designed for public consumption. The second letter that follows is of this type. These may be self-serving, misleading, or simply designed to float a trial balloon. Others are written to convey positions on current public issues; to convey personal views and feelings out of public discourse. The first letter below is of this type.

Personal Letter,
William Allen White to Judge J. A. Burnette,
Topeka, Kan., March 7, 1914

My Dear Judge:

Your letter was frank, and I liked it. I had a lot rather have a letter like that than a pollyfoxing letter, because your letter was all man, and while it gave me a bad morning, I am glad it came, and I think more of you for writing it than if you had ducked or sidestepped. The reason why you gave me a bad morning is that I got a look at myself through friendly eyes, and yet eyes that I know must be essentially kind toward me. I have had an idea that I was treating Bristow and Capper with the utmost fairness and consideration. I had no sort of an idea that I was abusing them. I do not remember that I have ever called Bristow a traitor, and I do not remember that I have ever called him a coward. I do think he did a dishonest thing to become a Republican merely to secure the traditional party vote. I think Capper is a little rabbity, but that is his nature and not the result of any particular combination of circumstances. He has caution developed where I have not and probably it would be better for me if I did have.

I have tried to make my position clear in this situation—that it is not for anybody's election, either to the Senate or as governor that I am striving. Personally, I have a high opinion of all the men running for governor, though I think Hodges [incumbent Democratic governor] has disappointed me by his petty partisan view of things, and yet I believe that even Hodges is honest and that Capper and Bristow and Allen and Murdock are square men. It is not a question of men with me. It is not even a question of the success or election of these men to any office. . . . If one believes that it is most important to elect a thoroughly competent, entirely honest, and unusually wise man United States senator from Kansas this year, there can be no question but that my course is wrong and that your course is right.

I do not believe, however, that the most important thing in politics right now is to elect anyone in particular. The most important thing I see in politics right now is to establish in this nation a party—even a minority party—having a common belief in political, economic and social advancement. A party that shall believe the same thing in Kansas, Oregon, Florida or Maine. There is no such party now. Under the old parties, there can be no such party. For they are factional and sectional. It is not a question of bad men or good men. There are just as many Progressives who mistreat their wives and tap tills as there are Republicans or Democrats. . . .

I have been fighting in a factional party for ten years, and so long as there is a . . . hope of organizing a non-factional, non-sectional party, as the Republican party was before it faced these new issues, I am going to make the fight for that party the chief consideration of my political activity. With me, it is not important that Bristow should be elected senator nor Murdock nor anyone else. Call it partisanship if you care to, call it party prejudice or party pride if you care to (and there is justice in the charge), but the fact remains that as I see the right I must follow it without compromise and without variableness or shadow of turning.

The end is, however, reasonably certain. Either this course on the part of the progressives all over the country will result in putting life into the progressive party and making it a genuine vital force among the parties, or it will repeat defeat for the Republican party until the reactionaries in that party will grow discouraged and quit it, when it will be a progressive party. But one thing is sure. Real progress in American politics will never come with the party divisions as they are. With each of the old parties half free and half controlled by reactionaries, there is too much lost motion. By the time the advocates of a proposition have won a primary, have nominated candidates and have stated the proposition in a party platform, they are worn out. Then, in the legislature or Congress they have to meet a lot of men who are of their own party who disbelieve in the proposition, and there the fight begins anew. As a result, the desired law when it finally comes often is a compromise. As a result, America is behind the civilized world in social and industrial legislation. Our political forms are more reactionary and less responsive to public opinion than they are in many a monarchy, and with all our boast of being the land of the free, we are behind civilization in too many things. It will be so just as long as the party system is what it is today, and to change that system, to smash it, many men will have to be sacrificed. I believe Kansas, for instance, is progressive. If Bristow had run as a Progressive, he would have had with him all the Progressives and all of the progressive Republicans, for Curtis [Charles Curtis, Bristow's opponent in the Republican primary] would have had the Republican nomination and the Republican party in Kansas would have been negligible. I told Bristow by letter, by wire and by word of mouth that Murdock was going to run, if Bristow did not run, and that I would support Murdock and not Bristow. So there was no deception. He knew just exactly where he was going. But he said to me: "Will, there are fifty thousand Republican voters who will vote for me on the Republican ticket, who will vote for Curtis, or for anyone else, and we need those votes to win." That I admit, if winning is the only thing you want. But I said: "In getting these fifty thousand voters who can't think, you will lose fifty thousand who do think—so there you are." He answered: "I'll not lose 'em." It is evident now that he will lose them.

But the whole difference between us hinges on these "fifty thousand voters who will vote for anyone on the Republican ticket." That is the drag on progress. They will sustain a reactionary in his .stand; they will sustain a progressive in his stand. But they will not sustain a progressive in his stand against party organization. They are the people in each party, who keep both parties half free and half conservative. This undigested, meaningless vote, must be broken up; must be made to think; must be made to take a stand on its own judgment. For when a progressive Republican finds that it is either his country or his party, these men who are governed "by habit, tradition and inheritance" may stand by the party. They are the slow boats that break the speed of the fleet. And my theme in glory is to blast the rock. If they stay in the Republican party, they must be jolted into knowing what they are there for, if the Progressives go back. And today these fifty thousand unthinking voters do not know anything about the issues.

The fifty thousand Kansas Progressives do know about the issues. Every vote there will back a man up in going the distance. Every Progressive voter knows why he is a Progressive. The Progressives appeal to the independent voter and will get a lot of them in Kansas—and a few Democrats; not as many as the fellows think, but a few. They will be the second party, and it is not impossible that they may land a few prizes. But that is unimportant, considering matters as I consider them, and as all the Progressive leaders I know consider things. We don't care what happens next autumn. We don't care what happens two years from now. We don't even care whether we finally get into the St. John [former governor of Kansas and for many years the regular presidential candidate of the Prohibition party] class, for our work will be accomplished. Others shall reap where we have sown, which is all right. We don't care to reap, but we do care that there shall be a harvest. We are now chiefly interested in planting the seed.

I have said all along—if you have read the Gazette as a penance for your sins, you may remember—that the Progressive party is no place for the fellows who want jobs.

The Progressives should enlist those who are willing to take long marches with hard bivouacs, and in the end only leave their unidentified political bones to mark the forward trail. We may become a great party. It is more than likely, but the problems which we have set forth will not be solved until either our party or some other party (and whatever comes it will not be the Democratic party, for Democracy is made irrevocably reactionary by the Negro question in the South)—until our party or some other party entirely reconstructed, entirely free of the unthinking votes and the reactionary faction, rises in the country, wholly consecrated to our ideas. I am fairly intimate with the Progressive leaders in this state and this nation. I talk with the Kansas leaders over the phone every day or two. I hear from the national leaders frequently. And I know they are not fooling me. I know that I share the common feelings as to our party, its aims and its destiny.

Open letter from William Allen White to Herbert B. Swope, New York *World,* September 17, 1921

An organizer of the Ku-Klux Klan was in Emporia the other day, and the men whom he invited to join his band at ten dollars per join turned him down. Under the leadership of Dr. J. B. Brickell and following their own judgment after hearing his story, the Emporians told him that they had no time for him. The proposition seems to be:

> Anti foreigners
> Anti Catholics
> Anti Negroes.

There are, of course, bad foreigners and good ones, good
Catholics and bad ones, and all kinds of Negroes. To make a case
against a birthplace, a religion, or a race is wickedly un-American
and cowardly. The whole trouble with the Ku-Klux Klan is that it is
based upon such deep foolishness that it is bound to be a menace
to good government in any community. Any man fool enough to be
Imperial Wizard would have power without responsibility and both
without any sense. That is social dynamite.

American institutions, our courts, our legislators, our executive
officers are strong enough to keep the peace and promote justice
and good will in the community. If they are not, then the thing to do
is to change these institutions and do it quickly, but always legally.
For a self-constituted body of moral idiots, who would substitute
the findings of the Ku-Klux Klan for the process of law to try to
better conditions, would be a most un-American outrage which
every good citizen should resent.

It is to the everlasting credit of Emporia that the organizer found
no suckers with $10 each to squander here. Whatever Emporia may
be otherwise, it believes in law and order, and absolute freedom
under the constitution for every man, no matter what birth or creed
or race, to speak and meet and talk and act as a free law-abiding
citizen. The picayunish cowardice of a man who would substitute
Klan rule and mob law for what our American fathers have died to
establish and maintain should prove what a cheap screw outfit the
Klan is.

(Source: Walter Johnson, *Selected Letters of William Allen White, 1899-1943*, New York:
Henry Holt, 1947, pp. 151-154; 220-221. Reprinted with permission of Barbara White
Walker.)

Journalism

As we know, journalism includes many different kinds of publications—newspapers, political magazines, fashion magazines, *Sports
Illustrated, TV Guide,* and even *The National Enquirer.* Because journalism takes so many forms and has many purposes, it collectively contains
a wealth of information and exerts broad influence. Historians have used
journalism—especially newspapers and political magazines and pamphlets—extensively over the years.

Examples of two types of journalism follow. Each must be
approached with caution, however; not because these two are more

suspect than others, but because all such sources must be so approached. Can you detect bias in either article? What about the authors' points of view? On what evidence, if any, does either author draw? What is the intent of each article; only to inform, to speculate, to promote action of some kind? Does the use of language by either author suggest their intentions? Who is the intended audience?

Tweed Days in St. Louis

The corruption of St. Louis came from the top. The best citizens— the merchants and big financiers—used to rule the town, and they ruled it well. They set out to outstrip Chicago. The commercial and industrial war between these two cities was at one time a picturesque and dramatic spectacle such as is witnessed only in our country. Businessmen were not mere merchants and the politicians were not mere grafters; the two kinds of citizens got together and wielded the power of banks, railroads, factories, the prestige of the city, and the spirit of its citizens to gain business and population. It was a close race. . . . It pressed Chicago hard. . . . But a change occurred. Public spirit became private spirit, public enterprise became private greed.

Along about 1890, public franchises and privileges were sought not only for legitimate profit and common convenience, but for loot. Taking but slight and always selfish interest in the public councils, the big men misused politics. The riff-raff, catching the smell of corruption, rushed into the Municipal Assembly, drove out the remaining respectable men, and sold the city—its streets, its wharves, its markets, and all that it had—to the now greedy business men and bribers. In other words, when the leading men began to devour their own city, the herd rushed into the trough and fed also. . . .

These creatures were well organized. They had a "combine" and legislative institution, which a grand jury has described as follows: "Our investigation, covering more or less fully a period of ten years, shows that, with few exceptions, no ordinance has been passed wherein valuable privileges or franchises are granted until those interested have paid the legislators the money demanded for action in the particular case. Combines in both branches of the Municipal Assembly are formed by members sufficient in number to control legislation. . . . So long has this practice existed, that such members have come to regard the receipt of money for action on pending measures as a legitimate perquisite of a legislator."

One legislator consulted a lawyer with the intention of suing a firm to recover an unpaid balance on a fee for the grant of a switch way. Such difficulties rarely occurred, however. In order to insure a regular and indisputable revenue, the combine of each house drew up a schedule of bribery prices for all possible sorts of grants, just such a list as a commercial traveler takes out on the road with him. There was a price for a grain elevator, a price for a short switch; side tracks were charged for by the linear foot . . . ; street improvement cost so much; wharf space was classified and precisely rated. As there was a scale for favorable legislation, so there was one for defeating bills. It made a difference in the price if there was opposition, and it made a difference whether the privilege asked was legitimate or not. But nothing was passed free of charge. Many of the legislators were saloon keepers—it was in St. Louis that a practical joker nearly emptied the House of Delegates by getting a boy to rush into a session and call out, "Mister, your saloon is on fire,"—but even the saloon keepers of a neighborhood had to pay to keep in their inconvenient locality a market which public interest would have moved.

. . .

The blackest years were 1898, 1899, and 1900. Foreign corporations came into the city to share in its despoliation, and home industries were driven out by blackmail. Franchises worth millions were granted without one cent of cash to the city, and with provision for only the smallest future payment; several companies which refused to pay blackmail had to leave; citizens were robbed more and more boldly; pay-rolls were padded with the names of non-existent persons; work on public improvements was neglected, while money for them went to the boodlers.

Some of the newspapers protested, disinterested citizens were alarmed, and the shrewder men gave warnings, but none dared make an effective stand. Behind the corruptionists were men of wealth and social standing, who, because of special privileges granted them, felt bound to support and defend the looters.

(Source: Claude H. Wetmore and Lincoln Steffens, "Tweed Days in St. Louis: Joseph W. Folk's Single-handed Exposure of Corruption, High and Low," *McClure's Magazine*, XIX, October 1902, 577–579.)

The Future of Radio

Those who have discussed radio broadcasting as a social force have recently confined themselves to its use in political campaigns. Under the circumstances this is natural; yet it is worth remembering that after November 4 radio will still be here. To what uses which have the slightest interest for intelligent people may we expect it to be put in the three years and ten months before the voice of the politician is again heard in the land?

In the belief of those most competent to judge, radio is not a mechanical fad which will sweep the country, as bicycle riding once did, and then disappear. While its present popularity is partly attributable to novelty, it is here to stay. As improvements are added (conceivably including radio transmission of motion pictures), it will become well nigh universal. The Department of Agriculture states that the number of receiving sets on farms has trebled in the past twelve months. Including home-made ones there are between three and four million of them in this country already, or one for each seven or eight families. It is easily within the bounds of possibility even now that a speaker may be listened to on some special occasion by a quarter or a third of the whole adult population.

It is also generally admitted that the radio is potentially a genuinely important medium of intellectual communication. Any one who will take the trouble to test it for himself may discover that (unless he is usually visual-minded) he can follow the drift of an argument quite as well or better by hearing a speaker on the ether than by reading his remarks in the next morning's paper. Despite the abnormality of listening to one whom you cannot see, it is common experience that better concentration is possible at the radio than in the public lecture hall with the distractions of a crowd. The speaker's "personal magnetism," if he has any, is enormously diminished in its power to affect the judgment of his auditors. Critical standards are preserved which are a useful assistance to independent thinking. Finally, the instant accessibility and ease of the radio are great incitements to the use of whatever intellectual opportunities it affords. Almost any owner of a receiving set will testify that at least during the first few weeks that he had it he listened to ten times as much oratorical and musical matter as during any equal period before.

But here comes the rub. In most parts of the country full 90 percent of the non-musical material on the air is sheer rubbish, not worth the attention of any one with more than an eight-year-old mind. The largest item of all on the program is, of course, jazz music. There is likewise a quantity of somewhat better music and occasionally a performance of real importance. If its usefulness were mainly as a musical instrument, the radio would have little social value—certainly not much more than the phonograph or the self-playing piano. It is when we consider it as a device for transmitting thought that we come both to the field of greatest potential usefulness, and the worst present failure.

Not only do the radio broadcasting stations give a disproportionately small amount of time to the spoken word, but the quality is in general appallingly bad. First and worst is the evil of paid advertising, most of which is not even acknowledged as such.

All sorts of commercial institutions hire lecturers and "rent time on the air" for discussion almost invariably dull and vulgar and usually smeared over with the demand that the auditors shall go and buy something. Some stations, we are glad to report, refuse to permit advertising; but the tendency is the other way.

Next to paid advertising, a common feature is broadcasting after-dinner speeches. Naturally, the merit of these depends on the men who make them; but in general it is fair to say that most are made by persons not worth hearing and that even the individual who has something to say is rarely in a mood to say it.

For the rest, these ethereal speakers are a job-lot of individuals who are willing to volunteer their services without charge: the broadcasters have not yet realized that it is just as impossible for them to secure competent speakers without payment as it would be to conduct a great university with a volunteer faculty, or a leading magazine with unpaid contributors. The corps of radio volunteers includes some self-advertising would-be publicists; a few professional patriots who are trying to scare the country back into the frame of mind of the eighteen eighties; special pleaders for charity bazaars, and the like. Some good speakers who should be willing to talk at least occasionally, speakers whom the radio audience would be glad to hear, are deterred by the arbitrary supposition of the managers that the listeners can't stand more than fifteen minutes of anything. Many others don't appear because they have never been asked.

This fact brings us to the heart of the problem and helps account for the failure of broadcasting as an intellectual force today. This remarkable invention, with potential powers second only to those of the printing press and with an audience already nearly as large as that of our entire public school system, is mainly under control of men unfitted by training and personality for posts of such importance. While there are a few exceptions, such as stations maintained by universities, it is generally true that the making of programs is in the hands of underpaid individuals, picked up at haphazard, usually musicians or men whose primary interest is music. They are admirably fitted to assemble orchestras, pianists and singers; but when it comes to lectures and addresses they are about as competent as Florenz Ziegfeld is to run Columbia University.

The development of motion pictures in the United States was held back half a decade because at first it was in the control of fly-by-nights, adventurers and reformed pushcart peddlers, not one in a hundred of whom had reached the social level where one takes one's hat off indoors. Radio broadcasting seems threatened by the same fate, and for somewhat the same reason: because a remarkable new educational device has suddenly developed as a sort of by-product of industry and is therefore in the hands of business men not only ignorant of its proper use, but indifferent as to whether it is used properly or not. . . .

This new and marvelous means of transmitting ideas cannot be allowed to go largely to waste as at present; public demand will force its more intelligent use even if those in charge of it continue blind to its opportunities and responsibilities.

(Source: Bruce Bliven, "The Future of Radio," *The New Republic*, XL, 1924, pp. 135-136.)

Supreme Court Decision

Laws, as seen through law enforcement, legal opinions, and court rulings, are important sources of information about a society. Laws are rules by which people live together. As such, they are good indicators of social values—how a society views itself; what it strives to be; the ideals that govern its daily existence. Oftentimes, individual behavior does not conform to these ideals, and it is at this point that the historian can discover much about what a society will tolerate; what its values are. In addition, there is often disagreement, particularly in a pluralistic society such as the United States, about what these ideals and rules should be. Accordingly, historians have long used court records and legal opinions as sources.

The document that follows was concerned with race relations in the United States. *Brown v. Topeka Board of Education* (1954) was a landmark decision in U.S. history. As you read it, note the facts of the case, the issues discussed, the arguments that are put forth, and the decision.

Brown v. Board of Education of Topeka (1954)
347 U.S. 483

WARREN, C. J., These cases come to us from the States of Kansas, South Carolina, Virginia, and Delaware. They are premised on different facts and different local conditions, but a common legal question justifies their consideration together in this consolidation opinion.

In each of the cases, minors of the Negro race, through their legal representatives, seek the aid of the courts in obtaining admission to the public schools of their community on a nonsegregated basis. In each instance, they had been denied admission to schools attended by white children under laws requiring or permitting segregation according to race. This segregation was alleged to deprive the plaintiffs of the equal protection of the laws under the Fourteenth Amendment. In each of the cases other than the Delaware case, a three-judge federal district court denied relief to the plaintiffs on the so-called "separate but equal" doctrine announced by this Court in *Plessy v. Ferguson,* 163 U.S. 537. Under that doctrine, equality of treatment is accorded when the races are provided substantially equal facilities, even though these facilities be separate. In the Delaware case, the Supreme Court of Delaware adhered to that doctrine, but ordered that the plaintiffs be admitted to the white schools because of their superiority to the Negro schools.

The plaintiffs contend that segregated public schools are not "equal" and cannot be made "equal," and that hence they are deprived of the equal protection of the laws. Because of the obvious importance of the question presented, the Court took jurisdiction. Argument was heard in the 1952 Term, and reargument was heard this Term on certain questions propounded by the Court.

Reargument was largely devoted to the circumstances surrounding the adoption of the Fourteenth Amendment in 1868. It covered exhaustively consideration of the Amendment in Congress, ratification by the states, then existing practices in racial segregation, and the views of proponents and opponents of the Amendment. This discussion and our own investigation convince us that, although these sources cast some light, it is not enough to resolve the problem with which we are faced. At best, they are inconclusive. The most avid proponents of the post–War Amendment undoubtedly intended them to remove all legal distinctions among "all persons born or naturalized in the United States." Their opponents, just as certainly, were antagonistic to both the letter and the spirit of the Amendments and wished them to have the most limited effect. What others in Congress and the state legislatures had in mind cannot be determined with any degree of certainty.

An additional reason for the inconclusive nature of the Amendment's history, with respect to segregated schools, is the status of public education at that time. In the South, the movement toward free common schools, supported by general taxation, had not yet taken hold. Education of white children was largely in the hands of private groups. Education of Negroes was almost nonexistent, and practically all of the race were illiterate. In fact, any education of Negroes was forbidden by law in some states. Today, in contrast, many Negroes have achieved outstanding success in the arts and sciences as well as in the business and professional world. It is true that public school education at the time of the Amendment had advanced further in the North, but the effect of the Amendment on Northern States was generally ignored in the congressional debates. Even in the North, the conditions of public education did not approximate those existing today. The curriculum was usually rudimentary; ungraded schools were common in rural areas; the school term was but three months a year in many states; and compulsory school attendance was virtually unknown. As a consequence, it is not surprising that there should be so little in the history of the Fourteenth Amendment relating to its intended effect on public education.

In the first cases in this court construing the Fourteenth Amendment, decided shortly after its adoption, the Court interpreted it as proscribing all state-imposed discriminations against the Negro race. The doctrine of "separate but equal" did not make its appearance in this Court until 1896 in the case of *Plessy v. Ferguson, supra,* involving not education but transportation. American courts have since labored with the doctrine for over half a century. In this Court, there have been six cases involving the "separate but equal" doctrine in the field of public education. In *Cumming v. County Board of Education,* 175 U.S. 528, and *Gong Lum v. Rice,* 275 U.S. 78, the validity of the doctrine itself was not challenged. In more recent cases, all on the graduate school level, inequality was found in that specific benefits enjoyed by white students were denied to Negro students of the same educational qualifications. *Missouri ex rel. Gaines v. Canada,* 305 U.S. 337; *Sipuel v. Oklahoma,* 332 U.S. 631; *Sweatt v. Painter,* 339 U.S. 629; *McLaurin v. Oklahoma State Regents,* 339 U.S. 637. In none of these cases was it necessary to re-examine the doctrine to grant relief to the Negro plaintiff. And in *Sweatt v. Painter, supra,* the Court expressly reserved decision on the question whether *Plessy v. Ferguson* should be held inapplicable to public education.

In the instant cases, that question is directly presented. Here, unlike *Sweatt v. Painter,* there are findings below that the Negro and white schools involved have been equalized, or are being equalized, with respect to buildings, curricula, qualifications and salaries of teachers, and other "tangible" factors. Our decision, therefore, cannot turn on merely a comparison of these tangible factors in the Negro and white schools involved in each of the cases. We must look instead to the effect of segregation itself on public education.

In approaching this problem, we cannot turn the clock back to 1868 when the Amendment was adopted, or even to 1896 when *Plessy v. Ferguson* was written. We must consider public education in the light of its full development and its present place in American life throughout the Nation. Only in this way can it be determined if segregation in public school deprives these plaintiffs of the equal protection of the laws.

Today, education is perhaps the most important function of state and local governments. Compulsory school attendance laws and the great expenditures for education both demonstrate our recognition of the importance of education to our democratic society. It is required in the performance of our most basic public responsibilities, even service in the armed forces. It is the very foundation of good citizenship. Today it is a principal instrument in awakening the child to cultural values, in preparing him for later professional training, and in helping him to adjust normally to his environment. In these days, it is doubtful that any child may reasonably be expected to succeed in life if he is denied the opportunity of an education. Such an opportunity, where the state has undertaken to provide it, is a right which must be made available to all on equal terms.

We come then to the question presented: Does segregation of children in public schools solely on the basis of race, even though the physical facilities and other "tangible" factors may be equal, deprive the children of the minority group of equal educational opportunities? We believe that it does.

In *Sweatt v. Painter, supra,* in finding that a segregated law school for Negroes could not provide them equal educational opportunities, this Court relied in large part on "those equalities which are incapable of objective measurement but which make for greatness in law school." In *McLaurin v. Oklahoma State Regents, supra,* the Court, in requiring that a negro admitted to a white graduate school be treated like all other students, again resorted to intangible considerations: "his ability to study, to engage in discussions and exchange views with other students, and, in general, to learn his profession." Such considerations apply with added force to children in grade and high schools. To separate them from others of similar age and qualifications solely because of their race generates a feeling of inferiority as to their status in the community that may affect their hearts and minds in a way unlikely ever to be undone. The effect of this separation on their educational opportunities was well stated by a finding in the Kansas case by a court which nevertheless felt compelled to rule against the Negro plaintiffs:

"Segregation of white and colored children in public schools has a detrimental effect upon the colored children. The impact is greater when it has the sanction of the law; for the policy of separating the races is usually interpreted as denoting the inferiority of the negro group. A sense of inferiority affects the motivation of a child to learn. Segregation with the sanction of law, therefore has a tendency to [retard] the educational and mental development of negro children and to deprive them of some of the benefits they would receive in a racial[ly] integrated school system."

Whatever may have been the extent of psychological knowledge at the time of *Plessy v. Ferguson,* this finding is amply supported by modern authority. Any language in *Plessy v. Ferguson* contrary to this finding is rejected. We conclude that in the field of public education the doctrine of "separate but equal" has no place. Separate educational facilities are inherently unequal. Therefore, we hold that the plaintiffs and others similarly situated for whom the actions have been brought are, by reason of the segregation complained of, deprived of the equal protection of the laws guaranteed by the Fourteenth Amendment. This disposition makes unnecessary any discussion whether such segregation also violates the Due Process Clause of the Fourteenth Amendment.

Because these are class actions, because of the wide applicability of this decision, and because of the great variety of local conditions, the formulation of decrees in these cases presents problems of considerable complexity. On reargument, the consideration of appropriate relief was necessarily subordinated to the primary question—the constitutionality of segregation in public education. We have now announced that such segregation is a denial of the equal protection of the laws. In order that we may have the full assistance of the parties in formulating decrees, the facts will be restored to the docket, and the parties are requested to present further argument on Questions 4 and 5 [dealing with detailed implementation of the decision] previously propounded by the Court for the reargument of this Term.

Political Speech

It is always difficult to deal with political documents. As you know, political statements are made for all sorts of reasons, not often the most important of which is to make an unambiguous statement. But consider the following document, the farewell address of President Dwight D. Eisenhower. Since Ike was leaving office and presumably had no intentions of seeking further political position, do you think that the speech might have been a firmer reflection of his actual beliefs? Is his warning of an emerging "military-industrial complex" convincing?

What evidence might you seek to determine whether his position (as stated here) was consistent with his own policies? What evidence might be available to suggest he might be warning Americans about the announced policies of his newly elected successor, John F. Kennedy? How would evidence of either influence your judgment about this document?

President Eisenhower's Farewell Address

Good evening, my fellow Americans:

First, let me express my gratitude to the radio and television networks for the opportunity to express myself to you during these past eight years and tonight.

Three days from now, after half a century in the service of our country, I shall lay down the responsibilities of office as, in traditional solemn ceremony, the authority of the President is vested in my successor.

This evening I come to you with a message of leave-taking and farewell, and to share a few final thoughts with you, my countrymen. . . .

We now stand ten years past the midpoint of a century that has witnessed four major wars among great nations. Three of these involved our own country. Despite these holocausts America is today the strongest, the most influential, and most productive nation in the world. Understandably proud of this pre-eminence, we yet realize that America's leadership and prestige depend, not merely upon our unmatched material progress, riches, and material strength, but on how we use our power in the interests of world peace and human betterment.

Throughout America's adventure in free government, our basic purposes have been to keep the peace; to foster progress in human achievement; and to enhance liberty, dignity, and integrity among people and among nations. To strive for less would be unworthy of a free and religious people. Any failure traceable to arrogance, or our lack of comprehension or readiness to sacrifice would inflict upon us grievous hurt both at home and abroad.

Progress toward these noble goals is persistently threatened by the conflict now engulfing the world. It commands our whole attention, absorbs our very beings. We face a hostile ideology—global in scope, atheistic in character, ruthless in purpose, and insidious in method. Unhappily the danger it poses promises to be of indefinite duration. To meet it successfully, there is called for, not so much the emotional and transitory sacrifices of crisis, but rather those which enable us to carry forward steadily, surely, and without complaint the burdens of a prolonged and complex struggle—with liberty the stake. Only thus shall we remain, despite every provocation, on our chartered course toward permanent peace and human betterment.

Crises there will continue to be. In meeting them, whether foreign or domestic, great or small, there is a recurring temptation to feel that some spectacular and costly action could become the miraculous solution to all current difficulties. A huge increase in newer elements of our defense; development of unrealistic programs to cure every ill in agriculture; a dramatic expansion in basic and applied research—these and many other possibilities, each possibly promising in itself, may be suggested as the only way to the road we wish to travel.

But each proposal must be weighed in the light of a broader consideration, the need to maintain balance in and among national problems—balance between the private and the public economy, balance between cost and hoped for advantage—balance between the clearly necessary and the comfortably desirable; balance between our essential requirements as a nation and the duties imposed by the nation upon the individual; balance between actions of the moment and the national welfare of the future. Good judgment seeks balance and progress; lack of it eventually finds imbalance and frustration.

The record of many decades stands as proof that our people and their government have, in the main, understood these truths and have responded to them well, in the face of stress and threat. But threats, new in kind or degree, constantly arise. I mention two only.

A vital element in keeping the peace is our military establishment. Our arms must be mighty, ready for instant action, so that no potential aggressor may be tempted to risk his own destruction.

Our military organization today bears little relation to that known by any of my predecessors in peacetime, or indeed by the fighting men in World War II or Korea.

Until the latest of our world conflicts, the United States had no armaments industry. American makers of plowshares could, with time and as required, make swords as well. But now we can no longer risk emergency improvision of national defense; we have been compelled to create a permanent armaments industry of vast proportions. Added to this, three and a half million men and women are directly engaged in the defense establishment. We annually spend on military security more than the net income of all United States corporations.

This conjunction of an immense military establishment and a large arms industry is new in American experience. The total influence—economic, political, even spiritual—is felt in every city, every state house, every office of the federal government. We recognize the imperative need for this development. Yet we must not fail to comprehend its grave implications. Our toil, resources and livelihood are all involved; so is the very structure of our society.

In the councils of government, we must guard against the acquisition of unwarranted influence, whether sought or unsought, by the military-industrial complex. The potential for the disastrous rise of misplaced power exists and will persist.

We must never let the weight of this combination endanger our liberties or democratic processes. We should take nothing for granted. Only an alert and knowledgeable citizenry can compel the proper meshing of the huge industrial and military machinery of defense with peaceful methods and goals, so that security and liberty may prosper together.

Akin to, and largely responsible for the sweeping changes in our industrial-military posture, has been the technological revolution during recent decades.

In this revolution, research has become central; it also becomes more formalized, complex, and costly. A steadily increasing share is conducted for, by, or at the direction of, the federal government.

Today, the solitary inventor, tinkering in his shop, has been overshadowed by task forces of scientists in laboratories and testing fields. In the same fashion, the free university, historically the fountainhead of free ideas and scientific discovery, has experienced a revolution in the conduct of research. Partly because of the huge costs involved, a government contract becomes virtually a substitute for intellectual curiosity. For every old blackboard there are now hundreds of new electronic computers.

The prospect of domination of the nation's scholars by federal employment, project allocations, and the power of money is ever present and is gravely to be regarded.

Yet, in holding scientific research and discovery in respect, as we should, we must also be alert to the equal and opposite danger that public policy could itself become the captive of a scientific-technological elite.

It is the task of statesmanship to mold, to balance, and to integrate these and other forces, new and old, within the principles of our democratic system—ever aiming toward the supreme goals of our free society.

Another factor in maintaining balance involves the element of time. As we peer into society's future, we—you and I, and our government—must avoid the impulse to live only for today, plundering, for our own ease and convenience, the precious resources of tomorrow. We cannot mortgage the material assets of our grandchildren without risking the loss also of their political and spiritual heritage. We want democracy to survive for all generations to come, not to become the insolvent phantom of tomorrow.

Down the long lane of the history yet to be written America knows that this world of ours, ever growing smaller, must avoid becoming a community of dreadful fear and hate, and be, instead, a proud confederation of mutual trust and respect.

Such a confederation must be one of equals. The weakest must come to the conference table with the same confidence as we do, protected as we are by our moral, economic, and military strength. That table, though scarred by many past frustrations, cannot be abandoned for the certain agony of the battlefield.

Disarmament, with mutual honor and confidence, is a continuing imperative. Together we must learn how to compose differences, not with arms, but with intellect and decent purpose. Because this need is so sharp and apparent I confess that I lay down my official responsibilities in this field with a definite sense of disappointment. As one who has witnessed the horror and the lingering sadness of war—as one who knows that another war could utterly destroy this civilization which has been so slowly and painfully built over thousands of years—I wish I could say tonight that a lasting peace is in sight.

Happily, I can say that war has been avoided. Steady progress toward our ultimate goals has been made. But, so much remains to be done. As a private citizen, I shall never cease to do what little I can to help the world advance along that road.

So—in this my last good night to you as your President—I thank you for the many opportunities you have given me for public service in war and peace. I trust that in that service you find some things worthy; as for the rest of it, I know you will find ways to improve performance in the future.

You and I—my fellow citizens—need to be strong in our faith that all nations, under God, will reach the goal of peace and justice. May we be ever unswerving in devotion to principle, confident but humble with power, diligent in pursuit of the nation's great goals.

To all the peoples of the world, I once more give expression to America's prayerful and continuing aspiration:

We pray that peoples of all faiths, all races, all nations may have their great human needs satisfied; that those now denied opportunity shall come to enjoy it to the full; that all who yearn for freedom may experience its spiritual blessings; that those who have freedom will understand, also, its heavy responsibilities; that all who are insensitive to the needs of others will learn charity; that the scourges of poverty, disease, and ignorance will be made to disappear from the earth, and that, in the goodness of time, all peoples will come to live together in a peace guaranteed by the binding force of mutual respect and love.

Now on Friday noon I am to become a private citizen. I am proud to do so. I look forward to it.

(Source: *Public Papers of the President: Dwight D. Eisenhower, 1960-1961,* Washington, D.C.: National Archives and Records Service, 1961, pp. 1036-1039.)

Secret Government Document

The following document was a memorandum written by George Ball, undersecretary of state, to President Lyndon Johnson in 1965. In it, Ball argued against further involvement in Vietnam. History proved Ball to be amazingly accurate in his assessment of the situation. What were Ball's arguments? How well did he support them? Do you think his position was carefully considered at the time by other actors in the decision? What counter arguments can you think of to respond to Ball? What other historical sources would shed light on why Ball's advice was not followed? Since this memo was made public only when *The Pentagon Papers* was leaked to the press and published, and therefore not a part of public discourse on Vietnam policy, do you think it would have made any difference if such information had been made public at the time of the decision?

George Ball Memorandum to President Johnson

(1) *A Losing War:* The South Vietnamese are losing the war to the Viet Cong. No one can assure you that we can beat the Viet Cong or even force them to the conference table on our terms, no matter how many hundred thousand *white, foreign* (U.S.) troops we deploy.

No one has demonstrated that a white ground force of whatever size can win a guerrilla war—which is at the same time a civil war between Asians—in jungle terrain in the midst of a population that refused cooperation to the white forces (and the South Vietnamese) and thus provides a great intelligence advantage to the other side. Three recent incidents vividly illustrate this point: (a) the sneak attack on the Da Nang Air Base which involved penetration of a defense perimeter guarded by 9,000 Marines. This raid was possible only because of the cooperation of the local inhabitants;

(b) the B52 raid that failed to hit the Viet Cong who had obviously been tipped off; (c) the search and destroy mission of the 173rd Air Borne Brigade which spent three days looking for the Viet Cong, suffered 23 casualties, and never made contact with the enemy who had obviously gotten advance word of their assignment.

(2) *The Question to Decide:* Should we limit our liabilities in South Vietnam and try to find a way out with minimal long-term costs?

The alternative—no matter what we may wish it to be—is almost certainly a protracted war involving an open-ended commitment of U.S. forces, mounting U.S. casualties, no assurance of a satisfactory solution, and a serious danger of escalation at the end of the road.

(3) *Need for a Decision Now:* So long as our forces are restricted to advising and assisting the South Vietnamese, the struggle will remain a civil war between Asian peoples. Once we deploy substantial numbers of troops in combat it will become a war between the U.S. and a large part of the population of South Vietnam, organized and directed from North Vietnam and backed by the resources of both Moscow and Peiping.

The decision you face now, therefore, is crucial. Once large numbers of U.S. troops are committed to direct combat, they will begin to take heavy casualties in a war they are ill-equipped to fight in a non-cooperative if not downright hostile countryside.

Once we suffer large casualties, we will have started a well-nigh irreversible process. Our involvement will be so great that we cannot—without national humiliation—stop short of achieving our complete objectives. *Of the two possibilities I think humiliation would be more likely than the achievement of our objectives—even after we have paid terrible costs.*

(4) *Compromise Solution:* Should we commit U.S. manpower and prestige to a terrain so unfavorable as to give a very large advantage to the enemy—or should we seek a compromise settlement which achieves less than our stated objectives and thus cut our losses while we still have the freedom of maneuver to do so.

(5) *Costs of a Compromise Solution:* The answer involves a judgment as to the cost to the U.S. of such a compromise settlement in terms of our relations with the countries in the area of South Vietnam, the credibility of our commitments, and our prestige around the world. In my judgment, if we act before we commit substantial U.S. troops to combat in South Vietnam we can, by accepting some short-term costs, avoid what may well be a long-term catastrophe. I believe we tended grossly to exaggerate the costs involved in a compromise settlement. An appreciation of probable costs is contained in the attached memorandum.

(6) *With these considerations in mind, I strongly urge the following program:*

(a) Military Program

(1) Complete all deployments already announced—15 battalions—but decide not to go beyond a total of 72,000 men represented by this figure.

(2) Restrict the combat role of the American forces to the June 19 announcement, making it clear to General Westmoreland that this announcement is to be strictly construed.

(3) Continue bombing in the North but avoid the Hanoi-Haiphong area and any targets nearer to the Chinese border than those already struck.

(b) Political Program

(1) In any political approaches so far, we have been the prisoners of whatever South Vietnamese government that was momentarily in power. If we are ever to move toward a settlement, it will probably be because the South Vietnamese government pulls the rug out from under us and makes its own deal *or* because we go forward quietly without advance prearrangement with Saigon.

(2) So far we have not given the other side a reason to believe there is *any* flexibility in our negotiating approach. And the other side has been unwilling to accept what *in their terms* is complete capitulation.

(3) Now is the time to start some serious diplomatic feelers looking towards a solution based on some application of a self-determination principle.

(4) I would recommend approaching Hanoi rather than any of the other probable parties, the NLF [National Liberation Front, or Viet Cong]—or Peiping. Hanoi is the only one that has given any signs of interest in discussion. Peiping has been rigidly opposed. Moscow has recommended that we negotiate with Hanoi. The NLF has been silent.

(5) There are several channels to the North Vietnamese but I think the best one is through their representative in Paris, Mai Van Bo. Initial feelers of Bo should be directed toward a discussion both of the four points we have put forward and the four points put forward by Hanoi as a basis for negotiation. We can accept all but one of Hanoi's four points, and hopefully we should be able to agree on some ground rules for serious negotiation—including no preconditions.

(6) If the initial feelers lead to further secret, exploratory talks, we can inject the concept of self-determination that would permit the Viet Cong some hope of achieving some of their political objectives through local elections or some other device.

(7) The contact on our side should be handled through a non-governmental cut-out (possibly a reliable newspaper man who can be repudiated).

(8) If progress can be made at this level a basis can be laid for a multinational conference. At some point, obviously, the government of South Vietnam will have to be brought on board, but I would postpone this step until after a substantial feeling out of Hanoi.

(9) Before moving to any formal conference we should be prepared to agree once the conference is started:

(a) The U.S. will stand down its bombing of the North

(b) The South Vietnamese will initiate no offensive operations in the South, and

(c) The DRV will stop terrorism and other aggressive action against the South.

(10) The negotiations at the conference should aim at incorporating our understanding with Hanoi in the form of a multinational agreement guaranteed by the U.S., the Soviet Union and possibly other parties, and providing for an international mechanism to supervise its execution.

Probable Reactions to the Cutting of Our Losses in South Vietnam

We have tended to exaggerate the losses involved in a complete settlement in South Vietnam. There are three aspects to the problem that should be considered. First, the local effect of our action on nations in or near Southeast Asia. Second, the effect of our action on the credibility of our commitments around the world. Third, the effect on our position of world leadership.

A. Free Asian Reactions to a Compromise Settlement in South Vietnam Would Be Highly Parochial.

With each country interpreting the event primarily in terms of (a) its own immediate interest, (b) its sense of vulnerability to Communist invasion or insurgency, and (c) its confidence in the integrity of our commitment to its own security based on evidence other than that provided by our actions in South Vietnam.

Within this framework the following groupings emerge:

(1) The Republic of China and Thailand—staunch allies whose preference for extreme U.S. actions including a risk of war with Communist China sets them apart from all other Asian nations;

(2) The Republic of Korea and the Philippines—equally staunch allies whose support for strong U.S. action short of a war with Communist China would make post-settlement reassurance a pressing U.S. need;

(3) Japan—it would prefer wisdom to valor in an area remote from its own interests where escalation could involve its Chinese or Eurasian neighbors or both;

(4) Laos—a friendly neutral dependent on a strong Thai-U.S. guarantee of support in the face of increased Vietnamese and Laos pressures.

(5) Burma and Cambodia—suspicious neutrals whose fear of antagonizing Communist China would increase their leaning toward Peiping in a conviction that the U.S. presence is not long for Southeast Asia; and

(6) Indonesia—whose opportunistic marriage of convenience of both Hanoi and Peiping would carry it further in its overt aggression against Malaysia, convinced that foreign imperialism is a fast fading entity in the region.

Japan
Government cooperation the essential in making the following points to the Japanese people:

(1) U.S. support was given in full measure as shown by our casualties, our expenditures and our risk taking;

(2) The U.S. record in Korea shows the credibility of our commitment so far as Japan is concerned.

The government as such supports our strong posture in Vietnam but stops short of the idea of a war between the U.S. and China.

Thailand
Thai commitments to the struggle within Laos and South Vietnam are based upon a careful evaluation of the regional threat to Thailand's security. The Thais are confident they can contain any threats from Indochina alone. They know, however, they cannot withstand the massive power of Communist China without foreign assistance. Unfortunately, the Thai view of the war has seriously erred in fundamental respects. They believe American power can do anything, both militarily and in terms of shoring up the Saigon regime. They now assume that we really could take over in Saigon and win the war if we felt we had to. If we should fail to do so, the Thais would initially see it as a failure of U.S. will. Yet time is on our side, providing we employ it effectively. Thailand is an independent nation with a long national history and, unlike South Vietnam, an acute national consciousness. It has few domestic Communists and none of the instability that plague its neighbors, Burma and Malaysia. Its one danger area in the northeast is well in hand so far as preventive measures against insurgency are concerned. Securing the Mekong Valley will be critical in any long-run solution, whether by the partition of Laos with Thai-U.S. forces occupying the western half or by some cover arrangement. Providing we are

willing to make the effort, Thailand can be a foundation of rock and not a bed of sand in which to base our political/military commitment to Southeast Asia.

With the exception of the nations in Southeast Asia, a compromise settlement in South Vietnam should not have a major impact on the credibility of our commitments around the world. . . . Chancellor Erhard has told us privately that the people of Berlin would be concerned by a compromise settlement of South Vietnam. But this was hardly an original thought, and I suspect he was telling us what he believed we would like to hear. After all, the confidence of the West Berliners will depend more on what they see on the spot than on [word illegible] news or events halfway around the world. In my observation, the principal anxiety of our NATO Allies is that we have become too preoccupied with an area which seems to them an irrelevance and may be tempted in neglect to our NATO responsibilities. Moreover, they have a vested interest in an easier relationship between Washington and Moscow. By and large, therefore, they will be inclined to regard a compromise solution in South Vietnam more as new evidence of American maturity and judgment than of American loss of face. . . . On balance, I believe we would more seriously undermine the effectiveness of our world leadership by continuing the war and deepening our involvement than by pursuing a carefully plotted course toward a compromise solution. In spite of the number of powers that have—in response to our pleading—given verbal support from feelings of loyalty and dependence, we cannot ignore the fact that the war is vastly unpopular and that our role in it is perceptively eroding the respect and confidence with which other nations regard us. We have not persuaded either our friends or allies that our further involvement is essential to the defense of freedom in the cold war. Moreover, the more men we deploy in the jungles of South Vietnam, the more we contribute to a growing world anxiety and mistrust.

In the short run, of course, we could expect some catcalls from the sidelines and some vindictive pleasure on the part of Europeans jealous of American power. But that would, in my view, be a transient phenomenon with which we could live without sustained anguish. Elsewhere around the world I would see few unhappy implications for the credibility of our commitments. No doubt the Communists will try to gain propaganda value in Africa, but I cannot seriously believe that the Africans care too much about what happens in Southeast Asia. Australia and New Zealand are, of course, special cases since they feel lonely in the far reaches of the

Pacific. Yet even their concern is far greater with Malaysia than with South Vietnam, and the degree of their anxiety would be conditioned largely by expressions of our support for Malaysia.

Earlier—Quite possibly President de Gaulle will make propaganda about perfidious Washington, yet even he will be inhibited by his much-heralded disapproval of our activities in South Vietnam.

South Korea

As for the rest of the Far East the only serious point of concern might be South Korea. But if we stop pressing the Koreans for more troops to Vietnam (the Vietnamese show no desire for additional Asian forces since it affronts their sense of pride) we may be able to cushion Korean reactions to a compromise in South Vietnam by the provision of greater military and economic assistance. In this regard, Japan can play a pivotal role now that it has achieved normal relations with South Korea.

(Source: Memorandum, "A Compromise Solution in South Vietnam," from Under Secretary of State George W. Ball for President Johnson, July 1, 1965, in *The Pentagon Papers*, Gravel Edition Volume IV, Boston: Beacon Press, 1971, pp. 615–619.)

Economic/Census Data

The practice of taking censuses is quite old, but the newly formed United States was the first country to begin taking systematic counts of its population every ten years. The Constitution adopted in 1787 called for a census to apportion taxes and representation. As a Census Report noted in 1908,

> The task of making the first enumeration of inhabitants was placed upon the President. Under this law the marshals of the several judicial districts were required to ascertain the number of inhabitants within their respective districts, omitting Indians not taxed, and distinguishing free persons . . . from all others; the sex and color of free persons; and the number of free males 16 years of age and over.
>
> The object of the inquiry last mentioned was, undoubtedly, to obtain definite knowledge as to the military and industrial strength of the country. This fact possesses special interest, because the Constitution directs merely an enumeration of inhabitants.

Over the years, the breadth of study of the Census Bureau has expanded. Now, a number of different censuses are undertaken in several cycles. Economic and business data have grown in importance. Tables 1 and 2 contain such information. Table 1 shows the composition of the U.S. labor force from 1800 to 1960. A great deal of economic history may be gleaned from this table. If you read this table from bottom to top, you will get a good sense of changes in particular categories (e.g., agricultural workers or teachers) over time. Look, for example, at the great growth in miners. What might this data suggest generally about economic changes or use of energy? If you read the table across from left to right, you will see the relative magnitude of each category, and compare it to the total work force or to other categories. Thus for 1800, for example, you can see that the 1.4 million farmers were 73 percent of the total labor force while in 1960 the 5.97 million farmers were just over 8 percent of the total. These changing relationships represent tremendous economic changes in the United States.

Table 2 gives much greater detail about the history of specific occupations between 1900 and 1970. Again, the table may be best read in two directions—from top to bottom and from left to right. There is particularly interesting information about the differences between men and women.

Table 1

Labor Force and Employment by Industry: 1800–1960 (in thousands of persons 10 years old and over)

| | Labor force | | | Employment | | | | Manufacturing | | | | Transport | | Service | |
| | Total | Free | Slave | Agri-culture | Fishing | Mining | Construc-tion | Total persons engaged | Cotton textile wage earners | Primary iron and steel wage earners | Trade | Ocean vessels | Rail-way | Teachers | Domestics |
Year															
1960	74,060	-------	-------	5,970	45	709	3,640	17,145	300	530	14,051	135	883	1,850	2,489
1950	65.470	-------	-------	7,780	77	901	3,029	15,648	350	550	12,152	130	1,373	1,270	1,995
1940	56.290	-------	-------	9,575	60	925	1,876	11,309	400	485	9,328	150	1,160	1,086	2,300
1930	48.830	-------	-------	10,560	73	1,009	1,988	9,884	372	375	8,122	160	1,659	1,044	2,270
1920	41.610	-------	-------	107,980	53	1,180	1,233	11,190	450	460	5,845	205	2,236	752	1,660
1910	37.480	-------	-------	11,770	68	1,068	1,949	8,332	370	306	5,320	150	1,855	595	2,090
1900	29.070	-------	-------	11,680	69	637	1,665	5,895	303	222	2,970	105	1,040	436	1,800
1890	23.320	-------	-------	9,960	60	440	1,510	4,390	222	149	2,960	120	750	350	1,580
1880	17.390	-------	-------	8,920	41	280	900	3,290	175	130	1,930	125	416	230	1,130
1870	12.930	-------	-------	6,790	28	180	780	2,470	135	78	1,310	135	160	170	1,000
1860	11.110	8,770	2,340	5,880	31	176	520	1,530	122	43	890	145	80	115	600
1850	8.250	6,280	1,970	4,520	30	102	410	1,200	92	35	530	135	20	80	350
1840	5.660	4,180	1,480	3,570	24	32	290	500	72	24	350	95	7	45	240
1830	4.200	3,020	1,180	2,965	15	22	-------	(NA)	55	20	-------	70	-------	30	160
1820	3.135	2,185	950	2,470	14	13	-------	(NA)	12	5	-------	50	-------	20	110
1810	2.330	1,590	740	1,950	6	11	-------	75	10	5	-------	60	-------	12	70
1800	1.900	1,370	530	1,400	5	10	-------	-------	1	1	-------	40	-------	5	40

Source: U.S. Department of Commerce, Bureau of the Census, *Historical Statistics of the United States: Colonial Times to 1970* (Washington, DC: U.S. Government Printing Office, 1975), Part 1, p. 139.

Table 2

Major Occupation Groups of the Experienced Civilian Labor Force, by Sex: 1900 to 1970 (In thousands of persons 14 years old and over, except as indicated. Census data for 1900, June 1; 1910, April 15; 1920, Jan. 1; 1930–1970, April 1.)

Major occupation group and sex	1970		1960		1950		1940	1930	1920	1910	1900
	16 years old and over	14 years old and over	1970 classification	1960 classification	1960 classification	1950 classification					
BOTH SEXES											
Total	[1]79,802	[2]80,603	[3]67,990	67,990	[4]59,230	58,999	51,742	48,686	42,206	37,291	29,030
White-collar workers	37,857	36,131	27,028	27,244	21,253	21,601	16,082	14,320	10,529	7,962	5,115
Professional, technical, and kindred workers	11,561	11,018	7,090	7,336	5,000	5,081	3,879	3,311	2,283	1,758	1,234
Managers, officials, and proprietors[5]	6,463	6,224	5,708	5,489	5,096	5,155	3,770	3,614	2,803	2,462	1,697
Clerical and kindred workers	14,208	13,457	9,431	9,617	7,132	7,232	4,982	4,336	3,385	1,987	877
Salesworkers	5,625	5,433	4,799	4,801	4,025	4,133	3,450	3,059	2,058	1,755	1,307
Manual and service workers	39,420	36,947	33,377	33,207	29,749	30,445	26,666	24,044	20,287	17,797	13,027
Manual workers	29,169	27,356	25,475	25,617	23,733	24,266	20,597	19,272	16,974	14,234	10,401
Craftsmen, foremen, and kindred workers	11,082	10,435	9,465	9,241	8,205	8,350	6,203	6,246	5,482	4,315	3,062
Operative and kindred workers	14,335	13,406	12,254	12,846	11,754	12,030	9,518	7,691	6,587	5,441	3,720
Laborers, except farm and mine	3,751	3,515	3,755	3,530	3,774	3,885	4,875	5,335	4,905	4,478	3,620
Service workers	10,251	9,591	7,902	7,590	6,015	6,180	6,069	4,772	3,313	3,562	2,626
Private household workers	1,204	1,143	1,817	1,825	1,492	1,539	2,412	1,998	1,411	1,851	1,579
Service workers, exc, private household	9,047	8,449	6,086	5,765	4,524	4,641	3,657	2,774	1,901	1,711	1,047
Farmworkers	2,448	2,345	4,132	4,085	6,858	6,953	8,995	10,321	11,390	11,533	10,888
Farmers and farm managers	1,428	1,350	2,528	2,526	4,325	4,375	5,362	6,032	6,442	6,163	5,763
Farm laborers and foremen	1,022	995	1,604	1,560	2,533	2,578	3,632	4,290	4,948	5,370	5,125
MALE											
Total	[1]49,455	[2]50,002	[3]45,686	45,686	[4]42,772	42,554	39,168	37,933	33,569	29,847	23,711
White-collar workers	19,428	18,693	15,316	15,413	12,798	12,974	10,434	9,564	7,176	6,019	4,166
Professional, technical, and kindred workers	6,917	6,621	4,366	4,543	3,025	3,074	2,271	1,829	1,275	1,032	800
Managers, officials, and proprietors[5]	5,386	5,189	4,864	4,695	4,408	4,456	3,356	3,321	2,612	2,312	1,623
Clerical and kindred workers	3,748	3,547	3,024	3,120	2,723	2,730	2,282	2,090	1,771	1,300	665
Salesworkers	3,378	3,336	3,063	3,055	2,642	2,715	2,525	2,323	1,518	1,376	1,079

Manual and service workers										
Manual workers	27,807	26,154	24,477	24,422	22,746	23,228	20,247	18,956	16,172	13,469	9,664
Craftsmen, foremen, and kindred workers	23,760	22,315	21,465	21,612	20,159	20,581	17,877	17,138	14,923	12,320	8,924
Operative and kindred workers	10,530	9,911	9,170	8,973	7,959	8,098	6,069	6,140	5,377	4,209	2,985
Laborers, except farm and mine	9,789	9,183	8,733	9,234	8,566	8,743	7,067	5,822	4,839	3,739	2,456
	3,440	3,221	3,562	3,405	3,634	3,740	4,742	5,177	4,707	4,372	3,482
Service workers	4,048	3,839	3,012	2,810	2,587	2,647	2,370	1,818	1,250	1,149	740
Private household workers	38	40	65	65	78	80	135	89	51	67	53
Service workers, exc, private household	4,010	3,800	2,947	2,745	2,509	2,568	2,235	1,729	1,199	1,082	687
Farmworkers	2,205	2,123	3,737	3,696	6,271	6,352	8,487	9,414	10,221	10,359	9,880
Farmers and farm managers	1,357	1,288	2,408	2,406	4,207	4,255	5,205	5,769	6,165	5,884	5,451
Farm laborers and foremen	848	835	1,329	1,290	2,064	2,097	3,282	3,645	4,056	4,475	4,429

FEMALE

Total	[1]30,347	[2]30,601	[3]22,304	[3]22,304	[4]16,507	16,445	12,574	10,752	8,637	7,445	5,319
White-collar workers	18,430	17,438	11,711	11,831	8,456	8,627	5,648	4,756	3,353	1,943	949
Professional, technical, and kindred workers	4,644	4,398	2,724	2,793	1,976	2,007	1,608	1,482	1,008	726	434
Managers, officials, and proprietors[5]	1,077	1,034	844	794	688	700	414	292	191	150	74
Clerical and kindred workers	10,461	9,910	6,407	6,497	4,408	4,502	2,700	2,246	1,614	688	212
Salesworkers	2,247	2,097	1,736	1,383	1,418	925	736	541	379	228	
Manual and service workers	11,612	10,793	8,900	8,786	7,003	7,217	6,419	5,088	4,115	4,327	3,363
Manual workers	5,409	5,041	4,010	4,006	3,574	3,685	2,720	2,134	2,052	1,914	1,477
Craftsmen, foremen, and kindred workers	552	524	295	268	246	253	135	106	105	106	76
Operative and kindred workers	4,546	4,223	3,521	3,612	3,188	3,287	2,452	1,870	1,748	1,702	1,264
Laborers, except farm and mine	311	295	193	125	140	145	133	158	199	106	137
Service workers	6,203	5,752	4,890	4,780	3,429	3,532	3,699	2,954	2,063	2,413	1,886
Private household workers	1,166	1,103	1,752	1,760	1,414	1,459	2,277	1,909	1,360	1,784	1,526
Service workers, exc, private household	5,037	4,649	3,139	3,020	2,015	2,073	1,422	1,045	703	629	359
Farmworkers	245	222	395	290	587	601	508	908	1,169	1,175	1,008
Farmers and farm managers	72	62	120	120	118	120	157	263	277	279	311
Farm laborers and foremen	173	160	275	270	469	481	351	645	892	895	697

[1] Includes 74,911 unemployed persons whose occupations were not reported: 14,781 males and 60,130 females.

[2] Includes 5,179,626 unemployed persons whose occupations were not reported; 3,032,524 males and 2,147,102 females.

[3] Includes 3,453,279 unemployed persons whose occupations were not reported; 2,155,586 males and 1,297,693 females.

[4] Includes 1,369,621 unemployed persons whose occupations were not reported; 907,615 males and 462,006 females.

[5] Except farm.

Source: U.S. Department of Commerce, Bureau of the Census, *Historical Statistics of the United States: Colonial Times to 1970* (Washington, DC: U.S. Government Printing Office, 1975), Part 1, pp. 139–140.

Directory of Organizations, Associations, and Government Agencies

5

LITERALLY HUNDREDS—if not thousands—of organizations have interests in U.S. history. Obviously, not all of those organizations or agencies could be listed here; we have tried to list all the major national organizations and agencies, as well as representative specialized agencies. We have listed organizations and agencies in three categories. First are those with general interests in U.S. history; they may specialize in a particular region, such as the South, or topic, such as education, but their interests cover the entire span of our nation's history.

State historical societies are the second category. Other state resources that might be of assistance include state archives, state humanities councils, and state preservation offices. Note that many localities also have historical societies providing a range of services. These may be accessed through local telephone directories.

The third category includes agencies or organizations specializing in U.S. history since 1865. These organizations can be particularly helpful in researching events or developments in that time span.

We have not included organizations focusing on the study of one individual (e.g., Theodore Roosevelt Association); organizations devoted to the study of one immigrant group (e.g., Polish-American Historical Society, Swedish-American Historical Society); presidential libraries, and museums, or restorations (e.g., Lyndon B. Johnson Library, Old Cowtown Museum), although all of these organizations can be helpful to teachers and students. Information about these types of organizations can be found in such other reference works as the *Encyclopedia of Associations* (Detroit, MI: Gale Research, annual) or *The Living History Sourcebook* (Nashville, TN: American Association for State and Local History, 1985).

General information for teachers and students can also be obtained through college and university departments of history, obviously too numerous to list here. A call to the department of a local institution can yield information on the specialties of faculty members and requirements for non-college students' use of the history library.

General Organizations and Agencies

Agricultural History Society (AHS)
Economic Research Service
U.S. Department of Agriculture
Washington, DC 20250
(202) 447-8183
Wayne D. Rasmussen, Executive Secretary

The Agricultural History Society has 1,400 members, composed of
historians, geographers, agricultural economists, farmers, and others
interested in the history of agriculture. The organization presents awards for
writing on agricultural history and sponsors an annual symposium in April
in conjunction with the meeting of the Organization of American Historians.
PUBLICATIONS: AHS publishes a quarterly, *Agricultural History,* as well as
the proceedings of its annual symposium.

American Association of Museums (AAM)
1225 I Street, NW, Suite 200
Washington, DC 20005
(202) 289-1818
Ed Able, Director

This national association has 9,000 members, including history museums,
historic houses and societies, and preservation projects, among other types
of museums. The association accredits museums and studies all aspects of
collection development, maintenance, and management. Its annual meeting
is held in June.
PUBLICATIONS: AAM publishes a monthly newsletter, *Aviso;* a bimonthly
journal, *Museum News;* and an annual museum directory. It also publishes
books on such topics as caring for collections, museums and the humanities,
and museum accreditation.

American Association for State and Local History (AASLH)
174 Second Avenue, North
Nashville, TN 37204
(615) 255-2971
Gerald George, Director

The stated purpose of this membership organization is "advancing
knowledge, understanding, and appreciation of local history in the United
States and Canada," but it also works in the areas of state, regional, and
even national and international history, particularly in relation to public
education about history. The association offers seminars, workshops, and
consultant services; its annual meeting is held in September.

PUBLICATIONS: AASLH publishes the monthly journal *History News*; the monthly newsletter *History News Dispatch*; and a series of technical reports on "everyday problems faced by museum and historical agency personnel." Other publications include the biennial *Directory of Historical Agencies in North America*, as well as numerous bibliographies, technical leaflets, guides, and educational materials, including videotapes.

American Folklore Society (AFS)
Maryland State Arts Council
15 West Mulberry Street
Baltimore, MD 21201
(301) 685-6740
Charles Camp, Executive Secretary

With more than 3,000 individual and institutional members, the American Folklore Society supports the collection, discussion, and publication of folklore. Although folklore from throughout the world is of interest to the society, North America is emphasized. The AFS annual meeting is held in October.

PUBLICATIONS: AFS publishes the *American Folklore Newsletter* six times per year; the quarterly *Journal of American Folklore*; and several irregular series, including *Memoirs Series*.

American Historical Association (AHA)
400 A Street, SE
Washington, DC 20003
(202) 544-2422
Samuel R. Gammon, Executive Director

The 13,000 members of this association include professional historians, educators, and others interested in historical study. The association holds an annual meeting in December, maintains an extensive library, and offers seminars on various historical topics.

PUBLICATIONS: AHA publishes the journal *American Historical Review* five times per year. It also publishes the proceedings of its annual meetings, as well as pamphlets on historical subjects.

American Indian Historical Society (AIHS)
1493 Masonic Avenue
San Francisco, CA 94117
(415) 626-5235
Jeanette Henry Costo, Executive Secretary

The American Indian Historical Society was founded in 1964 to promote study and understanding of the history of Native Americans. The organization sponsors classes, forums, and lectures; evaluates how Native

Americans are depicted in textbooks; and supports the rights of Indians. The society sponsors a triennial meeting.

PUBLICATIONS: The society publishes an annual volume entitled *The Indian Historian*. It also publishes a newspaper on an irregular basis and occasional books.

Association for Living Historical Farms and Agricultural Museums (ALHFAM)
National Museum of American History
Smithsonian Institution
Washington, DC 20650
(202) 357-2813
John T. Schlebecker, Secretary

Despite its title, this organization is now recruiting as members all museums or other organizations interested in the use of "living history" techniques to increase public understanding of the past. The association provides assistance to its members in living history interpretation through regional workshops. It also maintains an information bank and develops standards for living historical farms and museums.

PUBLICATIONS: ALHFAM publishes a bimonthly *Bulletin,* an annual convention proceedings, and a variety of booklets on topics of concern to members.

Association for the Study of Afro-American Life and History (ASALH)
1407 14th Street, NW
Washington, DC 20005
(202) 667-2822
Karen Robinson, Executive Director

The 12,000 members of this organization include historians, scholars, and students interested in the study of black American history and culture. The organization, which sponsors Afro-American History Month, collects manuscripts, promotes research and writing, and works for interracial harmony. The association's annual meeting is held in October. Its publishing arm holds a media festival every November.

PUBLICATIONS: ASALH publishes two quarterlies, *Journal of Negro History* and *Negro History Bulletin*. Its publishing arm also issues textbooks and monographs on related topics.

Bureau of the Census
U.S. Department of Commerce
Washington, DC 20233
(301) 763-4040
John G. Keane, Director

Calling itself "America's Fact Finder," the Bureau of the Census conducts the decennial census of U.S. population. It also conducts economic, agricultural, and government censuses every five years, as well as up to 250 smaller surveys each year. Topics covered include manufacturing, mining, retail trade, wholesale trade, service industries, transportation, and construction. The Bureau also collects data on other nations.

PUBLICATIONS: The Bureau of the Census publishes as many as 2,000 reports each year, in printed, microfiche, and computer tape form. It also publishes a variety of wall maps and educational materials. Help finding appropriate census information can be obtained by contacting the regional offices listed below.

California
Census Bureau Regional Office
11777 San Vicente Boulevard
Los Angeles, CA 90049
(213) 209-6612

Colorado
Census Bureau Regional Office
7655 West Mississippi Avenue
Denver, CO 80226
(303) 236-2200

Georgia
Census Bureau Regional Office
1365 Peachtree Street, NE
Atlanta, GA 30309
(404) 881-2274

Illinois
Census Bureau Regional Office
55 East Jackson Boulevard
Chicago, IL 60604
(312) 353-0980

Kansas
Census Bureau Regional Office
One Gateway Center
4th and State Streets
Kansas City, KS 66101
(913) 236-3731

Massachusetts
Census Bureau Regional Office
441 Stuart Street
Boston, MA 02116
(617) 565-7078

Michigan
Census Bureau Regional Office
231 West Lafayette
Detroit, MI 48226
(313) 226-4675

New York
Census Bureau Regional Office
26 Federal Plaza
New York, NY 10278
(212) 264-4730

North Carolina
Census Bureau Regional Office
230 South Tryon Street
Charlotte, NC 28202
(704) 371-6144

Pennsylvania
Census Bureau Regional Office
600 Arch Street
Philadelphia, PA 19106
(215) 597-8313

Texas
Census Bureau Regional Office
1100 Commerce Street
Dallas, TX 75242
(214) 767-0625

Washington
Census Bureau Regional Office
1700 Westlake Avenue, N
Seattle, WA 98109
(206) 442-7080

ERIC Clearinghouse for Social Studies/Social Science Education (ERIC/ ChESS)
2805 East Tenth Street, Suite 120
Indiana University
Bloomington, IN 47405
(812) 335-3838
John Patrick, Director

The ERIC Clearinghouse for Social Studies/Social Science Education
provides comprehensive information services in the area of social science
and history education. These services include low-cost user service products,
computer searches, and information-answering services.

PUBLICATIONS: The clearinghouse publishes a free newsletter, *Keeping Up*,
as well as reference sheets and digests on current topics. The clearinghouse

also publishes information analysis products, including the recent *Teaching History in the Elementary School.*

History of Science Society (HSS)
35 Dean Street
Worcester, MA 01609
(617) 793-5363
Michael Sokal, Executive Secretary

The 4,000 members of this society include educators, historians, scientists, and others studying the history of science and its influence on other aspects of culture. The organization presents several annual awards and meets annually in the fall.

PUBLICATIONS: HSS publishes a quarterly entitled *Isis,* as well as a quarterly newsletter and an annual publication, *Osiris.*

Immigration History Society (IHS)
Balch Institute
18 South Seventh Street
Philadelphia, PA 19106
(215) 925-8090
M. Mark Stolarik, Editor

This organization encourages interchange among historians, sociologists, economists, and others doing research in the field of human migration, particularly migration to the United States. Members meet twice each year in conjunction with the meetings of the Organization of American Historians and American Historical Association.

PUBLICATIONS: IHS publishes a semiannual *Immigration History Newsletter* as well as the semiannual *Journal of American Ethnic History.*

Library of Congress
10 First Street, SE
Washington, DC 20540
(202) 287-5000
Daniel J. Boorstin, Librarian of Congress

One of the world's largest libraries, the Library of Congress contains more than 50 million items. Its collection on U.S. history is one of the finest anywhere and includes the papers of 23 U.S. presidents. The library answers reference questions that cannot be handled by other libraries and provides referrals for questions on the history of science and technology.

PUBLICATIONS: One of the key resources for historical researchers is the Library of Congress publication *The National Union Catalog,* which lists every publication issued a Library of Congress card and the libraries that have it in their holdings. The Library of Congress has also published printed subject guides, which are of great assistance in historical research. Library of Congress bibliographic resources are computerized and are made available in microfiche form.

National Archives and Records Administration (NARA)
Pennsylvania Avenue and Eighth Street
Washington, DC 20408
(202) 523-3298
Don Wilson, Archivist

An independent agency of the federal government, the National Archives and Records Administration is the official depository for records of all federal agencies. As such, it has a huge collection of documentary materials related to U.S. history, going back to records of the Continental Congress in 1774.

PUBLICATIONS: NARA's key publication for the historical researcher is *Guide to the National Archives of the United States,* which describes the Archives' holdings. For many categories of records, NARA has published special guides and listings; examples include *Black History: A Guide to Civilian Records in the National Archives* and *Civil War Maps in the National Archives.* Microfilm reels of many records in the National Archives can be purchased from the Archives or can be viewed at Archives branches. Branches are found at the following locations:

California
National Archives Branch
Federal Records Center
24000 Avila Road
Laguna Niguel, CA 92677
(714) 831-4220

National Archives Branch
Federal Records Center
1000 Commodore Drive
San Bruno, CA 94066
(415) 876-9001

Colorado
National Archives Branch
Federal Records Center
Building 48, Federal Center
Denver, CO 80225
(303) 234-3187

Georgia
National Archives Branch
Federal Records Center
1557 St. Joseph Avenue

East Point, GA 30344
(404) 526-7477

Illinois
National Archives Branch
Federal Records Center
7358 South Pulaski Road
Chicago, IL 60629
(312) 353-8541

Massachusetts
National Archives Branch
Federal Records Center
380 Trapelo Road
Waltham, MA 02154
(617) 223-2657

Missouri
National Archives Branch
Federal Records Center
2306 East Bannister Road
Kansas City, MO 64131
(816) 926-7271

New Jersey
National Archives Branch
Federal Records Center
Building 22—MOT Bayonne
Bayonne, NJ 07002
(201) 858-7245

Pennsylvania
National Archives Branch
Federal Records Center
5000 Wissahickon Avenue
Philadelphia, PA 19144
(215) 438-5200

Texas
National Archives Branch
Federal Records Center
P.O. Box 6216
Fort Worth, TX 76115
(817) 334-5515

Washington
National Archives Branch
Federal Records Center
6125 Sand Point Way, NE
Seattle, WA 98115
(206) 442-4502

National Council on Public History (NCPH)
Department of History
West Virginia University
Morgantown, WV 26506
(304) 293-2421
Barbara J. Howe, Executive Secretary

This organization aims to encourage broader interest in history and to stimulate interest in history by promoting its use in society. The focus is nonacademic history—history that is brought to the public through museums and public displays. The organization serves as a clearinghouse, conducts training programs, and advises those seeking information on public history. The group has an annual spring conference.

PUBLICATIONS: NCPH publishes a quarterly newsletter, a quarterly journal, *The Public Historian,* and an irregular publication entitled *Directory of Academic and Training Programs.*

National Council for the Social Studies (NCSS)
3501 Newark Street, NW
Washington, DC 20016
(202) 966-7840
Frances Haley, Executive Director

The purpose of the National Council for the Social Studies is to improve social studies education, including history education, by setting guidelines and standards for the profession, providing leadership and leadership training opportunities, and by encouraging research. Consultant and workshop services are provided at negotiated fees. Letter and phone information requests are answered at no charge. An annual conference is held in November.

PUBLICATIONS: NCSS journals include *Social Education* and *Theory and Research in Social Education.* It also publishes a newsletter, *The Social Studies Professional,* a "How to Do It" series for teachers, and bulletins on topics of interest to the membership. Two bulletins of special note are *Teaching American History: New Directions* and *History in the Schools.*

National Endowment for the Humanities (NEH)
1100 Pennsylvania Avenue, NW
Washington, DC 20506
(202) 786-0435
Lynne V. Cheney, Chairman

This relatively new federal agency (established in 1965) aims to increase the influence of the humanities—primarily literature, history, and philosophy— on American thinking and life. It fulfills its mission by funding research, enhancement of proven humanities programs at the higher education level, and educational programs. Each year, NEH funds a number of summer institutes for elementary and secondary teachers of history; lists of these institutes are available from the agency.

PUBLICATIONS: Six times annually, NEH publishes the journal *Humanities.* It also publishes occasional reports such as the recent *American Memory: A Report on the Humanities in the Nation's Public Schools,* which helped to spark a resurgence of interest in history education. NEH also supports the development of many other works, although it does not publish these items.

National History Day
11201 Euclid Avenue
Cleveland, OH 44106
(216) 421-8803
Lois Scharf, Executive Director

This organization sponsors a program in which secondary students prepare projects for submission in local, state, and national competitions. The projects are judged by professional historians and teachers; winners are recognized at all levels. Each year's competition has a particular theme that students must address.

PUBLICATIONS: The organization annually publishes a collection of the winning papers from the competition.

National Park Service (NPS)
U.S. Department of the Interior
C Street between 18th and 19th, NW
Washington, DC 20240
(202) 343-1100
William Penn Mott, Director

In addition to administering the national park system, the National Park Service also oversees national monuments (e.g., Booker T. Washington National Monument), battlefields (e.g., Big Hole, site of the Nez Percé defeat in 1877), historic sites and parks (e.g., Fort Laramie in Wyoming), memorials and memorial parks (e.g., Chamizal Memorial in Texas), and military parks (e.g., Gettysburg, Pennsylvania).

PUBLICATIONS: NPS publishes informational brochures on all of the sites it administers, as well as other educational materials.

National Women's History Project (NWHP)
P.O. Box 3716
Santa Rosa, CA 95402
(707) 526-5974
Molly MacGregor, Director

As its name implies, this organization promotes education on the history of women through such activities as publication of resource catalogs on women's history, sponsorship of National Women's History Week in March, and publication of teaching materials on women's history. The staff conducts workshops and other training programs and offers internships. The organization also sponsors the Women's History Network.

PUBLICATIONS: The National Women's History Project publishes a variety of materials, including resource catalogs, a community organizing guide, bibliographies, curriculum guides, lesson plans, and posters.

Oral History Association (OHA)
P.O. Box 13734, NTSU Station
Denton, TX 76203
(817) 387-1021
Ronald E. Marcello, Executive Secretary

The Oral History Association has 1,400 individual and institutional members interested in the exchange of information on oral history, in encouraging the growth of oral history materials, and in the improvement of the discipline's techniques. The organization holds an annual colloquium in the fall.

PUBLICATIONS: Periodic publications include a quarterly newsletter, an annual membership directory, and the annual *Oral History Review.* OHA also publishes bibliographies, evaluation guidelines, and papers of special interest to its members.

Organization of American Historians (OAH)
112 North Bryan Street
Bloomington, IN 47401
(812) 335-7311
Joan Hoff-Wilson, Executive Secretary

The Organization of American Historians' mission is to promote historical research, study, and writing. It sponsors several award programs for historical writing, as well as maintaining a speakers bureau and operating a job registry. An annual meeting is held in April.

PUBLICATIONS: OAH publishes the bimonthly *Magazine of History,* targeted at teachers of American history; the quarterly *Journal of American History,* intended for a scholarly audience; and a newsletter.

Smithsonian Institution
1000 Jefferson Drive, SW
Washington, DC 20560
(202) 357-1300
Robert McCormick Adams, Secretary

The Smithsonian is perhaps best known for the museums it maintains, including the National Museum of American History and the National Air and Space Museum. The Smithsonian also conducts original research in the sciences, humanities, arts, and education and prepares and distributes many publications. The Smithsonian also offers educational programs for adults and children, with special emphasis given to preservice and inservice teacher training.

PUBLICATIONS: The Smithsonian publishes many books and reports. It publishes the monthly journal *Smithsonian*, as well as a quarterly newsletter for schools, *Art to Zoo*. This newsletter promotes the use of community resources in the classroom and contains ready-to-use instructional materials.

Social Science Education Consortium (SSEC)
855 Broadway
Boulder, CO 80302
(303) 492-8154
James R. Giese, Executive Director

The SSEC is dedicated to the improvement of social studies/social science education, including history education. Activities designed to implement that goal include curriculum development, teacher training, and dissemination of new teaching ideas and materials. The SSEC's Resource and Demonstration Center houses one of the nation's largest collections of curriculum materials in social studies and history, as well as the archives of many curriculum development projects of the 1960s and 1970s.

PUBLICATIONS: The SSEC publishes teacher resource and curriculum planning materials. Representative titles include *Lessons on the Constitution, Law in U.S. History, The Rise of Organized Labor,* and *Immigration: Pluralism and National Identity*.

Society of American Historians (SAH)
610 Fayerweather Hall
Columbia University
New York, NY 10027
(212) 280-2555
Kenneth T. Jackson, Executive Secretary

This society includes as members authors who have written at least one book on U.S. history that is recognized as being of high literary and scholarly quality. The society awards several prizes in the area of historical writing. Its annual meeting is held in April.

PUBLICATIONS: None

Society for History Education
California State University, Long Beach
Long Beach, CA 90840
(213) 985-4503
Augustus Cerillo, Jr., President

Members of this organization include high school and college teachers and librarians. The organization's goal is to support the work of historians who choose to teach by offering reprint, workshop, and other services.

PUBLICATIONS: The society publishes a newsletter, *Network News Exchange*, as well as a quarterly journal, *The History Teacher.*

Society for the History of Technology (SHOT)
Department of History
Duke University
Durham, NC 27706
(919) 684-2434
Aarne Vesilind, Secretary

This organization counts among its members 2,600 scholars, engineers, and institutions (including libraries and museums). Its purpose is to "encourage the study of the development of technology and its relations with society and culture." Through its training and award programs, SHOT encourages an interdisciplinary approach to study of the area. The organization's annual meeting is held in December.

PUBLICATIONS: SHOT publishes two quarterlies—a newsletter and the journal *Technology and Culture.*

Southern History Association (SHA)
Department of History
University of Georgia
Athens, GA 30602
(404) 542-8848
William F. Holmes, Secretary

This organization promotes the study of Southern history through research, preservation of historical records, and encouragement of state and local historical societies. The organization bestows awards for work in the area of Southern history. An annual meeting is held in November.

PUBLICATIONS: SHA publishes a quarterly journal, *Journal of Southern History.*

State Historical Societies

Each of the 50 states, as well as the District of Columbia, has a state historical society that offers services ranging from maintenance of museums, to publishing of newsletters, journals, and educational materials, to providing various training programs. The historical periods for which the state societies have extensive collections may vary from state to state. However, all are likely to have at least some material relevant to the period covered in this volume.

Alabama
Alabama Department of Archives and History
624 Washington Avenue
Montgomery, AL 36130
(205) 832-6510

Alaska
Alaska Historical Society
P.O. Box 100299
Anchorage, AK 99510
(907) 346-2410

Arizona
Arizona Historical Society
949 East Second Street
Tucson, AZ 85719
(602) 628-5774

Arkansas
Arkansas History Commission
1 Capitol Mall
Little Rock, AR 72201
(501) 682-6900

California
California Historical Society
2090 Jackson Street
San Francisco, CA 94109
(415) 567-1848

Colorado
Colorado Historical Society
1300 Broadway
Denver, CO 80203
(303) 866-3682

Connecticut
Connecticut Historical Society
1 Elizabeth Street
Hartford, CT 06105
(203) 236-5621

Delaware
Historical Society of Delaware
505 Market Street Mall
Wilmington, DE 19801
(302) 655-7161

District of Columbia
Columbia Historical Society
1307 New Hampshire Avenue, NW
Washington, DC 20036
(202) 785-2068

Florida
Florida Historical Society
University of South Florida Library
Tampa, FL 33620
(813) 974-3815

Georgia
Georgia Historical Society
501 Whitaker Street
Savannah, GA 31401
(912) 651-2128

Hawaii
Hawaiian Historical Society
560 Kawaiahao Street
Honolulu, HI 96813
(808) 537-6271

Idaho
Idaho State Historical Society
610 North Julia Davis Drive
Boise, ID 83702
(208) 384-2120

Illinois
Illinois State Historical Society
Old State Capitol
Springfield, IL 62706
(217) 782-4836

Indiana
Indiana Historical Society
315 West Ohio Street
Indianapolis, IN 46202
(317) 232-1882

Iowa
State Historical Society of Iowa
402 Iowa Avenue
Iowa City, IA 52240
(319) 335-3916

Kansas
Kansas State Historical Society
120 West Tenth Street

Topeka, KS 66612
(913) 296-3251

Kentucky
Kentucky Historical Society
300 West Broadway
Frankfort, KY 40601
(502) 564-3016

Louisiana
Louisiana Historical Society
203 Carondelet Street
New Orleans, LA 70130
(504) 588-9044

Maine
Maine Historical Society
485 Congress Street
Portland, ME 04101
(207) 774-1822

Maryland
Maryland Historical Society
201 West Monument Street
Baltimore, MD 21201
(301) 685-3750

Massachusetts
Massachusetts Historical Society
1154 Boylston Street
Boston, MA 02215
(617) 536-1608

Michigan
Historical Society of Michigan
2117 Washtenaw Avenue
Ann Arbor, MI 48104
(313) 769-1828

Minnesota
Minnesota Historical Society
690 Cedar Street
St. Paul, MN 55101
(612) 296-6980

Mississippi
Mississippi Historical Society
100 South State Street
Jackson, MI 39205
(601) 354-6218

Missouri
State Historical Society of Missouri
Hitt and Lowry Streets
Columbia, MO 65201
(314) 882-7083

Montana
Montana Historical Society
225 North Roberts
Helena, MT 59601
(406) 449-2681

Nebraska
Nebraska State Historical Society
1500 R Street
Lincoln, NE 68506
(402) 432-2793

Nevada
Nevada Historical Society
1650 North Virginia Street
Reno, NV 89503
(702) 789-0190

New Hampshire
New Hampshire Historical Society
30 Park Street
Concord, NH 03301
(603) 225-3381

New Jersey
New Jersey Historical Society
230 Broadway
Newark, NJ 07104
(201) 483-3939

New Mexico
Historical Society of New Mexico
P.O. Box 5819
Santa Fe, NM 87502

New York
New York Historical Society
170 Central Park West
New York, NY 10024
(212) 873-3400

North Carolina
Historical Society of North Carolina
University of North Carolina, Wilson Library
Chapel Hill, NC 27514
(919) 962-1345

North Dakota
State Historical Society of North Dakota
North Dakota Heritage Center
Bismarck, ND 58505
(701) 224-2666

Ohio
Ohio Historical Society
I-71 and Seventeenth Avenue
Columbus, OH 43211
(614) 466-1500

Oklahoma
Oklahoma Historical Society
2100 North Lincoln Boulevard
Oklahoma City, OK 73105
(405) 521-2491

Oregon
Oregon Historical Society
1230 Southwest Park Avenue
Portland, OR 97205
(503) 222-1741

Pennsylvania
Historical Society of Pennsylvania
1300 Locust Street
Philadelphia, PA 19107
(215) 732-6200

Rhode Island
Rhode Island Historical Society
52 Power Street
Providence, RI 02906
(401) 331-8575

South Carolina
South Carolina Historical Society
100 Meeting Street
Charleston, SC 29401
(803) 723-3225

South Dakota
South Dakota State Historical Society
Soldiers' and Sailors' Memorial Building
East Capitol Avenue
Pierre, SD 57501
(605) 773-3458

Tennessee
Tennessee Historical Society

War Memorial Building, Ground Floor
Nashville, TN 37219
(615) 742-6717

Texas
Texas Historical Commission
P.O. Box 12276, Capitol Station
Austin, TX 78711
(512) 475-3092

Utah
Utah State Historical Society
307 West Second Street
Salt Lake City, UT 84102
(801) 533-5961

Vermont
Vermont Historical Society, Inc.
State Street
Montpelier, VT 05602
(802) 828-2291

Virginia
Virginia Historical Society
428 North Boulevard
Richmond, VA 23221
(804) 358-4901

Washington
Washington State Historical Society
315 North Stadium Way
Tacoma, WA 98403
(206) 593-2830

West Virginia
West Virginia Historical Society
Department of Culture and History
State Capitol Complex
Charleston, WV 25305
(304) 348-2277

Wisconsin
State Historical Society of Wisconsin
816 State Street
Madison, WI 53706
(608) 262-9580

Wyoming
Wyoming State Archives and Historical Department
Barrett Building
Cheyenne, WY 82002
(307) 777-7518

Agencies or Organizations Specializing in U.S. History Since 1865

American Committee on the History of the Second World War (ACHSWW)
Department of History
Southern Illinois University
Carbondale, IL 62901
(618) 453-4391
Donald S. Detwiler, Secretary

The members of this organization include academic and government historians interested in the history of the Second World War. The organization is a member of an international committee on the history of the war. Both the national and international groups promote historical research, disseminate information, and sponsor conferences. Its annual meeting is held in conjunction with the meeting of the AHA.

PUBLICATIONS: ACHSWW publishes a semiannual newsletter, which contains information on archival and bibliographic resources of interest to its members.

Custer Battlefield Historical and Museum Association (CBHMA)
P.O. Box 39
Crow Agency, MT 59022
(406) 638-2382
Michael Downing, President

This organization includes 1,500 members interested in the Battle of the Little Big Horn. The organization's purpose is to "interpret the battle and educate the public concerning it." It offers summer educational programs, conducts archaeological research, and maintains a library.

PUBLICATIONS: CBHMA publishes a quarterly entitled *Battlefield Dispatch* as well as an annual volume, *Greasy Grass.*

Facing History and Ourselves National Foundation (FHONF)
25 Kennard Road
Brookline, MA 02146
(617) 232-1595
Margot Stern Strom, Executive Director

This organization was founded to help teachers and administrators infuse information about 20th-century genocide into the curriculum. Topics on which the organization focuses are the Holocaust, the genocide of the Armenians, contemporary racism, nuclear weapons, and anti-Semitism. The organization develops curriculum, offers consultation services, maintains a speakers bureau, and conducts training activities. It also maintains a library.

PUBLICATIONS: FHONF publishes a quarterly, *Facing History and Ourselves*. It also publishes such items as curriculum guides, bibliographies/ filmographies, and student writings.

National Association for Outlaw and Lawman History (NOLA)
Western Research Center
P.O. Box 3334
University of Wyoming
Laramie, WY 82071
(307) 766-4414
Gene M. Gressley, Director

This organization of writers, researchers, collectors, photographers, and historians collects material on lawmen and outlaws, and works to preserve historic sites and trails. The organization maintains an archive and library and sponsors competitions. The organization sponsors a summer "rendezvous."

PUBLICATIONS: NOLA publishes a newsletter six times yearly, as well as a quarterly magazine and special reports on topics of interest to the members.

Research Foundation for Jewish Immigration (RFJI)
570 Seventh Avenue
New York, NY 10018
(212) 921-3871
Herbert A. Strauss, Secretary

This foundation supports preparation, research, writing, and editing of the history of German-Jewish immigrants of the Nazi period and their resettlement and acculturation. The organization works closely with the Institut für Zeitgeschichte in Munich, West Germany. The foundation maintains an oral history collection on Jewish immigration to the United States since 1933.

PUBLICATIONS: RFJI publishes *Jewish Immigrants of the Nazi Period in the U.S.A.,* a series of reports. It is also the publisher of *International Biographical Dictionary of Central European Emigres, 1933–1945.*

Sons and Daughters of the Soddies (SDS)
P.O. Box 225
Colby, KS 67701
(913) 462-6787
Vernon Englehardt, President

This organization of 25,000 is dedicated to preserving documents, pictures, history, and items pertaining to the era of prairie settlement in North America (1840–1940). The organization maintains a library, from which they will supply pictures and other information to schools, libraries, and individuals. The group holds an annual meeting.

PUBLICATIONS: Publications of SDS include a newsletter and a booklet, *Sod Houses and Dugouts in North America.*

Western History Association (WHA)
University of Nevada
Reno, NV 89557
(702) 784-6852
William D. Rowley, Secretary-Treasurer

This association of 2,000 historians and others interested in the history of the West awards prizes for scholarship in the area. The association sponsors an annual meeting.

PUBLICATIONS: WHA publishes a bimonthly entitled *The American West,* as well as the *Western History Quarterly.*

Winter Soldier Archive
P.O. Box 9462, North Berkeley Station
Berkeley, CA 94709
(415) 527-0616
Clark C. Smith, Director

This relatively new organization, founded in 1980, collects oral histories from Vietnam veterans, as well as other materials concerning the Vietnam War. The organization also compiles medical statistics, maintains biographical archives, and provides speakers on topics related to the history of the Vietnam War.

PUBLICATIONS: The archive publishes two irregular items, *The Short Timer's Journal* and *Soldiering in Vietnam.* It also maintains an electronic database showing where herbicide spray missions were undertaken during the Vietnam War.

Reference Works

6

Atlases

American Expansion: A Book of Maps.
Randall D. Sale and Edwin D. Karn. Lincoln, NE: University of Nebraska
Press, 1979.
28 pp. $4.95. ISBN 0-8032-9104-3.

This brief atlas contains one map for each census year. The maps show
political boundaries at the time of the census, extension of settlement,
exploration, and location of land offices.

Atlas of American History.
James T. Adams, ed. New York: Scribner, 1985.
360 pp. $50. ISBN 0-684-18411-7.

This classic reference volume, now in its second revised edition, contains
maps prepared under the supervision of historians. Topics covered in the
maps include discovery, exploration, frontier posts, settlement, territorial
organization, and the extension of communications. An index contains
variant spellings of place names.

Comparative Atlas of America's Great Cities: Twenty Metropolitan Regions.
John S. Adams, ed. Minneapolis, MN: University of Minnesota Press, 1976.
500 pp. $95. ISBN 0-8166-0767-2.

This rich atlas focuses on the development of 20 of America's major
metropolitan areas. The numerous maps provide historical insights into
many aspects of the cities' developments.

Historical Atlas of the United States.
Clifford L. Lord and Elizabeth H. Lord. New York: Johnson Reprint, 1969
(reprint of 1953 ed.).
312 pp. $39. ISBN 0-384-33650-7.

The first section of this atlas contains general maps, the second focuses on the colonial period, and the third covers maps from 1775 to 1865. Political, economic, and social data are presented.

Historical Atlas of United States Congressional Districts, 1789–1983.
Kenneth C. Martis. New York: Free Press, 1982.
302 pp. $150. ISBN 0-02-920150-0.

This volume contains maps of congressional districts from the first Congress to the 97th. The members of each Congress are listed.

Railroad Maps of North America: The First Hundred Years.
Andrew M. Modelski. Washington, DC: Library of Congress, 1984.
186 pp. $28. ISBN 0-8444-0396-2.

This volume contains 92 maps related to the development of railroads in the United States. The maps are all historical maps from the Library of Congress collection.

These States United.
Chicago, IL: Rand McNally, 1985.
64 pp. $3. ISBN 0-528-17701-X.

This atlas, specifically designed for student use, includes 96 maps covering U.S. history from the pre-Columbian period to the present. The volume also includes tables, graphs, and an index.

United States History Atlas.
Maplewood, NJ: Hammond, 1985.
64 pp. $4.49. ISBN 0-8437-7465-7.

An atlas designed especially for students, the *United States History Atlas* aims to help students "discover the geographic and political influences underlying our nation's history and growth." Graphs on presidential elections, charts on the economy, and other materials supplement the maps.

Bibliographies and Printed Indexes

This listing of bibliographies and printed indexes is necessarily very selective. The bibliographies that are annotated are currently in print and cover a range of topics and periods in U.S. history. Hundreds more bibliographies and bibliographic guides are listed in the volumes we have included in the "Handbooks for Conducting Historical Research" section of this chapter. Students and teachers doing research should consult those handbooks for additional "leads" in searching for information. Note also that we have not listed print versions of indexes covered in the "Online Databases" section of the chapter. To determine whether those databases are available in print form, contact the suppliers.

The American Electorate: A Historical Bibliography.
Santa Barbara, CA: ABC-CLIO, 1984.
388 pp. $32.50. ISBN 0-87436-372-1.

More than 1,400 works are annotated in this bibliography, which covers the electoral process, the changing nature of the electorate, and reasons for voting.

American History: A Bibliographic Review.
Carol B. Fitzgerald, ed. Westport, CT: Meckler Publishing, annual.
Approx. 200 pp. $49.95.

This annual review publishes articles on bibliographic subjects of interest to historians, special bibliographies, and some reviews of books.

American Maritime History: A Bibliography.
Susan K. Kinnell and Suzanne R. Ontiveros, eds. Santa Barbara, CA: ABC-CLIO, 1986.
260 pp. $32.50. ISBN 0-87436-471-X.

This volume annotates 919 works on U.S. and Canadian maritime history. Topics include shipbuilding, piracy, sea disasters, the sea in literature, famous voyages, and many more.

The American Presidency: A Historical Bibliography.
Santa Barbara, CA: ABC-CLIO, 1984.
376 pp. $65.50. ISBN 0-87436-370-5.

This resource focuses not only on the presidency, but on the lives of the presidents, presidential elections, and the growth of the bureaucracy. More than 3,000 works are annotated.

America's Military Past: A Guide to Information Sources.
Jack C. Lane, ed. Detroit, MI: Gale, 1980.
280 pp. $62. ISBN 0-8103-1205-0.

This guide covers major "works dealing with American land and air forces without including any naval sources." Among the annotated works are government publications, books, and articles. The guide is arranged chronologically.

Bibliographic Guide to North American History.
Boston, MA: G. K. Hall, annual.
$150/year.

This guide lists the monographs and serials cataloged by the Research Libraries of the New York Public Library and the Library of Congress on an annual basis. Topic coverage includes Canada and the United States.

Bibliographies in American History: Guide to Materials for Research.
Henry P. Beers, ed. Woodbridge, CT: Research Publications, 1982.
978 pp. $260. ISBN 0-89235-038-5.

The first portion of this work is a standard bibliography originally published in 1942. The second part, which covers the years from 1942 to 1978, picks up where the first left off. Separately published books, bibliographies appearing in journals, and bibliographies appearing as parts of larger books are all included in this massive work.

Bibliography of American Naval History.
Paolo E. Coletta, ed. Annapolis, MD: Naval Institute Press, 1981.
453 pp. $15.95. ISBN 0-87021-105-6.

The author has annotated more than 4,500 books, documents, dissertations, theses, articles, essays, interviews, and works of fiction. The materials are arranged chronologically.

Bibliography on Southern Women.
Memphis, TN: Memphis State University Center for Research on Women, 1986.
37 pp. $2.50.

This bibliography is divided into three sections: scholarly historical works, personal narratives, and research studies on social conditions and indicators. The publisher plans to update the bibliography periodically.

Biography Index.
Bronx, NY: H. W. Wilson, quarterly.
$75/yr.

This index is a guide to biographical material appearing in periodicals and books. It serves both general and scholarly reference needs.

Book Review Digest.
Bronx, NY: H. W. Wilson, monthly except February and July.
Subscription rate is on a service basis; minimum rate is $95.

This subject and title index provides excerpts of and citations to reviews of fiction and nonfiction published in the United States. Reviews of books on history for the general reader are included, making the index especially useful for teachers.

The Democratic and Republican Parties in America: A Historical Bibliography.
Santa Barbara, CA: ABC-CLIO, 1984.
290 pp. $28. ISBN 0-87436-364-0.

This volume includes abstracts of more than 1,000 journal articles organized into five sections: party politics in America, the two-party system, the Republican ascendancy, the Democratic resurgence, and redefinitions and realignments.

Dickinson's American Historical Fiction.
Virginia B. Gerhardstein, ed. Methuen, NJ: Scarecrow, 1986.
368 pp. $27.50. ISBN 0-8108-1867-1.

This volume will be useful to teachers wishing to use historical fiction in their U.S. history courses. Students can also use the book to locate novels for pleasure reading or to deepen their understanding of a particular period.

Education Index.
Bronx, NY: H. W. Wilson, monthly (September–June).
Annual subscription rate determined by subscriber's periodical holdings; minimum rate is $80.

This index covers articles on education in English-language periodicals. Teachers can use this index to locate reviews of books, classroom materials, and teaching ideas.

The Female Experience in Eighteenth- and Nineteenth-Century America: A Guide to the History of American Women.
Jill Conway, ed. Princeton, NJ: Princeton University Press, 1985.
314 pp. $14.50. ISBN 0-691-00599-0.

This guide provides extensive annotated listings related to women's history in the 1700s and 1800s. The volume is a useful resource for those researching social history, as well as women's history.

Goldentree Bibliographies in American History.
Arthur Link, general ed. Arlington Heights, IL: Harlan Davidson, 1969–1981.
Variable lengths and prices.

Generally regarded as some of the finest bibliographies on particular periods or topics, this series includes the following titles of interest to teachers of early U.S. history:

The New South
American Social History Since 1860
The Gilded Age
The Progressive Era and the Great War
The New Era and the New Deal
The Second World War and the Atomic Age

The Great Depression: A Historical Bibliography.
Santa Barbara, CA: ABC-CLIO, 1984.
260 pp. $28. ISBN 0-87436-361-6.

This resource annotates nearly 1,000 articles on the Great Depression. All articles included were published between 1973 and 1982. The materials are organized into such chapters as "The Crash of '29 and Its Economic Aftermath," "The New Democratic Coalition and the Republican Response," and "The Culture of the Depression."

Introduction to United States Documents.
Joe Morehead, ed. Littleton, CO: Libraries Unlimited, 1983.
309 pp. $19.50. ISBN 0-87287-362-5.

This resource, a library school text, is a reference source for anyone interested in acquiring or gathering information via the numerous publications produced by the federal government.

Labor in America: A Historical Bibliography.
Santa Barbara, CA: ABC-CLIO, 1984.
307 pp. $69. ISBN 0-87436-397-7.

This resource contains more than 2,750 annotations of journal articles on the history of labor in the United States. Students researching labor or social history will find this source helpful.

The Living History Sourcebook.
Jay Anderson. Nashville, TN: American Association for State and Local History, 1985.
469 pp. $19.95. ISBN 0-910050-75-9.

This resource contains extensively annotated listings of museums, events, books, articles, magazines, organizations, suppliers, sketchbooks, films, and simulations related to living history and reenactments. Anecdotes from the author's own experience make this more interesting reading than a typical bibliography or resource guide.

Nuclear America: A Historical Bibliography.
Santa Barbara, CA: ABC-CLIO, 1984.
183 pp. $28. ISBN 0-87436-360-8.

This bibliography covers journal literature from 1973 to 1982. The more than 800 articles annotated cover nuclear weapons and nuclear energy from the early days at Oak Ridge to Three Mile Island.

Pamphlets in American History: A Bibliographic Guide to the Microform Collections.
Henry Barnard, ed. Sanford, NC: Microfilming Corporation of America, 1979–1984.
5 volumes of various lengths. $150 each.

This series serves as a bibliography of selected pamphlet literature, as well as a guide to the collection at the State Historical Society of Wisconsin. The volumes arc topically organized.

Progressive Reform: A Guide to Information Sources.
John D. Ruenker and Nicholas C. Burckel, eds. Detroit, MI: Gale, 1981.
300 pp. $62. ISBN 0-8103-1485-1.

This reference contains annotations of more than 1,600 works—books, articles, and dissertations—on the progressive era in the United States. The period covered spans roughly the years from 1890 to the end of World War I.

Religious Conflict in America.
Albert J. Menendez. New York: Garland Publishing, 1985.
500 pp. $20. ISBN 0-8240-8904-9.

This work lists books and articles dealing with religious conflict in our nation's history. The entries are arranged chronologically.

Review of Resources: Teaching Law and the Constitution.
Mary Elizabeth Glade, ed. Boulder, CO: Social Science Education Consortium, 1987.
149 pp. $14.95. ISBN 0-89994-320-9.

This publication provides analyses of 160 sets of materials on the Constitution, Bill of Rights, and the law. Also included are bibliographies of children's literature and films with constitutional content.

Selected Ethnic Literature: An Annotated Bibliography of Twelve Ethnic Groups.
Sharon Zirbes Fuller and H. Virginia Chacon, comps. Greeley, CO: Ukapress, 1986.
67 pp. $3.

This guide contains 329 briefly annotated entries on American ethnic groups. It also lists additional resources and ethnic holidays.

Sources for American Studies.
Jefferson B. Kellogg and Robert H. Walker, eds. Westport, CT: Greenwood Press, 1983.
766 pp. $45. ISBN 0-313-22555-9.

This volume contains a series of bibliographic essays on such topics as Afro-American studies, architectural history, economic history, folklore, immigration, and many more. Full citations are given for all sources mentioned in the essays.

Travels in America from the Voyages of Discovery to the Present: An Annotated Bibliography of Travel Articles in Periodicals.
Garold Cole. Norman, OK: University of Oklahoma Press, 1984.
291 pp. $48.50. ISBN 0-8061-1791-5.

The majority of travel narratives cited in this volume are from the eighteenth and nineteenth centuries. The more than 1,000 entries are grouped by region and date and are extensively indexed.

U.S. Cultural History: A Guide to Information Sources.
Philip I. Mitterling. Detroit, MI: Gale, 1980.
581 pp. $62. ISBN 0-8103-1369-3.

This volume contains numerous annotations of books and journal articles, all relating to cultural history. Sections include architecture and the arts, biography, economics, political and social thought, education, historiography, literature, and science and medicine, among others.

Women's Studies: A Recommended Core Bibliography.
Catherine R. Loeb, Susan E. Searing, and Esther F. Stineman, Littleton, CO: Libraries Unlimited, 1987.
238 pp. $23.50. ISBN 0-87287-598-9.

This broadly focused bibliography includes a section on history, as well as listings in such other subjects related to historical research as autobiography and other memoirs, language, and sociology.

Writings on American History: A Subject Bibliography of Books and Monographs.
James R. Masterson, comp. White Plains, NY: Kraus International, 1985.
10 volumes of various lengths. $1,300 for set. ISBN 0-527-98268-7.

Along with the previously published *Writings on American History: A Bibliography of Articles,* this massive set of guides provides comprehensive coverage of materials published between 1962 and 1973. Earlier editions of *Writings on American History* provided coverage of works from 1902 to 1962.

Biographical Dictionaries

Biographical Dictionary of Indians of the Americas.
Newport Beach, CA: American Indian Publications, 1984.
570 pp. $140. ISBN 0-317-17420-7.

This volume provides biographies of Native Americans from both North and South America.

Complete Book of U.S. Presidents.
William A. DeGregorio. New York: Dembner Books, 1984.
691 pp. $22.50. ISBN 0-934878-36-6.

This resource describes the U.S. presidents, devoting ten to twenty pages to each. Standard information is presented on each individual, along with interesting and unusual facts.

Concise Dictionary of American Biography.
New York: Scribner, 1980.
1,280 pp. $75. ISBN 0-684-16631-3.

Abridged from a much longer eight-volume work, this volume contains brief biographies of thousands of Americans, none of whom were alive at the time the volume was published. Notable people in all walks of life are included.

Dictionary of American Negro Biography.
Rayford W. Logan and Michael R. Winston. New York: Norton, 1983.
480 pp. $50. ISBN 0-393-01513-0.

This lengthy volume provides biographies of prominent black Americans from all periods of history.

Directory of American Scholars, Volume I: Historians.
Jacques Cattell Press, ed. New York: Bowker, 1982.
788 pp. $90. ISBN 0-8352-1478-8.

One of four volumes in the series, this book contains biographical information on some 9,000 historians. Personal information and data on publications and areas of specialization are provided.

Famous American Women: A Biographical Dictionary from Colonial Times to the Present.
Robert McHenry, ed. New York: Dover, 1983.
482 pp. $9.95. ISBN 0-486-24523-3.

This volume contains more than 1,000 biographical sketches of women in American history. The listings are presented alphabetically but are indexed by field and by women's organization.

Mujeres Celebres: A Biographical Encyclopedia of Hispanic Women.
Martha P. Cotera, ed. Santa Rosa, CA: National Women's History Project, in press.
$19.95.

This volume contains biographies and pictures of Hispanic women in history. Women from the United States, Latin America, the Caribbean, and Spain are included.

Notable American Women: 1607–1950.
Edward T. James and Janet W. James, eds. Cambridge, MA: Harvard University Press, 1971.
2,141 pp. $32.50. ISBN 0-674-62734-2.

This work was specifically written to fill in the gaps left by other biographical dictionaries, which tended to emphasize males. More than 1,300 women in various periods of U.S. history are included in this work.

Twentieth-Century American Historians.
Clyde N. Wilson, ed. Detroit, MI: Gale, 1983.
519 pp. $88. ISBN 0-8103-1144-5.

This resource offers lengthy essays on 59 writers of U.S. history who worked or are working in the twentieth century. Bibliographies of writings by these historians are included.

Webster's American Biographies.
Springfield, MA: Merriam-Webster, 1984.
1,233 pp. $18.95. ISBN 0-87779-253-4.

This well-known reference contains more than 3,000 entries covering prominent Americans from all historical periods. Native Americans, women, and western pioneers are among the traditionally neglected groups paid close attention in this book.

Who Was Who in America: A Series Providing Concise Biographies of the Outstanding Individuals of America's Past . . . from 1607 to the Present, Volume I: 1607–1897.
Chicago: Marquis, 1963.
1,396 pp. $67.50. ISBN 0-8379-0201-0.

The first in a series of nine volumes, this resource treats public figures in U.S. history from 1607 to 1897. The descriptions are somewhat more detailed than those provided in the *Concise Dictionary of American Biography* or *Webster's American Biographies.*

Dictionaries

Concise Dictionary of American History.
New York: Scribner, 1983.
1,140 pp. $70. ISBN 0-684-17321-2.

This greatly condensed version of the *Dictionary of American History* contains more than 6,000 entries covering U.S. history from prehistoric times to the 1980s.

Dictionary of American History.
Michael Martin and Leonard Gelber. Boston: Littlefield, Adams, 1981.
714 pp. $9.95. ISBN 0-8226-0124-9.

This compact reference includes more than 4,000 entries related to political, military, social, technological, and intellectual history. Slogans and sayings are also included.

Dictionary of Historical Terms.
Chris Cook. New York: Peter Bedrick Books, 1983.
304 pp. $22. ISBN 0-911745-16-5.

This book includes 2,000 terms used in examining U.S. and world history. Extensive cross-references are provided.

Dictionary of the Social Sciences.
Hugo F. Reading. New York: Methuen, 1977.
777 pp. $21.95. ISBN 0-7100-8642-3.

Terms related to research methodologies will be useful to students and teachers interested in developing skill in historical research.

The Encyclopedic Dictionary of American History.
Sluice Dock, CT: Dushkin, 1986.
344 pp. $9.95. ISBN 0-87967-605-1.

This volume includes more than 1,500 entries arranged alphabetically and extensively cross-referenced. Includes entries on people, events, and developments.

The Harlem Renaissance: An Historical Dictionary for the Era.
Bruce Kellner, ed. Westport, CT: Greenwood Press, 1984.
476 pp. $45. ISBN 0-313-23232-6.

This dictionary covers people, events, and locations relating to the "rich surge of black arts and letters" during the years between 1917 and 1935. Bibliographies are provided with all the articles; appendices provide chronologies, a glossary of Harlem slang, and a list of newspapers and other serials.

Yesterday and Today: A Dictionary of Recent American History, 1945 to the Present.
Stanley Hochman. New York: McGraw-Hill, 1979.
407 pp. $39.95. ISBN 0-07-029103-9.

This reference guide covers recent political, social, and cultural history in the United States. Arranged alphabetically, the entries cover events, movements, institutions, books, slogans, protests, and people that have shaped the American experience since World War II.

Encyclopedias, Almanacs, and Chronologies

The Almanac of American History.
Arthur M. Schlesinger, Jr., ed. New York: Putnam, 1983.
623 pp. $7.98. ISBN 0-399-51082-6.

This volume traces important events in U.S. history from the early arrival of European settlers to 1982. Each chronological section is introduced by a prominent U.S. historian. Events covered include not only military and political history but also art, culture, intellectual history, labor history, and more.

Almanac of American Women in the 20th Century.
Judith Freeman Clark. Englewood Cliffs, NJ: Prentice-Hall, 1987.
274 pp. $15.95. ISBN 0-13-022658-0.

This resource provides a chronology of events related to women's issues and women's accomplishments in such fields as the arts, science, labor, business, government, and law. Topical essays and brief biographies enliven the text.

Annals of America: 1493-1973.
Mortimer Adler, ed. Chicago: Encyclopaedia Britannica Educational Corporation, 1976.
23 volumes of various lengths. $459 for set. ISBN 0-87827-199-6.

The volumes in this series are arranged chronologically. Each volume presents a chronology of important events enhanced with primary source material related to those events.

Encyclopaedia Britannica.
Chicago: Encyclopaedia Britannica Educational Corporation, 1987.
$1,049 (includes free rolling book cart). ISBN 0-85229-444-1.

The *Encyclopaedia Britannica* is a sound general encyclopedia to use for broad summaries of historical topics and events.

Encyclopedia of American Economic History.
Glenn Porter, ed. New York: Scribner, 1980.
1,286 pp. $200. ISBN 0-684-16271-7.

This three-volume reference work includes entries on important events, people, and policies in economic history.

Encyclopedia of American Facts and Dates.
Gorton Carruth and Associates. New York: Crowell, 1979.
1,015 pp. $14.95. ISBN 0-690-01669-7.

A standard reference work, this volume is arranged chronologically. Topics covered include politics and government, war, books, art, architecture, science, economics, education, folklore, and many more.

Encyclopedia of American Foreign Policy.
Alexander De Conde, ed. New York: Scribner, 1978.
1,201 pp. $200. ISBN 0-684-15503-6.

This three-volume work contains 95 essays on "concepts, themes, large ideas, theories, and distinctive policies in the history of American foreign relations." Bibliographies, cross-references, and a biographical dictionary are included.

Encyclopedia of American History.
Richard B. Morris, ed. New York: Harper and Row, 1982.
1,285 pp. $29.45. ISBN 0-06-181605-1.

A standard work that is frequently revised, this volume is divided into four main parts: a basic chronology, a topical chronology, biographical sketches of 500 notable Americans, and a section on the structure of the federal government.

Encyclopedia of American Political History.
Jack P. Greene, ed. New York: Scribner, 1984.
1,420 pp. $200. ISBN 0-683-17003-5.

This three-volume work presents approximately 90 scholarly articles on "major issues, themes, institutions, processes, and developments as they have been manifest through the whole of United States history." Each article includes a bibliography.

Encyclopedia Americana.
Danbury, CT: Grolier, 1987.
$799 plus $23 shipping.

The *Encyclopedia Americana* is an excellent source of general information on history. It contains broad summaries of historical events and biographical sketches of important Americans suitable for use by students.

Encyclopedia of Black America.
W. Augustus Low and Virgil A. Clift. New York: McGraw-Hill, 1980.
992 pp. $76. ISBN 0-07-038834-2.

This work, arranged alphabetically, covers the black American experience from the colonial period to 1980. Education, employment, politics, agriculture, labor, medicine, literature, music, and many other topical areas.

Encyclopedia of Frontier and Western Fiction.
Jon Tuska and Vicki Piekarski. New York: McGraw-Hill, 1983.
384 pp. $24. ISBN 0-07-065587-1.

This reference will be useful to teachers who use historical fiction in their history courses. The guide provides information on more than 300 U.S. writers of the past 150 years, as well as some writers from Great Britain and Germany.

Harvard Encyclopedia of American Ethnic Groups.
Stephan Thernstrom, ed. Cambridge, MA: Harvard University Press, 1980.
2,001 pp. $70. ISBN 0-674-37512-2.

This massive work provides an alphabetical listing of American ethnic groups. Topics covered for each group are origins, migration, arrival, settlement, economic life, social structure, social organization, family and kinship, behavior and personal/individual characteristics, culture, religion, education, politics, intergroup relations, group maintenance, and individual ethnic commitment. A bibliography is also provided for each group.

International Encyclopedia of the Social Sciences.
New York: Free Press, 1977.
$310. ISBN 0-02-895700-8.

This reference work contains signed articles dealing with the social sciences and history. The articles contain illustrations, bibliographies, and cross-references. Contributors include leading scholars in their respective fields.

The Oxford History of the American People.
Samuel Eliot Morison. New York: New American Library, 1965.
*3 volumes of various lengths. $3.95–$4.95 each. ISBN 0-451-62192-1,
62408-4, and 62446-7.*

These volumes cover the history of the United States from the pre-Columbian period to the 1963 assassination of John F. Kennedy. Political, social, cultural, military, and economic history are covered.

The Timetables of American History.
Laurence Urdang, ed. New York: Simon and Schuster, 1981.
470 pp. $13.95. ISBN 0-671-25246-1.

This volume presents a chronology of U.S. history in tabular form. Columns cover history and politics, the arts, science and technology, and miscellaneous. The fact that events outside the United States are also included will help students gain a global perspective.

The Twentieth Century: An Almanac.
Robert H. Ferrell, ed. New York: World Almanac, 1985.
512 pp. $12.95. ISBN 0-345-32630-X.

This reference provides a chronological overview of events in the twentieth century. Both U.S. and world events are covered, as are scientific and technological advances. Brief biographies of important historical figures are provided.

Vietnam War Almanac.
Harry G. Summer. New York: Facts on File, 1985.
414 pp. $12.95. ISBN 0-8160-1017-X.

This almanac provides a brief history of Vietnam, a chronology of events in the war itself, and more than 450 brief articles on such topics as weapons, politicians in the United States and Vietnam, and protest movements. Additional sources of information are listed. The almanac includes a number of maps and more than 100 photographs.

Handbooks for Conducting Historical Research

Handbook for Research in American History: A Guide to Bibliographies and Other Reference Works.
Francis Paul Prucha. Lincoln, NE: University of Nebraska Press, 1987.
302 pp. $9.95. ISBN 0-8032-8719-4.

This is an extensive guide to information sources in U.S. history. The first part of the book deals with sources by type: library catalogs and guides, general bibliographies, book review indexes, and so on. The second part of the book is organized by subject area: political history, foreign affairs, military history, and so on.

Harvard Guide to American History.
Frank Freidel, ed. Cambridge, MA: Harvard University Press, 1974.
1,312 pp. $15. ISBN 0-674-37555-6.

A classic reference, this volume is organized into four sections: research methods and materials, biographies and personal records, comprehensive and area histories, and histories of special subjects.

Historian's Handbook: A Descriptive Guide to Reference Works.
Helen J. Poulton with Marguerite S. Howland. Norman, OK: University of Oklahoma Press, 1986.
300 pp. $10.95. ISBN 0-8061-1009-0.

The subtitle of this book accurately sums up its purpose and contents. It is somewhat different from other handbooks because the items cited are described, a feature that will make it useful to newcomers to historical research.

History: A Student's Guide to Research and Writing.
Robert Skapura and John Marlowe. Littleton, CO: Libraries Unlimited, 1988.
48 pp. $30 for set of 10. ISBN 0-87287-649-7.

This brief guide is designed to give students direction in beginning their research for reports and term papers. Steps in preparing a paper are also given.

The Modern Researcher.
Jacques Barzun and Henry F. Graff. New York: Harcourt Brace Jovanovich, 1985.
480 pp. $13.95. ISBN 0-15-562512-8.

This book focuses in detail on the process of conducting research and writing results. Students and teachers who use it not only will get direction in conducting their own research, but also will have a deeper understanding of how historians work.

A Student's Guide to History.
Jules R. Benjamin. New York: St. Martin's Press, 1987.
175 pp. $7.95. ISBN 0-312-77004-9.

This small handbook focuses not only on historical research but also on the use of history, reading history assignments and taking notes in class, studying for exams, writing book reviews and short papers. Thus it is a complete guide to the study of history and may be an especially suitable introduction for high school students.

Online Databases

The databases cited in this section are available through one or both of the following services:

BRS Information Technologies
1200 Route 7
Latham, NY 12110
(800) 468-0908

Dialog Information Services, Inc.
3460 Hillview Avenue
Palo Alto, CA 94304
(800) 3-DIALOG

Academic American Encyclopedia Database (AAED)
Supplier: Grolier Electronic Publishing
Availability: BRS: $20/hr.; citations: $.37 online, no offline charge
            DIALOG: $45/hr.; citations: no online charge, $.25 offline

This online edition of Grolier's academic encyclopedia provides teachers and students with 30,000 full-text entries, including tables, charts, cross-references, and bibliographic entries from the print version.

America: History and Life
Supplier: ABC-CLIO
Availability: DIALOG: $65/hr.; citations: no online charge, $.15 offline

This database indexes articles from almost 2,000 journals published worldwide. Books, book reviews, and dissertations are also indexed. The focus is the history and culture of the United States and Canada from prehistoric times to the present.

Arts and Humanities SEARCH
Supplier: The Institute for Scientific Information
Availability: BRS: $60/hr.; citations: $.39 online, no offline charge

This database focuses on arts and the humanities, including archaeology, architecture, dance, film, television, radio, folklore, history, language, linguistics, literature, music, philosophy, theater, and religion.

Biography Master Index
Supplier: Gale Research Company
Availability: DIALOG: $63/hr.; citations: $.55 online, $.65 offline

This is an index to biographical information from more than 600 publications, including biographical dictionaries, directories, and various kinds of handbooks.

Cendata
Supplier: U.S. Bureau of the Census
Availability: DIALOG: $36/hr.; citations: no online charge, $.20 offline

Cendata is a full-text database providing demographic and economic information from the Bureau of the Census. Also available via Cendata are the 20 most recent press releases from the Bureau of the Census.

Congressional Record Abstracts
Supplier: National Standards Association
Availability: DIALOG: $96/hr.; citations: $.15 online, $.25 offline

This database presents abstracts for each issue of the Congressional Record, the official journal of the legislative branch. This database will be of most interest to history students as a source of information on how current debates reflect enduring issues.

Dissertation Abstracts Online
Supplier: University Microfilms International
Availability: BRS: $34/hr.; citations: $.26 online, no offline charge
                 DIALOG: $72/hr.; citations: $.25 online, $.25 offline

This database provides access to virtually all doctoral dissertations accepted at North American universities since 1861. Only those dissertations added since 1980 have been abstracted, however. Information on ordering copies of the actual dissertations is supplied.

Educational Resources Information Center (ERIC)
Supplier: Office of Educational Research and Improvement
Availability: BRS: $16–$35/hr.; citations: $.11 online, no offline charge
                 DIALOG: $30/hr.; citations: $.10 online, $.14 offline

ERIC provides coverage of all areas of education, including history. Focus is on journal literature and "fugitive" documents not readily available elsewhere; these include locally developed materials, research reports, and conference papers, among others.

GPO Publications Reference File
Supplier: U.S. Government Printing Office
Availability: BRS: $26–$35/hr.; citations: $.07 online, no offline charge
             DIALOG: $35/hr.; citations: no online charge, $.10 offline

This database lists all documents for sale by the GPO. It can be used to locate and order government publications dealing with history, such as reports from the National Endowment for the Humanities or the U.S. Bureau of the Census.

Historical Abstracts
Supplier: ABC-CLIO
Availability: DIALOG: $65/hr.; citations: no online charge, $.15 offline

Articles from nearly 2,000 journals published worldwide are summarized and indexed. Focus is on history, social sciences, and humanities. Also cited are books and dissertations. Although the focus is not strictly the United States and Canada, students of U.S. history can use the database to gather information about events that impacted the United States.

Social SciSearch
Supplier: Institute for Scientific Information
Availability: BRS: $43.50–$64.50/hr.; citations: $.23 online, $.15 offline
             DIALOG: Nonsubscribers—$159/hr.; citations: $.20 online, $.25 offline. Subscribers—$62/hr.; citations: $.20 online, $.25 offline

This database allows researchers to trace citations both forward (i.e., find those works cited in a later work) and backward (i.e., find those works that have cited a particular previous work). Social and behavioral sciences are covered, as are interdisciplinary areas of study and approaches to history.

Periodicals

American Heritage: The Magazine of History
American Heritage (division of Forbes)
60 Fifth Avenue
New York, NY 10011
Bimonthly, plus issues in April and November. $24/yr.

This popular and lavishly illustrated journal covers a wide range of topics. For example, among the features in a recent issue were an analysis of the letters of General William Tecumseh Sherman; an article about the discovery of Machu Picchu; a memoir by historian Annie Dillard, who as a child was already intrigued by the French and Indian War; an article on the battle for Wake Island in World War II; and never-before-published photographs of FDR.

American Historical Review
American Historical Association
400 A Street, SE
Washington, DC 20003
5 times/yr. $43/yr.

This scholarly journal covers all periods of U.S. history as well as world history. Each issue contains five lengthy articles and a number of scholarly reviews.

American West
American West Publishing
3033 North Campbell Avenue
Tucson, AZ 85719
Bimonthly. $15/yr.

The official journal of the Western History Association, *American West* is written for both scholars and the general public. Each issue includes eight or nine articles on topics related to the West. The journal is illustrated.

Aztlan—International Journal of Chicano Studies Research
University of California, Los Angeles
Chicano Studies Research Center
405 Hilgard Avenue
Los Angeles, CA 90024
Semiannual. Individuals: $15/yr.; institutions: $20/yr.

Although the focus of this journal is broader than history, looking at contemporary concerns as well, it is of interest to students and teachers researching the history of Hispanics in the United States.

Ethnohistory
American Society for Ethnohistory
Arizona State Museum
University of Arizona
Tucson, AZ 85721
Quarterly. $10/yr.

This illustrated journal is "devoted to original research in the documentary history of the culture and movements of primitive peoples and related problems." Book reviews are included.

Great Plains Quarterly
Center for Great Plains Studies
1214 Oldfather Hall
University of Nebraska
Lincoln, NE 68588
Quarterly. $15/yr.

This journal focuses on issues related to the history and culture of the Great Plains, from earliest times to the present. Relevant books are reviewed.

Hispanic American Historical Review
Duke University Press
P.O. Box 6697
Durham, NC 27708
Quarterly. Individuals: $28/yr.; institutions: $45/yr.

Every issue of this scholarly journal includes four or five articles, with emphasis on the period from the seventeenth to nineteenth centuries. Critical book reviews are provided.

History News
American Association for State and Local History
172 Second Avenue North
Nashville, TN 37201
Monthly. Individuals: $40/yr.; students: $25/yr.; institutions: varies depending on annual budget (all rates include membership in AASLH)

History News includes articles on a range of topics of interest to museums, historians, and educators. Numerous announcements of programs and publications are included in the journal.

The History and Social Science Teacher
Grolier Publications
16 Overlea Boulevard
Toronto, Ontario, Canada M4H 1A6
Quarterly. Individuals: $16/yr.; students: $12/yr.; institutions: $19/yr.

This journal publishes articles on "curricular issues related to history, social sciences and social studies." For example, a recent issue included articles on the educational use of museums, local history, using pre-Columbian art to teach history, and researching social issues using databases.

Humanities
National Endowment for the Humanities
Superintendent of Documents
Government Printing Office
Washington, DC 20402
Bimonthly. $9/yr.

This journal, prepared by the National Endowment for the Humanities, carries scholarly articles, comments from prominent Americans on the value of the humanities in their own educations, and announcements of various NEH programs.

Journal of American History
Organization of American Historians
112 North Bryan Street
Bloomington, IN 47401
Quarterly. Individual: depends on income; students: $12/yr.; institutions: $80/yr. (all rates include membership in OAH)

This scholarly journal focuses exclusively on U.S. history, providing several scholarly articles and a large number of critical book reviews in each issue.

Journal of the History of Ideas
Temple University
Philadelphia, PA 19122
Quarterly. Individuals: $15/yr.; institutions: $25/yr.

This scholarly journal is devoted to intellectual and cultural history. Subjects treated include the history of philosophy, literature and the arts, the natural and social sciences, and religious, political, and social movements. At the secondary level, this journal is likely to be useful for advanced placement classes only.

Journal of Interdisciplinary History
MIT Press
28 Carleton Street
Cambridge, MA 02142
Quarterly. Individuals: $26/yr.; institutions: $60/yr.

This journal presents scholarly articles on interdisciplinary approaches to the study of history. Book reviews are included.

Journal of Social History
Carnegie-Mellon University Press
Schenley Park
Pittsburgh, PA 15213
Quarterly. $22/yr.

This scholarly journal includes interdisciplinary articles on social history topics, including women's history, history of the family, and history of various ethnic groups. Book reviews are included.

Journal of Southern History
Southern Historical Association
Rice University
P.O. Box 1892
Houston, TX 77251
Quarterly. $20/yr.

This highly regarded journal presents three or four scholarly articles in each issue. The focus is, as the title suggests, the history of the southern United States. Book reviews are also included.

Labor History
New York University
Bobst Library
70 Washington Square South
New York, NY 10012
Quarterly. Individuals: $21/yr.; institutions: $28/yr.

This journal focuses on the study of the history of work and the labor movement in the United States. A majority of the articles treat periods after 1865.

Magazine of History for Teachers of American History
Organization of American Historians
112 North Bryan Street
Bloomington, IN 47401
Quarterly. Individuals: $12/yr.; institutions: $17/yr.

This relatively new journal is designed to "address the interests and concerns of secondary history and social studies teachers." Each issue has a particular theme (e.g., development of nationalism, slavery, the frontier, the Constitution), presenting two or three articles on the theme along with three or four lesson plans complementing the articles. An interesting feature is a column in which secondary students discuss history topics.

Negro History Bulletin
Association for the Study of Afro-American Life and History
1407 14th Street, NW
Washington, DC 20005
Quarterly. Individuals: $25/yr.; institutions: $30/yr.

This journal treats the history of black Americans in three to six long articles per issue. Critical book reviews are also included in every issue.

New England Quarterly: A Historical Review of New England Life and Letters
New England Quarterly
Meserve Hall, 2nd Floor
Boston, MA 02115
Quarterly. $15/yr.

New England Quarterly is another highly regarded regional journal focusing on the history and culture of the region. In addition to four or five scholarly articles per issue, the journal provides critical book reviews.

Prologue: Journal of the National Archives
National Archives and Records Administration
Pennsylvania Avenue and Eighth Street
Washington, DC 20408
Quarterly. $12/yr.

This journal publishes scholarly articles based on records in the National Archives. Announcements on National Archives programs are also included in the journal.

Reviews in American History
The Johns Hopkins University Press
701 West 40th Street, Suite 275
Baltimore, MD 21211
Quarterly. Individuals: $18/yr.; students: $16/yr.; institutions: $45/yr.

This journal is devoted to reviews of scholarly historical writings, including 20 or more in each issue.

Signs: Journal of Women in Culture and Society
University of Chicago Press
P.O. Box 37005
Chicago, IL 60637
Quarterly. Individuals: $29/yr.; institutions: $58/yr.

This interdisciplinary journal treats new scholarship about women. Although the journal has a broad scope, many articles are of interest to students and teachers of U.S. history. For example, a special issue recently focused on women and the Constitution.

Social Education
National Council for the Social Studies
3501 Newark Street, NW
Washington, DC 20016

7 times/yr. Individuals: $40/yr.; students: $20/yr. (rates include membership in NCSS)

The official journal of NCSS, *Social Education* contains analytical articles as well as articles focusing on what and how to teach. All of the content areas comprising social studies are covered; several special sections in recent years have focused particularly on history.

Teaching History: A Journal of Methods
Emporia State University
Emporia, KS 66801
Semiannually. Individuals: $5/yr.; institutions: $10/yr.

This journal focuses on the teaching of history, in both high schools and colleges. The articles cover world history, as well as U.S. history. Critical book reviews are provided.

Technology and Culture
University of Chicago Press
P.O. Box 37005
Chicago, IL 60637
Quarterly. Individuals: $23.40/yr.; students: $16.15/yr.; institutions: $42.50/yr.

Prepared by the Society for the History of Technology, this journal focuses on "the development of technology and its relation with society and culture." Each issue includes two or three scholarly articles, reviews of museum exhibits related to technology, reports on conferences, and critical book reviews.

Women's Studies Quarterly
The Feminist Press
City University of New York
311 East 94th Street
New York, NY 10128
Quarterly. Individuals: $25/yr.; institutions: $35/yr.

This interdisciplinary journal covers issues and events related to women's studies and feminist education at all levels. Two issues each year have special themes (e.g., women and art; women and history; women, race and culture) and two are general. In addition to articles, course descriptions, and book reviews, the journal provides announcements of grants, scholarships, and other programs of interest.

Resources on Teaching History

The resources listed in this section are varied in their intent. Some were written to provide guidance or assistance to history teachers in improving their courses. Others, written in an attempt to reshape the curriculum in our schools, are usually not as directly helpful to teachers, but should be on the professional shelf of every school library because of the public debate and inquiry they have prompted.

Abrams, Eileen. **A Curriculum Guide to Women's Studies for the Middle School, Grades 5-9.**
New York: The Feminist Press, 1981.
60 pp. Paperbound. $6.95. ISBN 0-912670-94-0.

This guide for teaching about women in history and society can be used to plan a course on women or to plan for infusion into U.S. history and other courses.

Academic Preparation in Social Studies: Teaching for Transition from High School to College.
New York: College Entrance Examination Board, 1986.
112 pp. Paperbound. $6.95. ISBN 0-87447-224-5.

One of six sequels to the College Board's *Academic Preparation for College* (1983), this book suggests three changes in the content of social studies: (1) use of new findings in social history, (2) adoption of a worldwide perspective, and (3) more thorough incorporation of social studies concepts. The book describes how these three changes might be made in a program based on a core of world history, U.S. history, and U.S. government.

Banks, James A. **Multiethnic Education: Theory and Practice.**
Lexington, MA: Allyn and Bacon, 1981.
300 pp. Hardbound. $22.86. ISBN 0-205-07293-3.

This resource, by a leading proponent of multiethnic education, describes the history, rationale, and goals of multiethnic education; presents methodological issues and models; discusses characteristics of curricular reform; examines relationships to specific areas of the curriculum; and includes curriculum guidelines applicable to all areas.

Cheney, Lynne V. **American Memory: A Report on the Humanities in the Nation's Public Schools.**
Washington, DC: National Endowment for the Humanities, 1987.
35 pp. Paperbound. $4.

One of the reports contributing to the debate on the place of history in the curriculum, this booklet looks at problems with the current curriculum—too much emphasis on process, poor textbooks, and ill-prepared and overworked teachers. Three recommendations linked to these perceived problems conclude this essentially political document.

Commission on the Humanities. **The Humanities in American Life.**
Berkeley, CA: University of California Press, 1980.
205 pp. Paperbound. $5.95. ISBN 0-520-04183-6.

This report assesses the status of the humanities in the schools, in higher education, and in community and private life. It then makes recommendations for priorities and suggests methods of garnering support for the humanities.

Downey, Matthew T., ed, **"The Children of Yesterday."** *Social Education* 50 (April–May 1986): 260–293.
$5 for back issue of journal.

This special section of *Social Education* focuses on teaching about children in history. It includes an introduction to the benefits and possible pitfalls of teaching about children, several articles describing programs in which children are incorporated into the study of history, and an extensive annotated bibliography on the history of childhood.

Downey, Matthew T., ed. **History in the Schools.**
Washington, DC: National Council for the Social Studies, 1985.
54 pp. Paperbound. $7.25. ISBN 0-87986-049-9.

This document, the product of a one-day conference on the status of history education, looks at the place of history in the curriculum and concludes that it is still the dominant social studies subject. Problems in the curriculum, the methods and materials used in history classes, and preparation of history teachers are examined.

Downey, Matthew T., ed. **Teaching American History: New Directions.**
Washington, DC: National Council for the Social Studies, 1982.
115 pp. Paperbound. $8.75. ISBN 0-87986-043-X.

This volume looks at five areas of historical scholarship and their implications for the teaching of U.S. history. These areas are women, family, labor, Native Americans, and social history. For each, an essay on research in the area is followed by suggestions for classroom practice.

Finn, Chester E., Jr., Diane Ravitch, and Robert T. Fancher, eds. **Against Mediocrity: The Humanities in America's High Schools.**
New York: Holmes and Meier, 1984.
287 pp. Paperbound. $11.50. ISBN 0-8419-0945-8.

This collection examines the importance of humanities to education as a whole and discusses and provides case studies on the teaching of English, foreign languages, and history. Several articles are devoted to the education of teachers and improvement of teaching.

FitzGerald, Frances. **America Revised.**
New York: Random House, 1980.
256 pp. Paperbound. $5.95. ISBN 0-394-74439-X.

The author of this best-seller, a journalist, provides an analysis and critique of U.S. history textbooks and compares texts from different eras. FitzGerald's thesis is that national and educational politics have more influence on texts than does historical scholarship.

Haynes, Charles C. **Religious Freedom in America: A Teacher's Guide.**
Silver Spring, MD: Americans United Research Foundation.
108 pp. Paperbound. $2. ISBN 0-9617164-0-1.

This publication provides teachers with a variety of source materials for integrating the story of religious liberty into the curriculum. Background essays on religious freedom are followed by annotated lists of classroom materials for teaching about various topics and lists of other resources.

Hirsch, E. D., Jr. **Cultural Literacy: What Every American Needs to Know.**
New York: Random House, 1988.
268 pp. Paperbound. $6.95. ISBN 0-394-75843-9.

Hirsch's best-seller has four major components: a review of the research on reading, emphasizing the need for background information to read effectively; a discussion of why national language and culture are important in a pluralistic society; an analysis of how and why the schools have failed to develop cultural literacy and suggestions for addressing the problem; and the list of "what literate Americans know."

History–Social Science Framework for California Public Schools.
Sacramento, CA: California State Department of Education, 1988.
136 pp. Paperbound. $6. ISBN 0-8011-0712-1.

This new framework, which many expect to be a model for other states as well, proposes a substantially different curriculum arrangement than has been traditional for more than 50 years. Key differences include more emphasis on history and integration of biography, literature, and art with the teaching of history.

Howard, James, and Thomas Mendenhall. **Making History Come Alive.**
Washington, DC: Council for Basic Education, 1982.
99 pp. Paperbound. $5.50.

Yet another study on the status of history in the schools, this report concludes that "history is in trouble." The authors suggest reasons why history is important, why it is not taught as extensively as they believe it ought to be, and what the "irreducible minimum" of history instruction ought to be. Appendixes provide various aids for history teachers.

Keller, Clair W., and Denny L. Schillings, eds. **Teaching About the Constitution.**
Washington, DC: National Council for the Social Studies, 1987.
122 pp. Paperbound. $10.95. ISBN 0-87986-055-3.

This volume includes four brief scholarly essays on the origins and development of the Constitution, along with teaching activities related to the content in the essays. Most valuable are teaching activities on constitutional change, an area in which there is still room for additional instructional materials.

Kyvig, David E., ed. **Nearby History Series.**
Nashville, TN: American Association for State and Local History, 1986– .
3 books, 124–176 pp. Paperbound. $11.95 each. ISBN 0-910050-82-1, 84-8, and 88-0.

To date, this series includes three titles, although more will be published in the future. Each volume is subtitled "Exploring Their History" and focuses on one kind of place that can be explored in "doing" and teaching about local history. The first volume looks at local schools, the second at houses and homes, and the third at public places, such as parks, streets, and government buildings.

Metcalf, Fay D., and Matthew T. Downey. **Teaching Local History: Trends, Tips, and Resources.**
Boulder, CO: Social Science Education Consortium, 1977.
104 pp. Paperbound. $12.95. ISBN 0-89994-215-6.

This publication contains a variety of suggestions to help teachers introduce the study of local history. Topics covered include using the community as a historical resource; social, economic, and family history; architecture and public art; and folklore and cultural journalism.

Ravitch, Diane, and Chester E. Finn, Jr. **What Do Our 17-Year-Olds Know?**
A Report on the First National Assessment of History and Literature.
New York: Harper and Row, 1987.
302 pp. Hardbound. $15.95. ISBN 0-06-015849-2.

This much-publicized book reports the findings of a national assessment of
what 17-year-olds know about history and literature. It describes how and
why the assessments were done and presents the learning objectives for the
assessments. It describes how students did on the questions; looks at
correlations between such factors as parent education, sex, and ethnic
background and performance; and presents recommendations for remedying
the problem the assessment revealed—that students appear to know little
about history and literature.

Rosenzweig, Linda W., **"Teaching About Social History,"** *Social Education*
46 no. 5 (May 1982): 321-336.
$5 for back issue of journal.

This special section of *Social Education* presents two especially useful
articles. One presents an approach to integrating social history into history
courses, and the other looks at the use of social history in social science
courses. Two lists of resources for teaching social history are included.

Sewall, Gilbert T. **American History Textbooks: An Assessment of Quality.**
New York: Educational Excellence Network, Teachers College, 1987.
82 pp. Paperbound. $4.

Like several other reports listed in this section, this volume has provoked
considerable controversy. It provides a scathing critique of history textbooks
and suggests recommendations for their improvement. It should be noted
that no specific criteria for evaluating the texts were provided to the
reviewers, severely limiting the value of the study; still, the report is worth
reading because of the debate it has engendered.

Starr, Jerold M., ed., **"Teaching the Vietnam War,"** *Social Education* 52 no. 1
(January 1988): 23-57.
$5 for back issue of journal.

This special section of *Social Education* looks at why teachers should cover
Vietnam in their courses, how the war is covered in recent U.S. history
textbooks, training teachers to cover this topic, and a range of ideas for
teaching about the war. For example, one article describes a role play on the
origins of U.S. involvement in Vietnam while another describes a unit in
which students interviewed Vietnam veterans having various views on the
war and on the antiwar movement.

Women's History Curriculum Guide.
Santa Rosa, CA: National Women's History Project, n.d.
63 pp. Paperbound. $7.95. ISBN 0-938625-6920-7.

This K-12 curriculum guide provides background information for educators unfamiliar with the history of women in the United States, along with numerous suggestions for classroom use. Recommended supplementary instructional materials are listed.

Classroom Materials

Computer Software

American Foreign Policy
Source: Focus Media
            P.O. Box 865
            Garden City, NY 11530
Cost: 2 disks and guide, $119
Type: Tutorial
Grades: 7-12
Systems: Apple family

This package consists of four programs designed to develop students' understanding of U.S. foreign policy, from earliest times to the present. Titles of the programs are "The Emerging Nation Period," "From Isolationism to Imperialism," "From World War to Cold War," and "Super Powers in the Nuclear Age."

American History: Becoming a World Power
Source: Social Studies School Service
            P.O. Box 802
            Culver City, CA 90232
            (developed by Micro Learn/Word Associates)
Cost: 1 disk and guide, $39.95
Type: Tutorial
Grades: 7-12
Systems: Apple family, IBM PC/PCjr

The topics covered in this program are somewhat broader than the title might indicate, since it actually focuses on all events in the years between 1865 and 1912. Thus, Reconstruction, the frontier, industrialization, and urbanization are covered as well as expansionism and foreign policy.

American History Decades Games
Source: Social Studies School Service
P.O. Box 802
Culver City, CA 90232
(Developed by BrainBank)
Cost: Complete series of 3 disks and guides: $110; individual disk with guide: $39
Type: Game
Grades: 7–10
Systems: Apple family

Each disk contains five games that quiz students on the decades in which particular events in U.S. history occurred. Events related to politics, economics, science, technology, folklore, and art are included. The game can accommodate one to four players.

American History Keyword Series
Source: Focus Media
P.O. Box 865
Garden City, NY 11530
Cost: 3 disks and guides: $45 each
Type: Drill and practice
Grades: 7–12
Systems: Apple II family

These three disks help students review important vocabulary terms related to westward expansion, World War II, and changes in twentieth-century America. A variety of clues, such as definitions, examples, synonyms, and historical references, are provided to help students identify the terms.

The American People
Source: Focus Media
P.O. Box 865
Garden City, NY 11530
Cost: $45
Type: Game
Grades: 5–12
Systems: Apple II family, Commodore 64 and 128

Students compete to identify well-known Americans in the following categories: explorers, women, inventors, sports, the arts, and military leaders.

Choice or Chance?
Source: Rand McNally
P.O. Box 7600
Chicago, IL 60680

Cost: Complete series of 3 disks, guide, and masters for student
workbook: $111
Type: Simulation
Grades: 7-9
Systems: Apple II family, Atari 800

This program focuses on the relationship between geography and history.
Students examine problems caused by expansion and industrialization,
evaluate options, select an option, and compare the results they achieved
with what actually happened.

Decisions, Decisions: American History Series
Source: Tom Snyder Productions
90 Sherman Street
Cambridge, MA 02140
Cost: 2 programs, each containing 1 disk and guide: $89.95 each
Type: Simulation
Grades: 7-12
Systems: Apple family, IBM PC

These two simulations involve students in decision making about historical
issues. The two programs are titled "Urbanization: The Growth of Cities"
and "Immigration: Maintaining the Open Door." Connections are drawn
between historical and contemporary or future issues.

EasySearch: American Inventions
Source: Focus Media
P.O. Box 865
Garden City, NY 11530
Cost: Disk, guide, and workbook: $49
Type: Database
Grades: 5-9
Systems: Apple family

This database program allows students to search for information about
important inventions developed in the United States. Types of information
included are the inventor, the primary use and purpose of the invention, and
its original source of power.

European Theater and Pacific Theater
Source: Hartley Courseware
P.O. Box 419
Dimondale, MI 48821
Cost: 2 programs, each including 3 disks, 2 student books, and 1 guide,
$89.95 each

Type: Simulation
Grades: 10-12
Systems: Apple (64K), IBM PC (256K)

These two simulations help students understand the tactics used by the combatants in World War II. As students playing various groups attempt to "win" the war, they also learn why the war had such long-lasting effects.

Facts and Fallacies

Source: Hartley Courseware
             P.O. Box 419
             Dimondale, MI 48821
Cost: 2 disks and guide: $39.95 (Apple) or $49.95 (IBM)
Type: Drill and practice, game
Grades: 7-9
Systems: Apple family, IBM PC

This game provides a review of history facts. Questions are of varying difficulty, with more points awarded for more difficult questions.

Great American History Knowledge Race

Source: Focus Media
             P.O. Box 865
             Garden City, NY 11530
Cost: 2 disks, guide: $85
Type: Game
Grades: 9-12
Systems: Apple family, Commodore 64 and 128, IBM PC

This set of programs helps students review important historical facts. Categories related to later U.S. history include "Age of Imperialism," "Boom or Bust," "War and Cold War," and "America Today."

The HBJ Historian

Source: Harcourt Brace Jovanovich
             School Department
             6277 Sea Harbor Drive
             Orlando, FL 32821
Cost: 3 programs, each containing 2 disks, guide, copy masters,
             $156.60 each
Type: Tutorial
Grades: 7-12
Systems: Apple family (64K)

This series of programs puts students in the role of historical researchers, exploring hypotheses related to the following topics: "Boom Towns," "The Labor Movement Before 1915," and "The United States in Vietnam."

History 2 and History 3 (High School Skills Social Studies Instructional Series—Plato)

Source: Control Data Publishing
             3111 Sibley Memorial Drive
             Eagan, MN 55121
Cost: $115
Type: Tutorial, drill and practice
Grades: 9-12
Systems: IBM PC

This two-part program is designed to improve high school students' social studies skills. The first program deals with geographic expansion, economic expansion, and social expansion. The second program covers the quests for equality and security, changing lifestyles, and the future of the United States. (A third program—History 1—looks at the early years in U.S. history.)

The History of the U.S. Democomp Package

Source: Focus Media
             P.O. Box 865
             Garden City, NY 11530
Cost: set of 6 disks, guide, and workbook, $259
Type: Database (maps)
Grades: 5-12
Systems: Apple family (color monitor recommended)

This series of six programs includes dozens of colorful historical maps, many with overlays that show change over time. Graphs and charts are also included in the database, which is divided into the following six segments: "Explorers of North America," "The Thirteen Colonies," "Ownership of North America," "Territorial Expansion of the U.S.," "America Moves West," and "European Immigration to the U.S." The workbook helps students use the programs independently.

The Indian Wars

Source: Hartley Courseware
             P.O. Box 419
             Dimondale, MI 48821
Cost: set of 2 disks, guide, and 2 manuals: $89.95
Type: Simulation, tutorial
Grades: 10-12
Systems: Apple (64K), IBM (256K)

This simulation requires students to play the role of the U.S. Army or the Native American groups opposing it. They plan strategy and answer questions to gain strength.

Industrialism in America: An Economic History
Source: Focus Media
            P.O. Box 865
            Garden City, NY 11530
Cost: set of 2 disks and guide: $99
Type: Tutorial
Grades: 7–12
Systems: Apple family

This three-part program looks at the following topics: "The Industrial Revolution Comes to the U.S.," "The Age of Big Business," and "Industrial America in the 20th Century." Economic vocabulary and concepts are stressed as students learn about the historical development of our economic system.

Industrializing America: A Game of American Industrial Development
Source: Perfection Form Company
            1000 North Second Avenue
            Logan, IA 51546
Cost: 1 disk and guide, $39.95
Type: Simulation game
Grades: 7–12
Systems: Apple family

This program focuses on the growth and decline of key U.S. industries—the fur trade, railroads, iron and steel, oil, automobiles, power, textiles, and computers. Students play the role of investors, examining how historical developments affect their investments.

Living History
Source: Aquarius Instructional
            P.O. Box 128
            Indian Rocks Beach, FL 34635
Cost: 3 programs, each consisting of 1 disk and guide: $59.95 each
Type: Tutorial, drill and practice, game
Grades: 6–12
Systems: Apple family

These three programs present actual documents from U.S. history, along with vocabulary exercises, a game, and other activities designed to help students understand the importance of the documents presented. The first program covers the years from 1876 through World War I, the second from the end of World War I through World War II, and the third from the end of World War II through 1984.

MECC Dataquest: The Presidents

Source: MECC
            3490 Lexington Avenue North
            St. Paul, MN 55126
Cost: $49
Type: Database
Grades: 7–12
Systems: Apple (64K)

This package includes facts about the 40 U.S. presidents, their administrations, and events that took place while they were in office. Students must develop their own questions and criteria the computer will use to search for answers.

The Medalists Series

Source: Hartley Courseware
            P.O. Box 419
            Dimondale, MI 48821
Cost: 3 packages, each containing 1 disk and guide: $39.95 (Apple) or
          $49.95 (IBM)
Type: Game, drill and practice
Grades: 6–8
Systems: Apple family, IBM PC

Titles of interest in this series include "Presidents," "Black Americans," and "Women in History." The title, "The Medalists," refers to the designation given students when they achieve a designated score on the quiz/games.

Meet the Presidents

Source: Perfection Form
            1000 North Second Avenue
            Logan, IA 51546
            (Developed by Versa)
Cost: 2 disks, guide: $39.95
Type: Game, drill and practice
Grades: 4–9
Systems: Apple family

This program uses a game-show format to test students' knowledge of facts about the presidents. Entertaining graphics and music will stimulate student interest.

Oregon Trail

Source: MECC
            3490 Lexington Avenue North
            St. Paul, MN 55126

Cost: $29.95
Type: Simulation
Grades: 4-12
Systems: Apple (64K)

Perhaps the best-known piece of social studies software, *Oregon Trail* invites students to "relive the days of pioneers and covered wagons." Students make decisions and observe the consequences as they attempt to reach their destination—the Oregon Territory.

Presidential Profiles
Source: Opportunities for Learning
             20417 Nordhoff Street
             Chatsworth, CA 91311
Cost: $49.95
Type: Game
Grades: 5-12
Systems: Apple II family

This set of three games encourages students to learn, in-depth, about our nation's presidents. Timelines, facts about presidents, and visuals are incorporated into the games.

Quest for Files: Social Studies Series
Source: Mindscape
             3444 Dundee Road
             Northbrook, IL 60062
Cost: 2 disks and guides, $49.95 each
Type: Database, tutorial
Grades: 7-12
Systems: Apple II family (64K), IBM PC/PCjr

Titles of the two programs in this database series are "Families of the World: The Melting Pot" and "The American Presidency: Hail to the Chief." The programs encourage students to use the databases to test various hypotheses about the topic.

The Research Companion: Supreme Court Decisions
Source: Focus Media
             P.O. Box 865
             Garden City, NY 11530
Cost: 3 disks and guide: $119
Type: Simulation, database
Grades: 9-12
Systems: Apple with 64K

Part 1 of this program asks students to play the role of a law student or a legal assistant to a Supreme Court justice. With access to 60 landmark Supreme Court cases, students research important constitutional issues. The second part of the program gives students access to all the details of the relevant cases and allows the information to be printed.

Social Studies Data Bases

Source: Scholastic
          P.O. Box 7501
          Jefferson City, MO 65102
Cost: 3 disks, guide, student handbook, $79.95
Type: Data base
Grades: 7-12
Systems: Apple (64K), IBM PC, Tandy 1000

This program contains content files, instructions on how to create original files, and activities that teach students how to use data bases. Topics covered in the existing files are "The Expanding American Frontier," "Inventions and Technology," and "Twentieth Century America." The activities help students build files on U.S. presidents, local history, and pop culture and its history.

Timeliner

Source: Tom Snyder Productions
          90 Sherman Street
          Cambridge, MA 02140
Cost: $59.95
Type: Graphics
Grades: 5-12
Systems: Apple family

This program allows students or teachers to create their own timelines for display in the classroom. They simply input the dates and events they wish to display, and the computer produces a timeline drawn to scale. Several timelines can be combined for comparison and analysis.

Time Tunnel: American History

Source: Focus Media
          P.O. Box 865
          Garden City, NY 11530
Cost: 2 programs, each containing 1 disk and guide: $99 each
Type: Tutorial
Grades: 7-12
Systems: Apple family, Commodore 64, IBM PC, TRS-80

In each of these three-part programs, the second segment focuses on people from the period 1860-1920, and the third on people from 1920-1985. Among those covered are Henry Ford, W. E. B. DuBois, Emily Dickinson, Harry Truman, Jesse Owens, Helen Keller, and Rosa Parks. Students are given clues and must determine whom these clues describe.

U.S. Adventure

Source: K-12 MicroMedia
         6 Arrow Road
         Ramsey, NJ 07446
Cost: $39.95
Type: Game
Grades: 5-12
Systems: Apple family, Commodore 64, IBM PC

This program starts students in Delaware in 1787 and takes them on a cross-country geographic and historic tour. Students travel to the 50 states in the order of their admittance, discovering facts about each state and the nation as they proceed.

U.S. History

Source: Hartley Courseware
         P.O. Box 419
         Dimondale, MI 48821
Cost: $39.94 (Apple) or $49.95 (IBM)
Type: Drill and practice, game
Grades: 10-12
Systems: Apple family, IBM PC

This program provides a history review in a game format. Categories range from the early explorers to the present. The program can be used by individuals or groups.

Filmstrips, Slide Programs, and Media Kits

This section lists a selection of filmstrips, slide programs, recordings, and media kits covering the early years of U.S. history. Teachers should note that many filmstrips are now available on videocassette as well; the number is increasing rapidly. Check with the publisher regarding the availability of programs of interest in other formats. Also be careful when purchasing video materials that you do not already have the program in the filmstrip format.

America in the 1890s
Type: 4 photo resource files, 1 color filmstrip, 1 cassette, 4 worksheets, guide
Grades: 7–12
Length: Not applicable
Cost: $77
Source: Random House/Educational Enrichment Materials
             400 Hahn Road
             Westminster, MD 21157
Date: 1976

This multimedia kit looks at an era of social, economic, and political change. The sights, sounds, and key ideas of the period are presented.

America Divided: The Civil War and Reconstruction
Type: 4 color filmstrips, 4 cassettes, guide
Grades: 5–9
Length: 15 min. each
Cost: $140
Source: Encyclopaedia Britannica Educational Corporation
             425 North Michigan Avenue
             Chicago, IL 60611
Date: 1984

Titles in this series show its focus: "Sectional Differences and Slavery," "The Civil War: 1861-1864," "The Civil War: 1864-1865," and "Reconstruction." The discussion guide will aid teachers in developing student understanding of the causes and effects of the Civil War.

America Since World War II
Type: 8 color filmstrips, 8 cassettes, duplicating masters, guide
Grades: 10–12
Length: approx. 20 min. each
Cost: $240
Source: United Learning
             6633 West Howard Street
             Niles, IL 60648
Date: 1987

This up-to-date program gives students an overview of the 40 years since World War II ended—years that have reshaped U.S. life. Titles of individual programs are "The Superpowers Emerge," "Tension in the Nuclear Age," "The War in Vietnam," "Continued Involvement in Global Affairs," "New

Deal to New Federalism," "A Society in Upheaval," "Technology: On the Threshold of the Future," and "Economic Ups and Downs."

American Decades Series
Type: 7 kits, each containing 6 filmstrips, 3 cassettes, guide
Grades: 7–12
Length: approx. 15 min. each
Cost: $165 per set
Source: United Learning
            6633 West Howard Street
            Niles, IL 60648
Date: 1969–1981

Each set of programs in this series presents a detailed look at one decade in the twentieth century, from the teens to the seventies. To illustrate the kinds of topics presented, consider the individual titles in the set on the 1930s: *The Crash, The New Deal, On the Land, The Labor Movement, Prelude to War,* and *The Arts.*

The American Hero
Type: 3 color filmstrips, 3 cassettes, 52 worksheets, 8 transparencies,
            guide
Grades: 7–12
Length: Not applicable
Cost: $153
Source: Educational Audio Visual
            Pleasantville, NY 10570
Date: 1978

This multimedia kit looks at literary images of America's heroes and heroines to help students understand the American search for enduring values and heroic images. Among the literary figures examined are Hester Prynne, Huck Finn, Jay Gatsby, Holden Caulfield, and Rocky Balboa.

The American Woman: A Social Chronicle
Type: 6 color filmstrips, 6 cassettes, guide
Grades: 7–12
Length: approx. 15 min. each
Cost: $32 each or $150 for program
Source: Random House/Educational Enrichment Materials
            400 Hahn Road
            Westminster, MD 21157
Date: 1976

The six filmstrips together provide a chronological view of the history of women in the United States. Of particular interest to teachers of later U.S.

history are the following titles from the series: *Pioneer Woman and Belles of the Wild West; The Suffragist, the Working Woman, the Flapper; Breadlines, Assemblylines, Togetherness;* and *Liberation Now!*

America's 19th Century Wars: Triumph and Tragedy
Type: 6 color filmstrips, 6 cassettes, guide
Grades: 7–12
Length: approx. 15 min. each
Cost: $32 each or $150 for program
Source: Random House/Educational Enrichment Materials
             400 Hahn Road
             Westminster, MD 21157
Date: 1979

This series covers the War of 1812, the Mexican-American War, the Civil War (two filmstrips), the Indian Wars, and the Spanish-American War. For each war, information is provided on the background, the conflict itself, the way in which a resolution was negotiated, and the effects of the war on the United States.

America's Twentieth-Century Wars: The International Challenge
Type: 6 color filmstrips, 6 cassettes, guide
Grades: 7–12
Length: approx. 20 min. each
Cost: $32 each or $150 for set
Source: Random House/Educational Enrichment Materials
             400 Hahn Road
             Westminster, MD 21157
Date: 1979

This series explores U.S. involvement in four twentieth-century wars: World War I, World War II (two filmstrips), Korea, and Vietnam (two filmstrips). The causes of each conflict, the military strategies, public opinion, and outcome are all examined.

Black History in America
Type: 5 color filmstrips, 5 cassettes, guide
Grades: 7–12
Length: 20 min. each
Cost: $139
Source: Educational Design
             47 West 13th Street
             New York, NY 10011
Date: 1971

This five-part series is intended to provide a complete course in the history of black Americans. Three programs are of special interest to teachers of later U.S. history: *The Black Man in the Early 20th Century, The Black Revolution—Part I* (through 1965), and *The Black Revolution—Part II* (1966–1971).

Black Studies Resources
Type: 465 slides, guide
Grades: 7–college
Length: not applicable
Cost: $349
Source: Educational Design
            47 West 13th Street
            New York, NY 10011
Date: 1971

This massive slide collection includes primary-source documents, prints, drawings, engravings, and early photographs covering black history in the United States. Annotations are provided in the accompanying guide.

Building a Nation: The Story of Immigration
Type: 2 color filmstrips, 2 cassettes
Grades: 5–12
Length: 20 min. each
Cost: $62.95
Source: National Geographic Society
            Educational Services
            17th and M Streets, NW
            Washington, DC 20036
Date: 1983

This two-part program looks at the experiences of immigrants, including why they left their homelands and the obstacles they faced in the United States. The contributions of various immigrant groups to American life are also discussed.

The Building of the Panama Canal: "The Land Divided, the World United"
Type: 3 color filmstrips, 3 cassettes, guide
Grades: 7–12
Length: approx. 15 min. each
Cost: $40
Source: Multi-Media Productions
            P.O. Box 5097
            Stanford, CA 94305
Date: 1978

This set of filmstrips covers the building of the Panama Canal, from the first time the idea was discussed in the 1860s until its completion. The conditions workers on the canal endured are detailed, as are the engineering methods developed specifically for use in building the canal.

The Confident Years
Type:	5 color filmstrips, 5 cassettes, guide
Grades:	7–12
Length:	approx. 20 min. each
Cost:	$138
Source:	Random House/Educational Enrichment Materials
	400 Hahn Road
	Westminster, MD 21157
Date:	1985

This series looks at the 50 years of growth following the Civil War, focusing on the contrasts evident during the period—wealth and poverty, the promise of equality and the failure to make good on that promise, quiet peace and loud upheaval. Titles of the five programs are *Reconstruction, Riches, Roots, Reform,* and *Ragtime.*

The Cuban Missile Crisis: On the Edge of Apocalypse
Type:	2 color filmstrips, 2 cassettes, guide
Grades:	7–12
Length:	approx. 20 min. each
Cost:	$60
Source:	Random House/Educational Enrichment Materials
	400 Hahn Road
	Westminster, MD 21157
Date:	1981

This pair of filmstrips introduces students to the conflict between Communist and democratic nations that led to confrontation in Cuba. They view the debate on possible responses to Soviet missile placement and examine Kennedy's stance. Archival materials and reenactments are used to heighten interest.

Decades of History: The 20th Century
Type:	2 sets of 3 filmstrips, 3 cassettes
Grades:	7–12
Length:	18 min. each.
Cost:	$85.95 each set
Source:	National Geographic Society
	Educational Services
	17th and M Streets, NW
	Washington, DC 20036
Date:	1988

The first set of programs is entitled "The Early Years" and covers the 1920s, 1930s, and 1940s. The second set—"The Middle Years"—looks at the 1950s, 1960s, and 1970s. Social and political history are covered in these programs.

Developing the A-bomb: A Decision of Destiny

Type:	2 color filmstrips, 2 cassettes, guide
Grades:	7–12
Length:	20 min. each
Cost:	$60
Source:	Random House/Educational Enrichment Materials
	400 Hahn Road
	Westminster, MD 21157
Date:	1982

This pair of programs covers the research that led to development of the bomb, the Manhattan Project itself, and the dropping of the bomb on Hiroshima. The issues of nuclear proliferation, arms stockpiling, and the role of nuclear weapons in the cold war are briefly examined.

Famous Women of the West

Type:	1 color filmstrip, 1 cassette, guide
Grades:	7–12
Length:	13 min.
Cost:	$25
Source:	Multi-Media Productions
	P.O. Box 5097
	Stanford, CA 94305
Date:	1974

This program focuses on the women who helped settle the land west of the Mississippi. A range of outstanding women, including entertainers, politicians, teachers, and guides, are covered.

The Glory Days of the Railroad

Type:	4 captioned color filmstrips, 4 cassettes, guide (also available in captioned version without sound)
Grades:	4–10
Length:	approx. 15 min. each
Cost:	$45 each or $166 for set
Source:	Encyclopaedia Britannica Educational Corporation
	425 North Michigan Avenue
	Chicago, IL 60611
Date:	1985

This series looks at how the railroads united the nation. Titles of the four programs are *The Iron Horse, Workin' on the Railroad, The Great Train Robbers,* and *The Lonesome Whistle.*

The Great Depression
Type: 4 color filmstrips, 5 cassettes or LPs, worksheets, guide
Grades: 7–12
Length: not applicable
Cost: $186
Source: Educational Audio Visual
             Pleasantville, NY 10570
Date: 1973

This program focuses on the "economic and social conditions that contributed to the Depression, the inadequacy of the Hoover philosophy to cope with it, the coming of the New Deal and its departure from traditional handling of such crises, the effectiveness of its policies, and the universal disruption caused by the Depression." In addition to the filmstrips, the program provides a recorded discussion evaluating the New Deal's effectiveness and directions for a simulation.

The Great Depression: A Chronicle of the Lean Years
Type: 2 color filmstrips, 2 cassettes, guide
Grades: 7–12
Length: approx. 20 min. each
Cost: $60
Source: Random House/Educational Enrichment Materials
             400 Hahn Road
             Westminster, MD 21157
Date: 1982

This program covers the social and political events and changes of the 1930s, highlighting the voices of actual people who lived through that decade. The first filmstrip covers events through 1936, the second events from 1937 to the end of the decade.

Hiroshima Decision: Was the Use of the A-Bomb Necessary?
Type: Color filmstrip, cassette, 10 photographs, guide
Grades: 7–12
Length: 20 min.
Cost: $39.50
Source: Social Studies School Service
             P.O. Box 802
             Culver City, CA 90232
Date: not available

This filmstrip focuses on Truman's decision to use the atomic bomb against Japan. Background information on development of atomic weapons is also provided.

The History of the Black Man in the United States
Type: 4 color filmstrips, 4 cassettes, guide
Grades: 7–12
Length: approx. 20 min. each
Cost: $176
Source: Educational Audio Visual
Pleasantville, NY 10570
Date: 1970

These four programs look at four aspects of black American life in the twentieth century. Titles of the programs are *Harlem Renaissance, The Black Man in the Depression, Racism and the Kerner Commission Report,* and *Black Protest Movements.*

Immigration: The Dream and the Reality
Type: 6 color filmstrips, 6 cassettes, guide
Grades: 4–8
Length: approx. 10 min. each
Cost: $29 each or $140 for set
Source: Clearvue
5711 North Milwaukee Avenue
Chicago, IL 60646
Date: 1982

This series presents the stories of immigrants who came to the United States between the Civil War and World War I. Titles of the programs are *The Dream, The Reality, No Irish Need Apply, Little Italy, You Belong to Germany,* and *The Japanese Nightmare.*

Immigration: Growth of a Nation
Type: 2 color filmstrips, 2 cassettes, guide
Grades: 7–12
Length: approx. 20 min. each
Cost: $460
Source: Random House/Educational Enrichment Materials
400 Hahn Road
Westminster, MD 21157
Date: 1986

This two-part program looks at the major turning point in the story of immigration—the great flood of immigrants who came between 1880 and 1920. Their impact and the hardships they faced are examined.

Leaders in American History
Type: 3 sets of 4 color filmstrips and 4 cassettes, guide
Grades: 4-9
Length: approx. 13 min. each
Cost: $37 each, $133 for one set, or $359 for series
Source: Encyclopaedia Britannica Educational Corporation
             425 North Michigan Avenue
             Chicago, IL 60611
Date: 1977-1979

Each of these filmstrips uses historic photographs and original documents to enhance a biographical study of a leader in social justice, social reform, or American industrialization. Individuals covered in the series are Clarence Darrow, Franklin D. Roosevelt, John L. Lewis, Earl Warren, Jane Addams, Eugene Debs, Horace Mann, Elizabeth Cady Stanton, Thomas Edison, Henry Ford, Cyrus McCormick, and John D. Rockefeller.

Legacies: An Audio Introduction to the History of Women and the Family in America
Type: 9 audio cassettes, book, guide
Grades: 9-adult
Length: 9 hours
Cost: $50
Source: The Annenberg/CPB Project
             1111 16th Street, NW
             Washington, DC 20036
Date: 1987

This series of programs looks at the history of women and the family in the years from 1607 to 1870. Because of the social history approach taken, these materials would be valuable supplements to texts taking a political/military approach.

Manifest Destiny
Type: 2 color filmstrips, 1 cassette
Grades: 11-12
Length: approx. 17 min. each
Cost: $49
Source: Eye Gate Media
             3333 Elston Avenue
             Chicago, IL 60618
Date: 1971

This program surveys expansionist policies from 1781 to the closing of the frontier, looking particularly at why the United States chose to advance its boundaries.

Mark Twain's America

Type:	Color captioned filmstrip
Grades:	5–8
Length:	10 min.
Cost:	$17
Source:	Clearvue
	5711 North Milwaukee Avenue
	Chicago, IL 60646
Date:	1965

This filmstrip examines the ways in which the United States changed during Mark Twain's lifetime—1835–1910. Growth of the population and changes in transportation are a particular focus.

Martin Luther King, Jr. and the Civil Rights Movement: Barriers Fall

Type:	2 color filmstrips, 2 cassettes, guide
Grades:	7–12
Length:	20 min. each
Cost:	$60
Source:	Random House/Educational Enrichment Materials
	400 Hahn Road
	Westminster, MD 21157
Date:	1984

This two-part program traces not only the work of Dr. King but also the larger struggle for civil rights, from the abolition of slavery to the present. The filmstrip presents news photos depicting the activities of civil rights workers, as well as reaction by segregationists.

McCarthyism: Era of Fear

Type:	2 color filmstrips, 2 cassettes, guide
Grades:	7–12
Length:	20 min. each
Cost:	$60
Source:	Random House/Educational Enrichment Materials
	400 Hahn Road
	Westminster, MD 21157
Date:	1981

This set of materials presents a study of propaganda and confrontation. News photos and actual taped excerpts of testimony at the Army-McCarthy hearings lend authenticity to the program.

Muckrakers and Reformers

Type:	1 color filmstrip, 1 cassette
Grades:	11–12

Length: 18 min.
Cost: $32
Source: Eye Gate Media
             3333 Elston Avenue
             Chicago, IL 60618
Date: 1971

Muckrakers and Reformers presents actual pages from *Puck, McClure's,* and *Collier's* to illustrate the goals of the muckrakers. Similarities in rhetoric between the early 1900s and the present can be drawn.

Muckraking
Type: 2 color filmstrips, 2 cassettes or LPs
Grades: 7–12
Length: 20 min. each
Cost: $97
Source: Educational Audio Visual
             Pleasantville, NY 10570
Date: 1979

This program traces the history of the muckraking tradition from the days of Ida Tarbell, Lincoln Steffens, and others to the coverage of Watergate. Muckraking in television and radio is also covered.

Ongoing Issues in American Society
Type: 5 sets of 3 color filmstrips, 3 cassettes, and guide
Grades: 7–12
Length: 12–15 min. each
Cost: $37 each, $100 for each set, or $450 for series
Source: Encyclopaedia Britannica Educational Corporation
             425 North Michigan Avenue
             Chicago, IL 60611
Date: 1977–1980

Each set in this series focuses on one enduring public issue—immigration, the presidency, the problem of cities, U.S. business, and the American consumer. Each filmstrip in a set examines a different aspect of the problem. For example, the programs in the set on cities are *Boston, 1765: The Stamp Act Riot; Chicago, 1890s: Machine Politics;* and *Los Angeles, 1965: The Watts Riot.*

Patterns of Civilization: America
Type: 4 color filmstrips, 4 cassettes, guide
Grades: 7–8
Length: approx. 15 min. each
Cost: $106

Source: Random House/Educational Enrichment Materials
400 Hahn Road
Westminster, MD 21157
Date: 1974

This four-part program looks at four major themes in U.S. history: immigration, industrialization, poverty, and dissent. The material is enriched through excerpts from writings of the nation's founders. Historic prints and contemporary graphics are combined to provide visual interest.

Post World War II America: A Unit of Study
Type: 6 color filmstrips, 6 cassettes, guide, duplicating masters
Grades: 5-9
Length: approx. 15 min. each
Cost: $200
Source: United Learning
6633 West Howard Street
Niles, IL 60648
Date: 1987

This six-part series covers political, social, and economic events and trends since 1945. Titles of the programs are *The Cold War, The Vietnam Conflict, Trouble in Foreign Lands, The Political Scene, Society Changes,* and *Science and Technology.*

The Presidency: Decisions of Destiny
Type: 5 color filmstrips, 5 cassettes, guide
Grades: 7-12
Length: approx. 20 min. each
Cost: $178
Source: Random House/Educational Enrichment Materials
400 Hahn Road
Westminster, MD 21157
Date: 1982

These five filmstrips look at key decisions faced by five presidents. The titles reveal the decisions examined: *Theodore Roosevelt Builds a Canal, Franklin Roosevelt Fights the Depression, Truman Acts in Korea, Eisenhower Intervenes in Little Rock,* and *Kennedy Confronts the Soviet Union.* A second set of filmstrips, looking at decisions made by earlier presidents, is also available.

Presidents and Precedents
Type: 10 filmstrips, 10 cassettes, guide, 10 duplicating masters, wall chart
Grades: 7-12
Length: approx. 20 min. each

Cost: $214
Source: Random House/Educational Enrichment Materials
            400 Hahn Road
            Westminster, MD 21157
Date: 1976

This multimedia kit pairs early and later presidents, examining how decisions became models for future problem solving and decision making. Pairs covered are Washington and Truman, Jackson and Lincoln, Jefferson and Wilson, the two Roosevelts, Monroe and Kennedy.

Presidents of the United States
Type: 8 filmstrips, 8 cassettes
Grades: 5–12
Length: 16–17 min. each
Cost: $226.60
Source: National Geographic Society
            Educational Services
            17th and M Streets, NW
            Washington, DC 20036
Date: 1980

These programs look at the personalities, early lives, families, and administrations of the following presidents: Theodore and Franklin Roosevelt, Wilson, Hoover, Truman, Eisenhower, Kennedy, and Johnson. An earlier series looks at presidents of the eighteenth and nineteenth centuries.

Prohibition: Can Morality Be Legislated?
Type: 2 color filmstrips, 1 cassette, guide
Grades: 9–12
Length: 15 min. each
Cost: $30
Source: Multi-Media Productions
            P.O. Box 5097
            Stanford, CA 94305
Date: 1975

These programs trace the spirit of temperance throughout U.S. history, look at its victory in enactment of Prohibition, the results of Prohibition, and the decision to repeal it. Archival photographs and cartoons comprise much of the programs.

Reconstruction
Type: 2 color filmstrips, 2 cassettes or LPs
Grades: 7–12
Length: 20 min. each

Cost: $97
Source: Educational Audio Visual
            Pleasantville, NY 10570
Date: 1979

This program provides an in-depth look at Reconstruction. The first filmstrip looks at Lincoln's plan for Reconstruction, the Radicals, life in the postwar South, the impeachment of Johnson, and the 1868 election. The second program shows both the achievements and failures of Reconstruction, covering the scalawags and carpetbaggers, rise of the Ku Klux Klan, and the 1876 election.

The Rise of the American Labor Movement: Toil and Struggle
Type: 2 color filmstrips, 2 cassettes, guide
Grades: 7-12
Length: 20 min. each
Cost: $60
Source: Random House/Educational Enrichment Materials
            400 Hahn Road
            Westminster, MD 21157
Date: 1984

The first part of this two-part program looks at how industrialization and immigration combined to create "the climate in which unionism was born." The second part looks at the Great Depression as the "testing ground" for the labor movement. Challenges facing labor and management today are also covered.

Settling the West
Type: 6 color filmstrips, 6 cassettes, guide
Grades: 7-9
Length: approx. 15 min. each
Cost: $28 each or $133 for program
Source: Random House/Educational Enrichment Materials
            400 Hahn Road
            Westminster, MD 21157
Date: 1971

This series looks at how the land gained through the Louisiana Purchase was settled in the years from 1803 to 1869. Individual filmstrips look at *The Trailblazers, The Miners, Wagon Trains to Railroads, The Cattlemen, The Farmers,* and *Growth of Towns and Cities.*

The Sixties: The Best of Times, the Worst of Times
Type: 2 color filmstrips, 2 cassettes, guide
Grades: 7-12

Length: 20 min. each
Cost: $60
Source: Random House/Educational Enrichment Materials
400 Hahn Road
Westminster, MD 21157
Date: 1981

These filmstrips provide a broad view of four major events in the 1960s: civil rights, space exploration, the Vietnam War, and the counterculture. Students are encouraged to reflect on the balance of successes and failures.

Social Reform Movements
Type: 4 color filmstrips, 4 cassettes or LPs
Grades: 7-12
Length: approx. 20 min. each
Cost: $176
Source: Educational Audio Visual
Pleasantville, NY 10570
Date: 1973

This set of filmstrips examines the origins, nature, and character of reform in America. The first filmstrip looks at *The Reform Tradition in America.* The second looks at early reform efforts (1830-1860). The third focuses on *The Progressive Era,* while the fourth looks at *The 1930s.*

Space, Sputnik, the Moon and Beyond
Type: 2 color filmstrips, 2 cassettes, guide
Grades: 7-12
Length: 20 min. each
Cost: $60
Source: Random House/Educational Enrichment Materials
400 Hahn Road
Westminster, MD 21157
Date: 1987

This presentation opens with a history of the scientific developments that made space travel possible—from the work of Galileo to Goddard to the Soviets' launching of *Sputnik* and the eventual U.S. moon landing. The second part of the package examines space exploration that has occurred since the moon landings. A reappraisal of the shuttle program and an examination of alternate technologies conclude the program.

The Spanish-American War
Type: 2 color filmstrips, 1 cassette
Grades: 11-12
Length: 17 min. each

Cost: $49
Source: Eye Gate Media
           3333 Elston Avenue
           Chicago, IL 60618
Date: 1971

This program analyzes the mood of the American people in the 1880s and 1890s, examining how that mood led to the war with Spain and the eventual emergence of the United States as a world power. The influence of the media is also covered.

The Story of Great American Inventors
Type: 6 filmstrips, 3 cassettes
Grades: 4–9
Length: approx. 12 min. each
Cost: $36 each or $141 for set
Source: Eye Gate Media
           3333 Elston Avenue
           Chicago, IL 60618
Date: 1977

These six biographical programs provide a perspective on American inventions and their impact on history. Titles of the individual programs are *Whitney, Howe and Singer: Inventors of New Machines; McCormick, Deere and Glidden: Inventors in Agriculture; Henry, Vail and Morse: Inventors of New Communications; Westinghouse and Morgan: Inventors of New Safety Devices; Edison and Latimer: Inventors in Electricity;* and *Selden, Duryea, Olds and Ford: Inventors of Automobiles.*

Supreme Court Cases
Type: 2 programs, 1 containing 3 cassettes and 1 containing 4 cassettes
Grades: 10–12
Length: not applicable
Cost: $45 for 3-cassette set and $60 for 4-cassette set
Source: Educational Audio Visual
           Pleasantville, NY 10570
Date: 1969 and 1975

These cassettes present Supreme Court cases that have significantly affected U.S. history. A narrator briefly introduces each case, the arguments for both sides are presented, and a condensation of the Court's decision is given; when appropriate, excerpts from dissenting opinions are given. One program of three cassettes focuses on civil liberties cases, beginning with *Dred Scott* and ending with *Miranda.* The second set looks at cases between 1969 and 1974.

Supreme Court Decisions That Changed the Nation
Type: 6 color filmstrips, 6 cassettes, 6 guides
Grades: 7-12
Length: approx. 20 min. each
Cost: $59 each or $277 for program
Source: Center for Humanities
P.O. Box 1000
Mount Kisco, NY 10549
Date: 1986

This series examines seven landmark Supreme Court cases. Of particular interest to teachers of later U.S. history are programs on *Plessy v. Ferguson, Brown v. Topeka Board of Education, Gideon v. Wainwright,* and *Miranda v. Arizona.* Students learn not only about the substance of the cases and their impact on the United States but also about the workings of the Supreme Court.

U.S. History Through Architecture
Type: 4 color filmstrips, 4 cassettes, guide
Grades: 7-12
Length: approx. 20 min. each
Cost: $154
Source: Social Studies School Service
P.O. Box 802
Culver City, CA 90232
(produced by McIntyre)
Date: 1977

This series looks at four periods of U.S. history by examining the architecture of each. The periods covered are the colonial, federal, eclectic, and international.

The United States as World Leader
Type: 8 color filmstrips, 8 cassettes or LPs, document packets, guide
Grades: 7-12
Length: not applicable
Cost: $287
Source: Educational Audio Visual
Pleasantville, NY 10570
Date: 1968

This comprehensive program traces the evolution of our nation's position in world affairs since the turn of the century. Titles of the individual programs are *Entering the World Scene: To 1913, The Road to War: To 1917, The War and the Treaty: 1917-1919, Aloof From World Affairs: 1919-1933, The Gathering Storm: 1933-1941, World War II: 1941-1945, The Burden of Responsibility: 1945-1953,* and *Uneasy Coexistence: 1953-1963.*

The United States as a World Power: From the 1890s to the 1970s
Type: 3 color filmstrips, 3 cassettes
Grades: 5-12
Length: 17 min. each
Cost: $85.95
Source: National Geographic Society
             Educational Services
             17th and M Streets, NW
             Washington, DC 20036
Date: 1981

This series of three programs looks at major diplomatic efforts, military conflicts, and foreign policies that have "defined the role the nation plays in international affairs." The filmstrips are divided chronologically, with the first covering the years to 1921, the second 1921 to 1945, and the third the period since World War II.

The Watergate Scandal: People, Power, and Politics
Type: 2 color filmstrips, 2 cassettes, guide
Grades: 7-12
Length: 20 min. each
Cost: $60
Source: Random House/Educational Enrichment Materials
             400 Hahn Road
             Westminster, MD 21157
Date: 1985

This set of programs traces the Watergate scandal from the discovery of the burglary to the eventual resignation of President Nixon. The long-term effects of the episode are examined by those directly involved in the story.

Westward Movement
Type: 5 color filmstrips, 5 cassettes, guide, duplicating masters
Grades: 5-9
Length: approx. 15 min. each
Cost: $170
Source: United Learning
             6633 West Howard Street
             Niles, IL 60648
Date: 1985

This unit includes filmstrips with the following titles: *The First Frontier, Early Frontier Life, Moving Deep Into the Interior, Settling Western Lands,* and *Sodbusters, Cowboys, and Indians.* An interesting feature is use of folk songs to illustrate aspects of pioneer life.

Where Historians Disagree

Type: 4 sets each including 2 color filmstrips, 2 cassettes, and guide
Grades: 7-12
Length: approx. 20 min. each
Cost: $60 per set
Source: Random House/Educational Enrichment Materials
             400 Hahn Road
             Westminster, MD 21157
Date: 1986

Each two-filmstrip set in this series looks at an event in U.S. history about which historians have differing theories or interpretations. Topics applicable to the later years of U.S. history are the success or failure of Reconstruction, the New Deal, the Japanese attack on Pearl Harbor, and the origins of the cold war.

Women in American History

Type: 6 color filmstrips, 6 cassettes, 6 guides, duplicating masters
Grades: 7-12
Length: approx. 15 min. each
Cost: $139
Source: Educational Activities
             P.O. Box 392
             Freeport, NY 11520
Date: 1973

This series looks at women's contributions, as well as their struggles for equality and justice. Vignettes from the lives of well-known women, as well as excerpts from primary source documents, give students a firsthand look at women's roles in various periods of history.

World War I and World War II

Type: 2 sets of 5 color filmstrips, 5 cassettes, guide
Grades: 7-12
Length: approx. 20 min. each
Cost: $138 for each set
Source: Random House/Educational Enrichment Materials
             400 Hahn Road
             Westminster, MD 21157
Date: 1986, 1972

Posters, cartoons, combat photographs, and eyewitness drawings provide the visual materials for these programs; the narration is supplemented by excerpts from speeches, poems, and letters home. The result is a detailed treatment of each of the world wars. The treatment of World War II focuses more heavily on military strategy than does the program on World War I, which looks more closely at personal experiences.

Games, Simulations, and Dramatizations

American History Re-creations
Grades: 8–12
Playing time: 3–4 hours for each re-creation
Participants: 15–35
Cost: $35 for each set of 5 re-creations
Publisher: Interact
                 P.O. Box 997
                 Lakeside, CA 92040

Students re-create such historical events as the trial of Andrew Johnson, the Philippine islands annexation debate, the establishment of a quota system for immigration in the early 1920s, the 1940 debate over U.S. neutrality, the Cuban missile crisis, and the trial of William Calley.

Causes of World War II
Grades: 8–12
Playing time: 1 or more hours per game
Participants: 6–36
Cost: $6 each or $17 for set of three games
Publisher: Social Studies School Service
                 P.O. Box 802
                 Culver City, CA 90232
                 (developed by H.M.S. Historical Games)

This set of three games focuses on the causes of World War II, with the first game focusing on events from 1919–1933, the second on 1933–1936, and the third on 1937–1941. The games focus on decision making.

Collision
Grades: 7–12
Playing time: 8–12 hours
Participants: 15–35
Cost: $16
Publisher: Interact
                 P.O. Box 997
                 Lakeside, CA 92040

This resource simulates the conflicts between Native Americans and the U.S. government. Students learn about the history of individual Native American groups, as well as current issues facing the government in its relationship with Native Americans.

Equality
Grades:	4–8
Playing time:	15–20 hours
Participants:	20–35
Cost:	$16
Publisher:	Interact
	P.O. Box 997
	Lakeside, CA 92040

Students analyze five short essays on black history, role play incidents between minority groups, and participate in a school board meeting on desegregation. During the debriefing, students have the opportunity to analyze their own views on racial problems.

Fifties
Grades:	7–12
Playing time:	10–30 hours
Participants:	15–35
Cost:	$16
Publisher:	Interact
	P.O. Box 997
	Lakeside, CA 92040

Students take the role of historians of the 1950s, examining both big events of the decade (the McCarthy hearings) and social phenomena (the Beatniks, Davy Crockett rage). As families, they plan an ideal 1950s weekend. They also interview someone who grew up in the decade and examine yearbooks from the 1950s.

Games and Strategies for Teaching U.S. History
Grades:	8–12
Playing time:	variable
Participants:	variable
Cost:	$15
Publisher:	J. Weston Walch
	P.O. Box 658
	Portland, ME 04104

This book includes a number of games and simulations for use in U.S. history classes. Among these are team games, board games, debates, and mock trials.

Gateway
Grades:	7–12
Playing time:	10–16 hours
Participants:	20–35

Cost: $16
Publisher: Interact
                P.O. Box 997
                Lakeside, CA 92040

Gateway involves three learning experiences that help students define "American" and analyze the goals of our pluralistic society: they simulate the immigrant experience of the early twentieth century, hold congressional hearings on immigration restrictions, and examine a group of students' call to teach ethnic studies instead of U.S. history.

Great American Confrontations
Grades: 7–12
Playing time: 1 day for each confrontation
Participants: 10–35
Cost: $12 for each confrontation
Publisher: Interact
                 P.O. Box 997
                 Lakeside, CA 92040

Each confrontation involves students in presenting a "television show"—panel, debate, interview, game-show competition—on an event from U.S. history. Reformers, politicians, and industrialists from the Progressive Era participate in a debate, the programs of the New Deal are put on trial, a congressional committee convenes in Arizona to investigate charges related to the internment of Japanese-Americans, and key issues of the 1960s and 1970s are debated.

Great American Lives
Grades: 7–12
Playing time: 1–2 hours for each biography
Participants: 10–35
Cost: $10 for each biography
Publisher: Interact
                 P.O. Box 997
                 Lakeside, CA 92040

This series uses a "This is Your Life" format to familiarize students with the lives of Elizabeth Cady Stanton, Eleanor Roosevelt, John Kennedy, and Martin Luther King, Jr.

Great Women Biographical Card Games
Grades: 3–adult
Playing time: 20 min.
Participants: 3–6
Cost: $7 for each set

Publisher: National Women's History Project
               P.O. Box 3716
               Santa Rosa, CA 95402

Three sets of cards acquaint players with the lives of *Foremothers* (Susan B. Anthony, Harriet Tubman, Sojourner Truth, etc.), *Founders and Firsts* (Clara Barton, Elizabeth Blackwell, Amelia Earhart, etc.), and *Poets and Writers* (Louisa May Alcott, Harriet Beecher Stowe, Phillis Wheatley, etc.).

Herstory
Grades: 8-12
Playing time: 15-23 hours
Participants: 20-35
Cost: $16
Publisher: Interact
              P.O. Box 997
              Lakeside, CA 92040

Students work in male-female teams to study role expectations and marital customs throughout U.S. history. Optional activities allow students to study prominent women and learn more about the Seneca Falls Convention.

Homefront
Grades: 7-12
Playing time: 10-20 hours
Participants: 16-35
Cost: $16
Publisher: Interact
              P.O. Box 997
              Lakeside, CA 92040

This unit looks at U.S. society during World War II. Students join teams that examine recreation/entertainment, socioeconomic problems, daily life/ education, and work. They also undertake community research projects to learn more about the era.

Homestead
Grades: 5-8
Playing time: 10-13 hours
Participants: 20-35
Cost: $40
Publisher: Interact
              P.O. Box 997
              Lakeside, CA 92040

In this simulation, students act as families homesteading after the Civil War. They must choose their land, plant crops, raise livestock, and cut timber.

Those families who are not "cut out to be farmers" may decide to establish businesses. In the last half of the simulation, students create a frontier community, hold elections, build roads, and pay taxes.

Involvement Part II: 1885-1945
Grades:	9-12
Playing time:	1-2 hours per simulation
Participants:	20-30
Cost:	$10
Publisher:	Social Studies School Service
	P.O. Box 802
	Culver City, CA 90232

This resource includes instructions for brief simulations related to farming, imperialism, World War I, the stock market, the Great Depression, and World War II.

Judgment
Grades:	8-12
Playing time:	8-10 hours
Participants:	15-35
Cost:	$16
Publisher:	Interact
	P.O. Box 997
	Lakeside, CA 92040

This simulation looks at President Truman's decision to use the atomic bomb in the war against Japan. The simulation is set in a trial in which students must decide whether Truman is guilty of "war crimes." Analogies are drawn with contemporary situations.

Mission
Grades:	7-8
Playing time:	10-13 hours
Participants:	20-35
Cost:	$16
Publisher:	Interact
	P.O. Box 997
	Lakeside, CA 92040

This role play focuses on U.S. foreign policy in Vietnam. Students play hawks, doves, and moderates working to influence presidential decisions.

Panic
Grades:	8-12
Playing time:	15-23 hours

Participants: 24–35
Cost: $16
Publisher: Interact
                    P.O. Box 997
                    Lakeside, CA 92040

This simulation helps students understand the reaction to the depression of the 1930s, emphasizing the great contrast between that decade and the prosperous 1920s. In an interesting twist, a simulation involving inflated grades is used to develop student understanding of the emotional reactions in particular.

Peace
Grades: 8–12
Playing time: 12–20 hours
Participants: 15–35
Cost: $16
Publisher: Interact
                    P.O. Box 997
                    Lakeside, CA 92040

The focus of this unit is the range of decisions faced by President Wilson during World War I. Students practice writing skills through publishing of newspapers propagandizing their positions. Use of logical reasoning is stressed.

Progressive Era
Grades: 7–12
Playing time: 4 hours
Participants: 13–37
Cost: $17.50
Publisher: Social Studies School Service
                    P.O. Box 802
                    Culver City, CA 90232

Teams of students develop programs related to nine problems the United States faced in the 1890s: business monopolies, corruption in government, women's rights, conservation, city problems, labor problems, consumerism, farm problems, and unequal distribution of wealth. Elected representatives study the practicality of proposed solutions.

The Spanish-American War
Grades: 7–12
Playing time: 5 hours
Participants: 32–105

Cost: $17.50
Publisher: History Simulations
               P.O. Box 2775
               Santa Clara, CA 95051

Students represent pressure groups with particular positions on war with Spain. They try to win others over to their views before a decision for war or peace is made.

Strike
Grades: 8–12
Playing time: 10–12 hours
Participants: 20–35
Cost: $16
Publisher: Interact
                 P.O. Box 997
                 Lakeside, CA 92040

Focusing on the history of U.S. labor relations, this simulation helps students understand the evolution of labor-management relations over the past 100 years.

20 Short Plays for American History Classes
Grades: 6–9
Playing time: variable
Participants: variable
Cost: $15
Publisher: J. Weston Walch
                 P.O. Box 658
                 Portland, ME 04104

This resource contains 20 easy-to-use plays, 14 of which are brief plays that can be prepared for and read in one class period, six of which can be staged for more formal presentation.

U.S. History Classroom Games
Grades: 7–12
Playing time: variable
Participants: 2–35
Cost: $6 for each game
Publisher: Social Studies School Service
                 P.O. Box 802
                 Culver City, CA 90232
                 (developed by H.M.S. Historical Games)

This series of flexible games covers numerous topics in U.S. history, including the Chisholm trail, building the steel empire, the stock market crash, inventions during the Industrial Revolution, and development of the U.S. economy.

Womanspeak

Grades:	9–adult
Playing time:	1 hour
Participants:	12
Cost:	$3.25
Publisher:	National Women's History Project
	P.O. Box 3716
	Santa Rosa, CA 95402

This play shows a contemporary woman in search of her historical roots. Such women as Sojourner Truth, Susan B. Anthony, Margaret Sanger, and Eleanor Roosevelt speak to her about the tradition of women in U.S. history.

Posters, Study Prints, and Other Visual Aids

Achievements of American Women

Grades:	7–12
Description:	8 two-color 12″ × 18″ posters
Cost:	$4.95 for set
Publisher:	Hayes School Publishing
	321 Pennwood Avenue
	Wilkinsburg, PA 15221

Each of these eight posters presents candid photographs and biographical information about women who have achieved in one of the following fields: firsts, science, art and literature, performing arts, government, social reform, sports, common women.

American History Images on File

Grades:	7–12
Description:	3 books, each containing 300 reproducible images with annotations
Cost:	$95 each
Publisher:	Facts on File
	460 Park Avenue South
	New York, NY 10016

The first book in this series, *The Faces of America,* contains portraits and biographies of settlers, writers, politicians, artists, musicians, reformers, and sports figures. The second, *Key Issues in American Constitutional History,* contains annotated prints, drawings, paintings, photographs, and maps related to such topics as abolition, federalism vs. regionalism, women's rights, labor, and urbanization. Both of these volumes cover the full range of U.S. history, while the third volume presents images related specifically to the *American Civil War and the Reconstruction.*

American History Transparency Books
Grades: 7–12
Description: 9 books, each containing 12 full-color transparencies, 28
                duplicating masters, and a teacher's guide
Cost: $9.95 each
Publisher: Milliken Publishing
                P.O. Box 21579
                St. Louis, MO 63132

Each book in the series looks at a particular event or era in U.S. history. Although a majority of the events fall in the earlier years of the nation, the years from 1865–1890 and 1890–1900 are the focus of two books. The full-color transparencies present maps, diagrams, and drawings.

American Indian
Grades: 7–12
Description: 18 full-color transparencies, 47 overlays, teacher's guide
Cost: $174
Publisher: Social Studies School Service
                P.O. Box 802
                Culver City, CA 90232

This resource provides information on Native Americans' culture, discoveries, migrations, and lifestyles throughout the span of U.S. history. Archaeological, anthropological, sociological, and historical perspectives are presented.

American Studies Series
Grades: 5–12
Description: 10 full-color 50″ × 50″ wall maps
Cost: $288 with tripod; $348 with disc base or multiroller
Publisher: Rand McNally
                P.O. Box 7600
                Chicago, IL 60680

Each of these full-color wall maps includes quotations, charts, and pictures, along with the maps. Topics include the western frontier in the late 1800s, expansion of the United States beyond its territorial boundaries, immigration, World War I and World War II, and population mobility.

American Timeline Series
Grades: 7–12
Description: 4 books, each containing a foldout timeline, 28 duplicating masters, and a teacher's guide
Cost: $5.95 each
Publisher: Milliken Publishing
              P.O. Box 21579
              St. Louis, MO 63132

These four books look at *Industrial America, Entering the 20th Century, World War II to the 80s,* and *Future Problems and Alternatives.* The timelines presented can be removed for display in the classroom.

American West Wallcharts
Grades: 4–12
Description: 24 full-color 14½″ × 19″ wall charts
Cost: $29.75 for set
Publisher: Social Studies School Service
              P.O. Box 802
              Culver City, CA 90232

These 24 charts depict the history of the American West. They focus on the following topics: pioneers, cowboys, gunfighters, Indians, and the Indian wars. Each chart is organized around a single concept and can be used to stimulate class discussion.

Americans Who Changed Our History
Grades: 9–12
Description: 100 black-and-white 8½″ × 11″ photographs with essays on reverse
Cost: $21.95 for set
Publisher: J. Weston Walch
              P.O. Box 658
              Portland, ME 04104

These 100 black-and-white study prints show photographs of Americans from various eras of history; those pictured contributed in the political, social, technological, economic, and reform fields. On the back of each photograph is a brief biography of the pictured man or woman.

A Cartoon History of U.S. Foreign Policy
Grades: 7–adult
Description: 52 black-and-white 11″ × 14″ cartoons with guide

Cost: $49.50
Publishei: Documentary Photo Aids
              P.O. Box 956
              Mt. Dora, FL 32757

These 52 cartoons illustrate how the United States became involved in international affairs. Such events as the War of 1812, Monroe Doctrine, Berlin Airlift, and Vietnam War are covered.

A Cartoon History of Watergate

Grades: 7-adult
Description: 34 black-and-white 11″ × 14″ cartoons with guide
Cost: $32
Publisher: Documentary Photo Aids
                P.O. Box 956
                Mt. Dora, FL 32757

This resource presents editorial cartoons related to the specifics of the Watergate affair and its significance in the history of the 1970s.

Chief Briefs

Grades: 5-12
Description: 2 sets of full-color 11″ × 17″ posters, one containing 12 posters, the other 15 posters
Cost: $17.95 for set of 12, $19.95 for set of 15
Publisher: Perfection Form Company
                1000 North Second Avenue
                Logan, IA 51546

Each poster presents a caricature of a president, along with a humorous story or little-known fact about the president. The first set depicts presidents from Fillmore through McKinley, the second Theodore Roosevelt through Reagan (a third set showing the earliest presidents is also available).

Congressional Districts of the 100th Congress of the United States

Grades: 7-adult
Description: Wall map with guide
Cost: $4.75
Publisher: Government Printing Office
                Superintendent of Documents
                Washington, DC 20402
                (developed by the U.S. Bureau of the Census)

This wall map shows the congressional districts in the first, 25th, 50th, 75th, and 100th Congresses, allowing students to examine population grov .h and distribution, as well as shifts in political power. A guide with background information and suggested activities is provided with the map.

Events to Remember
Grades: 7–12
Description: 66 black-and-white 11″ × 14″ photographs with guide
Cost: $62
Publisher: Documentary Photo Aids
                P.O. Box 956
                Mt. Dora, FL 32757

This set of photographs presents scenes related to the Korean War, the operations of the United Nations, the assassination of President Kennedy, the Vietnam War, and the U.S. space program.

Famous Indians Posters
Grades: 5–12
Description: set of 12 three-color 17″ × 22″ posters with 32-page booklet
Cost: $21.95
Publisher: Perfection Form Company
                1000 North Second Avenue
                Logan, IA 51546

Each poster in the series depicts a famous Native American leader. The accompanying booklet provides biographies and additional illustrations.

The Feminist Revolution
Grades: 7–12
Description: 26 black-and-white 11″ × 14″ photographs with guide
Cost: $24.50
Publisher: Documentary Photo Aids
                P.O. Box 956
                Mt. Dora, FL 32757

This collection covers the women's movement from its earliest days, when it struggled for abolition as well as women's rights, through the crusade for voting rights, to the work of the "new" feminists.

The Great Depression
Grades: 7–12
Description: 32 black-and-white 11″ × 14″ photographs with guide
Cost: $30.50
Publisher: Documentary Photo Aids
                P.O. Box 956
                Mt. Dora, FL 32757

This set of materials, which includes both photographs and cartoons, examines the events of the Depression, as well as the ways in which people coped with personal and societal difficulties.

Immigration
Grades: 7–12
Description: 40 black-and-white 11″ × 14″ photographs with guide
Cost: $38
Publisher: Documentary Photo Aids
                P.O. Box 956
                Mt. Dora, FL 32757

The "New Immigrants" of the late nineteenth and earlier twentieth centuries are the focus of this collection. The photographs show in detail the steps through which the immigrants had to pass as they arrived in the country and proceeded through Ellis Island.

Indians of the Plains
Grades: 7–12
Description: 46 black-and-white 11″ × 14″ photographs with guide
Cost: $43.50
Publisher: Documentary Photo Aids
                P.O. Box 956
                Mt. Dora, FL 32757

This collection depicts the history, culture, and society of the Plains Indians, as well as their clashes with the U.S. government and white settlers.

Key Supreme Court Decisions
Grades: 7–12
Description: 13 transparencies, 31 overlays, teacher's guide
Cost: $120
Publisher: Social Studies School Service
                P.O. Box 802
                Culver City, CA 90232

This set of transparencies shows the effects of major Supreme Court decisions on U.S. government and life. Of special interest to teachers of later years in U.S. history are transparencies on New Deal cases, released time cases, civil rights, apportionment, and due process.

Map History of the United States
Grades: 7–12
Description: 8 full-color 11″ × 17″ posters
Cost: $8.95
Publisher: Social Studies School Service
                P.O. Box 802
                Culver City, CA 90232
                (developed by Scholars Press)

This set of eight posters shows the expansion of the United States by presenting maps of the nation in 1790, 1803, 1821, 1848, 1863, 1896, 1917, and 1959.

Negro Experience in America
Grades: 7–12
Description: 49 black-and-white 11″ × 14″ photographs
Cost: $46.50
Publisher: Documentary Photo Aids
                P.O. Box 956
                Mt. Dora, FL 32757

This set includes 49 photographs depicting the black experience in the United States from the slave trade to the present. A booklet on interpreting photographs in the classroom is provided free with the set.

North American Timeline
Grades: 4–12
Description: 7 full-color 31″ × 11½″ posters
Cost: $8.95
Publisher: Social Studies School Service
                P.O. Box 802
                Culver City, CA 90232
                (developed by Instructor)

These seven posters can be attached to form an 18-foot timeline of U.S. history from 1565 to the present. A detailed written timeline elaborates on the events pictured. Blank space is provided to allow students to add events.

The Panama Canal
Grades: 7–12
Description: 14 black-and-white 11″ × 14″ photographs with guide
Cost: $13.50
Publisher: Documentary Photo Aids
                P.O. Box 956
                Mt. Dora, FL 32757

This collection documents the digging of the Panama Canal, a feat that had previously been attempted several times. The massive scale of the effort is highlighted.

Presidents of the United States, Vice Presidents of the United States, and Wives of Presidents
Grades: 5–12
Description: 3 black-and-white 20″ × 28″ posters
Cost: $4.95 each

Publisher: Social Studies School Service
P.O. Box 802
Culver City, CA 90232
(developed by Waterwheel Press)

Each of these posters depicts the individuals indicated by its title—the 39 U.S. presidents, 43 vice presidents, and 44 first ladies.

Territorial Growth and History of the United States
Grades: 5–9
Description: 19 full-color transparencies with overlays
Cost: $150
Publisher: Eye Gate Media
3333 Elston Avenue
Chicago, IL 60618

This set of transparencies includes maps of territorial expansion, maps related to events (such as the Spanish-American War) that resulted in territorial expansion, and maps showing geographical information about the United States to allow students to examine the kind of land that was added during various periods of expansion.

Women and the Constitution Bulletin Board Kit
Grades: 8–12
Description: Packet including historical photographs and documents, suggestions for organizing a bulletin board, background information, mats for photos, and bunting
Cost: $10
Publisher: National Women's History Project
P.O. Box 3716
Santa Rosa, CA 95402

This kit provides all the materials and ideas needed to create a discussion-stimulating bulletin board on women and the Constitution. Numerous additional posters and visuals on women in U.S. history are available from this publisher.

Supplementary Print Materials

The materials listed in this section are varied in terms of their content, approach, and intent. Some materials were developed specifically for classroom use, while others were written for general audiences but are also appropriate for secondary students. The listing is, of course, selective. All of the potential print resources on this period of U.S. history would fill several volumes themselves. Those selected are of high quality, address a range of subjects, and represent a wide sampling of publishers and authors. Note that no historical fiction is included, although that is another category of materials with utility in the history classroom.

The American Image: Photographs From the National Archives.
New York: Pantheon, 1979.
191 pp. Paperbound. $10. ISBN 0-394-73815-2.

This book presents more than 200 photographs selected from the National Archives collection. The photographs cover the years from 1860 to 1960, presenting famous faces (e.g., Clara Barton, Frederick Douglass, Franklin Roosevelt) as well as working people of all races.

American Letters.
Lakeside, CA: Interact, 1987.
Five 35-page paperbound books, sold in sets of 35; $25 for each set or $105 for all five sets.

These innovative materials involve students working in pairs to research, write, and exchange letters related to events of the twentieth century. For example, a young man fighting in World War I writes home about his experiences; his girlfriend writes back about life on the homefront. Each set of booklets covers a different era: 1900–1913, 1914–1929, 1930–1945, 1946–1960, and 1961–1975.

Arizzi, Mavis. **Thinking About American History Through Historical Fiction.**
Culver City, CA: Social Studies School Service (developed by Book Lures), 1985.
30 pp. Paperbound. $4.95.

This activity book presents exercises to help students in grades 5–9 use historical fiction to appreciate the American heritage. Some of the activities focus on particular works of fiction, while others can be applied to any novel with a historical setting.

Banks, James, and Cherry A. Banks. **March Toward Freedom: A History of Black Americans.**
Belmont, CA: Fearon Education, 1978.
200 pp. Paperbound. $9. ISBN 0-8224-4406-2.

This chronological history is written at a grade 6 reading level, but in a style that makes it of interest to all secondary students. The text covers the

African heritage of black Americans, as well as events from their arrival in the Americas to the late 1970s.

Bender, David, **The Vietnam War: Opposing Viewpoints.**
St. Paul, MN: Greenhaven Press, 1984.
200 pp. Paperbound. $6.95. ISBN 0-89908-324-2.

One of the popular *Opposing Viewpoints* series, this book presents articles espousing varying views on the causes, problems, consequences, and lessons of the Vietnam War. The final chapter offers opposing views on whether the current situation in Central America parallels the earlier experience in Vietnam.

Billington, Roy A., and Martin Ridge. **American History After 1865.**
Totowa, NJ: Littlefield, Adams, 1981.
368 pp. Paperbound. $9.95. ISBN 0-8226-0027-7.

This work provides an outline of U.S. history from Reconstruction to the Reagan era. Key topics appear in bold type, while important events, dates, and names are italicized and underlined. These design features make the book especially useful for review.

Binder, Frederick M., and David M. Reimers. **The Way We Lived: Essays and Documents in American Social History. Volume II: Since 1865.**
Lexington, MA: D. C. Heath, 1988 (in press).
Paperbound. $12. ISBN 0-0669-09031-XC.

Suitable for advanced placement students, this resource provides essays on social history trends and topics. Each essay is followed by a collection of primary source materials that elaborate on the essay.

Breil, Ann, and others. **Basic Skills in United States History.**
Dubuque, IA: Wm. C. Brown Publishers, 1988.
294 pp. Spiralbound. $34.95. ISBN 0-697-02592-6.

This book of activities is designed to help middle school and high school students develop reading, study, research, information acquisition, and social participation skills while learning U.S. history content. Approximately half of the 52 activities provided deal with the post–Civil War years.

Brown, Bernard E. **Great American Political Thinkers. Volume II: Modern America/Since Civil War and Industrialism.**
New York: Avon, 1983.
464 pp. Paperbound. $4.95. ISBN 0-380-83923-7.

Brown surveys U.S. political thought from the Civil War, using the writings of such individuals as Eugene V. Debs, Hannah Arendt, and Martin Luther

King, Jr. to illuminate a range of topics, including religious freedom and democracy, women's rights, progressivism and reform, and others.

Brownstone, David M., Irene M. Franch, and Douglass L. Brownstone. **Island of Hope, Island of Tears.**
New York: Penguin, 1986.
307 pp. Paperbound. $7.95. ISBN 0-8149-0882-9.

The words of immigrants are used to help the readers understand the experience of coming to the United States. The intellectual and emotional impact of the experience are emphasized. The book is suitable for all secondary students and adults.

Cababe, Louise, and others. **U.S. History, Book 2.**
Dubuque, IA: Wm. C. Brown Company, 1987.
281 pp. Spiralbound. $34.95. ISBN 0-697-02259-5.

This book contains 36 supplementary lessons and five unit tests expanding on topics covered in textbooks, providing more information or helping students examine the topic from a different perspective. Many lessons involve using source material and/or completing worksheets. The lessons cover the period from 1876.

Claypool, Jane. **The Worker in America: Issues in American History.**
New York: Watts, 1985.
120 pp. Hardbound. $10.90. ISBN 0-531-04933-7.

This supplementary student text examines the evolution of the U.S. economic system, as well as the problems and triumphs of U.S. workers. Special attention is devoted to immigrant, black, and women workers and their efforts to overcome discrimination.

Cummins, D. Duane and William Gee White, series editors. **Inquiries into American History.**
Mission Hills, CA: Glencoe, 1980.
5 books, 216-240 pp. each. Paperbound. $4.71 each. ISBN 0-02-652780-4, 652820-7, 652860-6, 652900-9, and 652940-8.

Each of these books looks in depth at a particular era, event, or region. Titles related to later U.S. history are: *Reconstruction: 1865-1877, Industrialism: The American Experience, American Foreign Policy: 1789-1980, Contrasting Decades: The 1920s and 1930s,* and *Combat and Consensus: The 1940s and 1950s.*

Combs, Eunice A. and Laurel R. Singleton. **Our Nation: Its Past and Present.**
Boulder, CO: Graphic Learning Corporation, 1986.

220-pp. three-ring binder (ISBN 0-87746-033-7), 232-pp. spiralbound teacher's guide (ISBN 0-87746-034-5), 30 laminated desk maps, and 30 marking pens. $325.

This activity-based program for students in grades 5–8 covers events from the earliest days of U.S. history to the present. Emphasis is placed on learning map and globe, social studies reading, thinking/problem solving, research, and citizenship skills while learning about the history of the United States.

Curti, Merle, Isadore Starr, and Lewis Paul Todd. **Living American Documents.**
Orlando, FL: Harcourt Brace Jovanovich, 1971.
368 pp. Paperbound. $7.20. ISBN 0-15-371886-2.

This collection of primary source materials is organized chronologically, presenting documents related to the colonial period, the creation of the new nation, the conflict between the North and South, Reconstruction and expansion, and the modern era, in which the United States has been a world leader.

Davidson, James West, and Mark H. Lytle. **After the Fact: The Art of Historical Detection.**
Atlanta, GA: Random House, 1986 (2nd ed.).
400 pp. Paperbound. $15. ISBN 0-394-35475-3.

This unusual supplement uses 14 dramatic episodes in U.S. history to demonstrate how historians go about their work—"historical detective work" as it were. Skills covered include selection of evidence, document analysis, and oral interviews.

Dollar, Charles, and Gary Reichard. **American Issues: A Documentary Reader.**
Atlanta, GA: Random House, 1988.
496 pp. Paperbound. $10.95. ISBN 0-676-35607-9. (Teacher's guide, paperbound, $6.95, ISBN 0-676-35627-3.)

This collection includes more than 200 sources, including primary sources, secondary sources, and illustrations (maps, paintings, cartoons, etc.). The materials have been selected to focus on such recurring themes as race/ethnic relations and the evolution of democratic institutions, as well as to develop students' ability to participate in historical inquiry.

Esper, George. **The Eyewitness History of the Vietnam War: 1961–1975.**
New York: Ballantine, 1983.
209 pp. Paperbound. $11.95. ISBN 0-345-30865-4.

This chronological history is well illustrated with more than 400 Associated Press photographs of the Vietnam War and the student protests against it. The narrative is supplemented with excerpts from the diaries and letters of soldiers who served in Vietnam.

Family: Past and Present.
Sturbridge, MA: Old Sturbridge Village, 1986.
Paperbound. $6.95.

This sourcebook contains a range of activities that help students look at family composition, functions, and roles. Such documentary material as census records, journals, and vital records are used in the lessons, which focus on change over time.

Ferrero, Pat, Elaine Hedges, and Julie Silber. **Hearts and Hands: The Influence of Women and Quilts on American Society.**
Santa Rosa, CA: National Women's History Project, 1988.
112 pp. Paperbound. $19.95. ISBN 0-938625-8700-3.

This resource looks at the role of women and quilts in important events of the nineteenth century: abolition, the Civil War, westward expansion, temperance, and suffrage. The full-color photographs and unusual approach should capture the interest of high school students.

Forging the Nation: A Brief History of the United States From 1865.
Logan, IA: Perfection Form, 1985.
120 pp. Paperbound. $5.60 (includes free 28-p. paperbound teacher's guide).

This secondary-level workbook chronicles the history of the United States from Reconstruction to the present. Illustrated with drawings, maps, and photographs, the book contains 12 units, each focusing on a particular period and providing narrative, a glossary, and exercises.

Frazier, Thomas R. **Voices of America: Readings in American History.**
Boston, MA: Houghton Mifflin, 1985.
304 pp. Paperbound. $11.76. ISBN 0-395-18608-2.

This collection of supplementary readings contains a variety of sources addressing salient issues in each time period. The readings are generally brief and are followed by questions to help students deepen their understanding of the document. Many readings focus on the experience of the "common people."

Ganley, Albert, Thomas Lyons, and Gilbert Sewall. **After Hiroshima: America Since 1945.**
Wellesley Hills, MA: Independent School Press, 1985.
356 pp. Paperbound. $8.25. ISBN 0-88334-121-2.

This supplementary text covers foreign relations and domestic affairs since World War II. Highlighted phrases are designed to help students find information efficiently as they use the resource. The book may be of interest to teachers because one of the authors is the writer of a much-publicized report excoriating history textbooks.

Giddings, Paula. **When and Where I Enter: The Impact of Black Women on Race and Sex in America.**
New York: Bantam, 1985.
408 pp. Paperbound. $8.95. ISBN 0-553-34225-8.

Giddings provides an analysis of the role of black women in the struggles for black and women's rights in the twentieth century. Although the book may be too difficult for students, teachers may wish to share excerpts from the speeches, diaries, and letters of black women provided in the text.

Gluck, Sherna Berger. **From Parlor to Prison: Five American Suffragists Talk About Their Lives.**
New York: Monthly Review Press, 1985.
300 pp. Paperbound. $10. ISBN 0-85345-676-3.

Five women involved in the struggle to gain the vote for women were interviewed for this book, which explores how social and individual circumstances can combine to create a political movement.

Goldinger, Carolyn, ed. **Presidential Elections Since 1789.**
Washington, DC: Congressional Quarterly, 1987 (4th ed.).
245 pp. Paperbound. $11.95. ISBN 0-87187-431-8.

This book provides a wealth of statistical data on presidential elections, including information on the electoral college and electoral votes (1879-1984), the popular vote (1824-1984), party conventions (1831-1984), and primaries (1912-1984).

Gordon, Irving L. **American History.**
New York: Amsco, 1989 (2nd ed.).
770 pp. Paperbound. $9.25. ISBN 0-87720-852-2.

This review text in U.S. history is presented in outline form, with important events or ideas in bold type and narrative generally brief. Each of the book's ten units ends with a series of questions to check for understanding.

Gordon, Lois, and Alan Gordon. **American Chronicle: Six Decades in American Life, 1920-1980.**
New York: Atheneum, 1987.
575 pp. Paperbound. $16.95. ISBN 0-689-11901-1.

This almanac presents an overview of each decade covered, along with information on each individual year. This information includes quotes from well-known people, snippets from ads, lists of popular songs, movies, books, and so on; sports statistics; a list of developments in science and technology; and a "Kaleidoscope" of other facts. Students should find much to fascinate them—and perhaps draw them into deeper investigation—in the volume.

Guide to the Study of Childhood, 1820–1920.
Rochester, NY: Margaret Woodbury Strong Museum, 1985.
Paperbound. $6.

This resource aims to give secondary students a better understanding of local, family, and cultural history in the nineteenth century. The book includes children's letters, photographs, advertisements, and other primary sources, as well as suggested activities.

Heffner, Richard D. **A Documentary History of the United States.**
New York: New American Library, 1985 (4th ed.).
352 pp. Paperbound. $4.95. ISBN 0-451-62413-0.

This collection presents documents from the Declaration of Independence to recent Supreme Court decisions. The author provides annotations that explain the significance of the various documents to U.S. history.

Hofstadter, Richard. **The Progressive Movement: 1900 to 1915.**
New York: Touchstone, 1986.
185 pp. Paperbound. $6.95. ISBN 0-671-62824-0.

Hofstadter has collected 36 primary source documents that focus on how the progressive reformers attacked and sought remedies for problems of the early 1900s. Writings by Ida Tarbell, Louis Brandeis, Jane Addams, and Upton Sinclair are included.

Hoxie, Frederick E., ed. **Indians in American History.**
Arlington Heights, IL: Harlan Davidson, 1988.
330 pp. Paperbound. $9.95. ISBN 0-88295-855-0.

This edited collection of papers, several of which were written by Indian authors, covers the full chronological span of the Native American experience. Articles related to the later years in U.S. history include "How the West Was Lost," "The Curious Story of Reformers and the American Indian," "American Imperialism and the Indians," and "The Struggle for Indian Civil Rights."

Hughes, Glenn E., Norman D. Miller, and Stephen L. Volkening. **Reading American History.**
Glenview, IL: Scott, Foresman, 1987 (rev. ed.).

148 pp. Paperbound. $6.28. ISBN 0-673-22237-5. (Teacher's edition: 148 pp., paperbound, $8.35, ISBN 0-673-22238-9.)

This workbook for students in grades 7 and 8 teaches reading skills in the context of content from the standard U.S. history curriculum. The 148 exercises, which focus on understanding the main idea, learning the vocabulary, and reading maps and graphs, are arranged chronologically, from "Reasons for Exploration" to "Baseball Attendance."

Hughes, Langston, Milton Meltzer, and C. Eric Lincoln. **A Pictorial History of Black Americans.**
New York: Crown, 1983 (5th ed.).
400 pp. Hardbound. $19.95. ISBN 0-517-55072-5.

This resource contains more than 1,200 illustrations depicting the economic, political, social, and cultural changes black Americans have undergone since arriving in North America in 1619.

Hymowitz, Carol, and Michaele Weissman. **A History of Women in America.**
New York: Bantam, 1978.
400 pp. Paperbound. $4.95. ISBN 0-553-24928-2.

This general history begins with European colonization and progresses to the women's movement of the 1970s. The book focuses on how women of all classes shaped the life and culture of the United States.

Industrial Era: Creative Activities for Teaching American History.
Stockton, CA: Stevens and Shea, 1983.
30 pp. Unbound reproducibles. $12.95.

This set of reproducibles provides puzzles, games, and valuing exercises for learning about the Industrial Era. Decision-making skills are stressed through such activities as deciding on a solution to the Pullman strike. The activities are suitable for students in grades 5-9.

Israel, Fred L., ed. **The Peoples of North America Series.**
Edgemont, PA: Chelsea House, 1986-1988.
15 books, approx. 90 pp. each. $16.95 each or $241.50 for complete set.

This series designed for students in grades 6 and up covers the history, culture, religion, customs, education, holidays, dress, and contemporary life of the following American ethnic groups: the Amish, Japanese-Americans, Chinese-Americans, Mexican-Americans, Italian-Americans, Irish-Americans, Arab-Americans, Slovak-Americans, Korean-Americans, Swedish-Americans, Greek-Americans, French-Americans, Danish-Americans, Jewish-Americans, and Scotch-Irish-Americans.

Jordan, Teresa. **Cowgirls: Women of the American West.**
New York: Anchor, 1984.
310 pp. Paperbound. $10.95. ISBN 0-385-14511-X.

Jordan provides an oral history focusing on the cowgirl experience from the 1870s to the present. Viewpoints represented are the rancher's daughter, the mother/daughter tradition, the husband/wife team, women alone, women ranchhands, and professional rodeo performers.

Klose, Nelson. **United States History: Volume 2.**
Santa Barbara, CA: Barrons, 1983 (4th ed.).
488 pp. Paperbound. $8.95. ISBN 0-8120-2251-3.

This review text uses an outline format to present information on U.S. history from 1865 to the present. Each chapter includes a chronology, a reading list, and review questions, as well as the outline of events.

Kuzirian, Eugene, and Larry Madaras. **Taking Sides: Clashing Views on Controversial Issues in American History, Volume II: Reconstruction to the Present.**
Sluice Dock, CT: Dushkin, 1985.
300 pp. Paperbound. $8.95. ISBN 0-87967-568-3.

The authors look at opposing viewpoints on 15 issues, such as the following: Was Reconstruction a total failure? Was the U.S. labor movement conservative? Have antitrust laws preserved competition in the U.S. economic system? Was U.S. policy toward Japan and Japanese-Americans motivated by racial prejudice?

Lake, Steven A. **The American Centuries.**
Glenview, IL: Decisionmakers, 1985.
2 books, 78–82 pp. each, drilled and bound with brads, $29.95 each.

Each volume in this set contains 20 lessons for one period of U.S. history: 1800–1899 and the twentieth century (a third volume looks at events to 1799). In each lesson, students assume the role of a historical figure and make a decision about an issue or problem in U.S. history. A variety of instructional activities are included.

Lavender, David. **The Great West: American Heritage Library.**
Boston, MA: Houghton Mifflin, 1985.
468 pp. Paperbound. $8.95. ISBN 0-8281-0481-6.

Illustrated with numerous photographs, drawings, and maps, this text details the history of America's western frontier. Topics covered include pioneer life, gold rushes, railroads, land booms, and outlaws.

Lawrence, Bill. **Fascinating Facts From American History.**
Portland, ME: J. Weston Walch, 1982.
271 pp. Spiralbound. $9.95.

This book presents brief anecdotal articles providing human interest, debunking historical myths, and presenting other "sidelights" of history to stimulate the interest of students in grades 9–12.

Lawrence, Bill. **A Social History of America.**
Portland, ME: J. Weston Walch, 1986.
226 pp. Spiralbound. $8.95.

This resource provides an easy-to-read anecdotal account of the lives of everyday Americans. Topics covered include family life, social life, recreation, health and diet, fads, and jobs.

Lawson, Robert, ed. **Watchwords of Liberty: A Pageant of American Quotations.**
Boston, MA: Little, Brown, 1986 (rev. ed.).
115 pp. Paperbound. $7.95. ISBN 0-316-51754-2.

This collection of more than 50 quotations is presented in a unique story form and illustrated with entertaining drawings. The book is suitable for students in grades 5–12.

Lengel, James B., and Gerald Danzer. **Law in American History.**
Glenview, IL: Scott, Foresman, 1983.
263 pp. Paperbound. $8.54. ISBN 0-673-11690-1. (Teacher's guide: 72 pp., paperbound, $3.72, ISBN 0-673-11691-X.)

Important legal events from ten major periods of U.S. history have been chosen as the focal points of ten chapters in this text. For example, one chapter examines the application of law to economic changes in the age of industrialization. Many instructional activities are suggested to deepen and extend student understanding.

Levy, Tedd, and Donna Collins Krasnow. **A Guidebook for Teaching United States History: Mid-Nineteenth Century to the Present.**
Newton, MA: Allyn and Bacon, 1979.
504 pp. Paperbound. $29.95. ISBN 0-205-06496-5.

This comprehensive resource is designed "to provide practical ideas and resources for developing student understanding of significant historical events and processes." To that end, the authors provide a general introduction to teaching U.S. history, along with numerous teaching activities for the following topics: industrialization, the frontier, the rise of cities, international relations, the changing role of the government in domestic affairs, and current and future challenges.

Lewin, Stephen, and Ted Silveira. **United States History: Volume II: The Twentieth Century.**
Belmont, CA: Fearon Education, 1986.
91 pp. Paperbound. $4.50. ISBN 0-8224-7682-7.

This worktext presents basic concepts from junior and senior high school history courses at a grade 5 reading level. Illustrated with historic black-and-white photographs and artworks, the book covers the world wars, the twenties, the Great Depression, and civil rights, among other topics.

Litwak, Leon, ed. **The American Labor Movement.**
New York: Touchstone, 1986.
176 pp. Paperbound. $6.95. ISBN 0-671-62827-5.

This collection provides brief commentaries on the U.S. labor movement's development from 1860 to the 1950s. It also presents more than 60 primary sources, including the testimony of workers and employers and editorials.

Lockwood, Alan L., and David E. Harris. **Reasoning With Democratic Values: Ethical Problems in United States History.**
New York: Teachers College Press, 1985.
350 pp. Paperbound. $11.95. ISBN 0-8077-6095-1. (Teacher's guide: 176 pp., paperbound, $11.95, ISBN 0-8077-6101-X.)

This unique teaching resource presents 28 historical "episodes" that presented ethical dilemmas for individual citizens or decision makers. This volume includes episodes beginning with the era of expansion and ending with the present (a companion volume presents episodes from the earlier period in the nation's history). The teacher's guide presents detailed instructions for using the episodes to develop students' reasoning skills and commitment to democratic values.

Maddox, Robert James. **Annual Editions: American History, Volume II: Reconstruction Through the Present.**
Sluice Dock, CT: Dushkin, annual.
256 pp. Paperbound. $8.95.

These resources, published annually, contain articles from such sources as *American History Illustrated, Saturday Review, Smithsonian, Early American Life,* and other periodicals. Topics are varied, covering all periods within the scope of the volume.

Maher, C. **American History Project File.**
Portland, ME: J. Weston Walch, 1982.
156 cards. $12.

This set of cards presents 156 creative projects to help students explore U.S. history. Projects involve reading, writing, research, and self-expression.

Manchester, William. **The Glory and the Dream: A Narrative History of America, 1932–1972.**
New York: Bantam, 1975.
1,408 pp. Paperbound. $15.95. ISBN 0-553-34285-1.

This massive work is written in a style that is accessible to high school students. It covers not only events of the focus period but also information related to "national character." Detailed biographical sketches of key figures are presented.

Meltzer, Milton. **The Black Americans: A History in Their Own Words.**
New York: Crowell, 1984 (rev. ed.).
306 pp. Hardbound. $13.50. ISBN 0-690-04419-4.

This condensed version of the original three-volume work contains letters, speeches, memoirs, and testimonies regarding the black experience in the United States. Both individual lives and the struggle for political and economic equity are chronicled. The book is suitable for grades 7 and up.

Morrison, Joan, and Charlotte Fox Zabusky. **American Mosaic: The Immigrant Experience in the Words of Those Who Lived It.**
New York: New American Library, 1980.
480 pp. Paperbound. $8.95. ISBN 0-452-00590-6.

This book presents the first-person accounts of more than 140 people who immigrated to the United States between 1901 and 1980. Some of the immigrants are well known (Lynn Redgrave, Nguyen Cao Ky), but others are "common" people from a wide range of countries (Vietnam, USSR, Nigeria, India, Cuba, Germany, South Africa, Mexico).

Nurse, Ronald J. **The Development of American Foreign Policy.**
Orlando, FL: Harcourt Brace Jovanovich, 1980.
192 pp. Paperbound. $10.45. ISBN 0-15-379-206-X. (Teacher's guide: 96 pp., paperbound, $2.25, ISBN 0-15-379-232-9.)

This readable supplementary text presents a "lively survey" of the development of U.S. foreign policy from 1776 to 1980. A section of primary sources concludes the volume. The teacher's guide suggests a range of instructional strategies for use with the text.

O'Neill, William L. **Coming Apart: An Informal History of America in the 1960s.**
New York: Times Books, 1972.
480 pp. Paperbound. $9.95. ISBN 0-8129-6223-0.

This work examines the people, events, and movements of the 1960s. Covered are such topics as the Warren Report, Ralph Nader and consumerism, the women's movement, Cesar Chavez, and the Hell's Angels. The book is suitable for mature high school students.

O'Reilly, Kevin. **Critical Thinking in History.**
South Hamilton, MA: Critical Thinking Press, 1983–1984.
2 books, each containing 86 pp. Paperbound. $2.95 each. (2 teacher's guides, each containing 156 pp., paperbound, $12.95 each.)

These units, which focus on *Reconstruction/Gilded Age/Populism/ Progressivism* and *America Becomes a World Power/The Depression Era/The Cold War/Issues and Changes in the 1950s and 1960s,* are designed to help students evaluate historical evidence, recognize assumptions, analyze interpretations, and use data to assess hypotheses. The teacher's guides present detailed plans for presenting the material. Teacher training in use of the materials is available.

Perspectives: Readings on Contemporary American Government.
Arlington, VA: Close Up Foundation, 1987 (8th ed.).
258 pp. Paperbound. $14. ISBN 0-932765-04-1.

This anthology, while designed for use in government classes, also provides material of interest to history teachers and students, particularly in the section on the Constitution. Other topics covered are the presidency, the Congress, the judiciary, the media, the bureaucracy, interest groups, and the American people.

The Public Issues Series: Immigration: Pluralism and National Identity and **The Rise of Organized Labor: Workers, Employers, and the Public Interest.**
Boulder, CO: Social Science Education Consortium, 1988.
2 books. 68 pp. each. Paperbound. $2.50 each. ISBN 0-89994-332-2 and 333-0 (with teacher's guides).

Originally developed by the Harvard Social Studies Project in the 1960s, the Public Issues Series focuses on enduring public issues and the development of analysis and discussion skills. These two units are among the first in the revision of the series. The subtitle of each unit suggests the issues on which students focus as they read and analyze primary and secondary sources. Analogies are drawn with contemporary events.

Reid, William, Jr. **American Crafts: A Reproducible Guide for 100 Projects.**
Portland, ME: J. Weston Walch, 1986.
265 pp. Spiralbound. $18.

The projects described in this resource give students a feeling for the
everyday lives of Americans in various periods of history. The projects are
organized into five sections: "Folk Art and Crafts of the American Indians,"
"Folk Art and Crafts of the Colonial Era," "Folk Art and Crafts of the
Young Republic," "Folk Art and Crafts of the Victorian Period," and "Folk
Art and Crafts of the Modern Era."

Reid, William, Jr. **Popular Music in American History.**
Portland, ME: J. Weston Walch, 1981.
221 pp. Spiralbound. $8.95.

This resource provides activities to help students "understand American
history through their knowledge of song" and vice versa. Music and
activities are provided throughout the book.

Riley, Glenda. **Inventing the American Woman: A Perspective on Women's
History, Volume 2, 1866 to the Present.**
Arlington Heights, IL: Harlan Davidson, 1987.
176 pp. Paperbound. $8.95. ISBN 0-88295-838-0.

This book combines recent scholarship on women's history, biographical
data, statistics, and narrative on social history to describe the role of women
in U.S. life since 1866. The text is suitable for students in grades 9 and up, as
well as adults.

Rosenzwieg, Linda W., and Peter N. Stearns. **Themes in Modern Social
History.**
Pittsburgh, PA: Carnegie-Mellon University Press, 1985.
*225 pp. Paperbound. $8.95. ISBN 0-88748-059-4 (with 13-p. teacher's
guide).*

This supplementary text is organized around themes reflecting the
everyday lives of ordinary people who lived in four different time periods:
preindustrial society (1600–1780), early industrial society (1780–1870),
mature industrial society (1870–1950), and advanced industrial society
(1950–present). The themes covered are work and leisure, family and
childhood, health and medicine, and crime and law enforcement. Source
material is provided in each section.

Schlesinger, Arthur M., Jr., ed. **The Almanac of American History.**
New York: Putnam, 1983.
623 pp. Hardbound. $10.25. ISBN 0-399-51082-6.

An excellent research resource for students, this volume is divided into five sections, each introduced by a prominent U.S. historian. The sections cover founding the nation, testing the union, forging the nation, expanding resources, and emerging as a world power. Many biographies and short essays on special topics are included.

Scott, John Andrew. **The Ballad of America: The History of the United States in Song and Story.**
Carbondale, IL: Southern Illinois University Press, 1983 (rev. ed.).
439 pp. Paperbound. $14.95. ISBN 0-8093-1061-9.

This text attempts to "show how the story of the American people is revealed in their song." Popular songs of various eras are presented, along with narrative that places the songs in their historical and geographic contexts.

Shaping American Democracy: U.S. Supreme Court Decisions.
Albany, NY: New York State Bar Association, 1985.
89 pp. Paperbound. $8.95.

This resource booklet briefly examines a number of Supreme Court cases dealing with issues of capital punishment, civil rights, freedom of assembly, free speech, freedom of the press, religious freedom, separation of powers, search and seizure, and voting rights. The cases range from *Chisholm v. Georgia* in 1793 to *New York v. Quarles* in 1984.

SIRS/National Archives Supplementary Teaching Units.
Boca Raton, FL: Social Issues Resource Series, 1985.
7 kits, each containing a teacher's guide, activities, and documents, $35.00 each.

Prepared in cooperation with the National Archives, these teaching kits provide about 50 reproductions of historical documents, along with activities for developing student understanding. Topics of the kits are *The Progressive years—1898-1917, World War I—The Home Front, The 1920s, The Great Depression and the New Deal, World War II—The Home Front, The Truman Years—1945-1953,* and *Peace and Prosperity—1953-1961.*

Slosson, Preston W. **Pictorial History of the American People.**
Essex, CT: Gallery Press, 1985 (rev. ed.).
328 pp. Hardbound. $14.98.

This well-illustrated text focuses on the social history of the United States from precolonial days to 1984. Titles of some of the sections of the book include "Utopias in the Backwoods," "The Day of the Cowboy," and "American Science and Invention."

Smith, Gary, John Zola, and Jaye Zola. **Teaching About U.S. History: A Comparative Approach.**
Denver, CO: Center for Teaching International Relations, 1988 (rev. ed. in press).
Paperbound. $21.95.

This book presents more than 30 activities employing a comparative approach to the study of U.S. history. The activities use a broad range of strategies, including data collection, interviews, decision-making games, and use of community resources. Activities are suitable for students in grades 6-12.

Smith, Melinda R., ed. **Law in U.S. History: A Teacher Resource Manual.**
Boulder, CO: Social Science Education Consortium, 1983.
335 pp. Spiralbound. $19.95. ISBN 0-89994-281-4.

This collection contains more than 35 activities designed to develop legal issues and themes in secondary U.S. history courses. Especially timely are the numerous activities that focus on development of vital constitutional issues over time.

Space: The Last Frontier.
Logan, IA: Perfection Form, 1988.
56 pp. Paperbound. $3.50.

This workbook chronicles "the significant events in the history of air and space travel from Kitty Hawk to *Challenger.*" The book includes not only workbook-style exercises but also text reading to expand students' knowledge.

Stallone, Carol N., ed. **Faces and Phases of Women.**
Seneca Falls, NY: National Women's Hall of Fame, 1983.
76 pp. Paperbound. $6.95. ISBN 0-9610622-0-7.

This resource for students in grades 5-9 includes biographies and sketches of 31 women who have been inducted into the National Women's Hall of Fame. Among these are Margaret Sanger, Margaret Mead, Amelia Earhart, Rachel Carson, and Mary McLeod Bethune. A set of posters is also available from the publisher.

Stoler, Mark, and Marshall True. **Explorations in American History, Volume II: Since 1865.**
Atlanta, GA: Random House, 1987.
192 pp. Paperbound. $8. ISBN 0-394-35471-5 (with teacher's guide).

This book introduces research and writing skills in the context of U.S. history. Such skills as analysis of sources, using the library, and forming hypotheses are developed.

Strasser, Susan. **Never Done: History of American Housework.**
New York: Pantheon, 1982.
365 pp. Paperbound. $11.95. ISBN 0-394-51024-0.

This history covers American household technology and ideas about
housework in a style that makes it suitable for students in grades 9 and up.
The author analyzes the relationship of housework and the housewife's role
to economic and demographic changes in the United States. The influence of
advertising and commercial interests is covered.

Suter, Coral, and Marshall Croddy. **American Album: 200 Years of
Constitutional Democracy.**
Los Angeles, CA: Constitutional Rights Foundation, 1986.
139 pp. Paperbound. $12.50 (with teacher's guide).

This publication contains eight units arranged chronologically from the
Constitution's first implementation in the late eighteenth century to the civil
rights movement of the 1960s. The material, which is designed specifically
for infusion in secondary U.S. history courses, is presented through a wide
array of teaching strategies.

Terkel, Studs. **The Good War: An Oral History of World War II.**
New York: Ballantine, 1984.
591 pp. Paperbound. $4.95. ISBN 0-394-53103-5.

Following his pattern in many other books, which would also be useful in
high school U.S. history courses, Terkel presents excerpts from interviews
organized around various subtopics related to his theme. In this work, the
subtopics used to organize the material include reactions to Pearl Harbor,
race relations, D-Day, the world immediately after the war, and others.

Ver Steeg, Clarence L., Richard Hofstadter, and Beatrice K. Hofstadter, eds.
**Great Issues in American History, Volume III: From Reconstruction to the
Present Day.**
New York: Vintage, 1982.
602 pp. Paperbound. $8.95. ISBN 0-394-70842-3.

The editors have presented a variety of primary source materials related to
major political controversies in U.S. history. Included are speeches, debates
in Congress, letters, political pamphlets, and other materials presenting both
sides of the controversies covered.

Voices of Freedom: Sources in American History.
Englewood Cliffs, NJ: Prentice Hall, 1987.
176 pp. Paperbound. $10.94. ISBN 0-139-43655-3.

This collection of primary source materials focuses on "real-life" experiences of Americans. Included are letters, poetry, diaries, songs, drawings, and other kinds of source materials, each with background information and reading review questions to help students interpret and analyze the source.

Weatherford, Doris. **Foreign and Female: Immigrant Women in America, 1840–1930.**
New York: Schocken, 1987.
288 pp. Paperbound. $18.95. ISBN 0-8052-4017-9.

This work profiles women from every major European ethnic group, examining their day-to-day experiences—where they lived, what they ate, how they felt about men, children, marriage, and divorce. Excerpts from letters enliven the presentation.

Weiner, Lynn Y. **From Working Girl to Working Mother: The Female Labor Force in the United States, 1820–1980.**
Chapel Hill, NC: University of North Carolina Press, 1986.
187 pp. Paperbound. $8.95. ISBN 0-8078-1612-4.

This text focuses on changes in social attitudes, women's self-image, and economic necessity and how they have impacted women's participation in the work force. Beginning with entry of single women into the labor force in the 1820s and proceeding to the post–World War II era of working mothers, the text provides a readable narrative suitable for students in grades 9 and up.

Whiteaker, Larry. **The Individual and Society in America.**
Orlando, FL: Harcourt Brace Jovanovich, 1979.
176 pp. Paperbound. $9.45. ISBN 0-15-379-208-6. (Teacher's guide: 96 pp., paperbound, $2.25, ISBN 0-15-379-234-5.)

This supplementary text for grades 9–12 looks at four periods of change in U.S. history, examining the goals, beliefs, and government of Puritan New England; growth of individualism in the 1800s; urban life in the early 1900s; and the post–World War II society.

Whitney, Sharon. **The Equal Rights Amendment.**
New York: Watts, 1984.
128 pp. Hardbound. $14.95. ISBN 0-531-04768-7.

This text for students in grades 9 and up explores the personalities and organizations on both sides of the issue of the Equal Rights Amendment. The author traces the history of the amendment from colonial times to 1984. Strategies used to advance the amendment since it was first introduced in Congress in 1923 are detailed.

Whittemore, Thomas. **The Vietnam War: A Text for Students.**
Cambridge, MA: Cambridgeport Press, 1988.
172 pp. Paperbound. $10.75. ISBN 0-944348-00-9.

This student text presents a straightforward narrative on the historical
background of the Vietnam War, how the level of U.S. involvement escalated,
who fought in Vietnam, and the impact of the war on U.S. society.

Zinn, Howard. **A People's History of the United States.**
New York: Harper and Row, 1980.
614 pp. Paperbound. $8.95. ISBN 0-06-090792-4.

This resource focuses on the role of the powerless in U.S. history. Coverage
of the views and experiences of indentured servants, women, Native
Americans, blacks, and the poor provides a unique view of U.S. history.

Textbooks

This section includes basal textbooks specifically designed for the
secondary market. Texts written for the college market and marketed to
secondary teachers are not included, although teachers in advanced
placement courses may find such texts suitable for their students. The
texts in this section include both those that cover only the period
emphasized in this volume and those that provide a general survey of
U.S. history. In examining texts that cover only the later years of U.S.
history, teachers should be cautious, in that many such texts are mildly
revised versions of the second half of another text, expanded with
primary sources or other features. This is not to suggest that packaging a
text in this manner is not a legitimate marketing strategy; it is merely to
indicate that teachers should be fully aware of what they are buying.

Berkin, Carol, and Leonard Wood. **Land of Promise: A History of the
United States, Volume II: From 1865.**
Glenview, IL: Scott, Foresman, 1986.
*608 pp. Hardbound. $22.90. (A teacher's annotated edition, teacher's resource
book, and test generator package are available to supplement the text.) ISBN
0-673-13374-5.*

Land of Promise surveys U.S. history from the end of the Civil War to the
Reagan years. Although the primary focus is on political, economic, and
military developments, social history and such subjects as women and
minorities are given adequate treatment. Special features on "The

Geographic Setting" link history and the environment. A lengthy section entitled "Documents, Artifacts, Exhibits, and Other National Treasures" concludes the text. *Land of Promise* is also available as a single-volume survey of U.S. history from the earliest times to the present; that volume does not have the extensive document section at the end.

Bidna, David B., Morris S. Greenberg, and Jerold H. Spitz. **We the People: A History of the United States.**
Lexington, MA: D. C. Heath, 1982.
639 pp. Hardbound. $23.61. (An annotated teacher's edition, activities book, and evaluation program are available to supplement the text.) ISBN 0-669-04484-9.

We the People is designed for average and below-average junior high school students and thus has a controlled reading level and uses stories and graphics to stimulate interest. The text covers events from pre-Columbian times through the election of President Reagan. Social and cultural aspects of history receive ample attention.

Boorstin, Daniel, and Brooks Mather Kelley. **A History of the United States.**
Englewood Cliffs, NJ: Prentice Hall, 1986 (rev. ed.).
752 pp. Hardbound. $24.48. (A teacher's resource book, computer test bank, and critical thinking skill transparencies are available to supplement the text.) ISBN 0-663-37997-0.

This high school text provides comprehensive coverage of events in U.S. history. The text focuses most heavily on a chronological presentation of political and military history, but also examines economic, social, and cultural developments. The authors of this text are probably the most distinguished historians currently writing for the school market.

Branson, Margaret Stimman. **America's Heritage.**
Englewood Cliffs, NJ: Prentice Hall, 1986.
658 pp. Hardbound. $23.91. (A teacher's resource book, student workbook, and critical thinking skill transparencies are available to supplement the text.) ISBN 0-663-40907-1.

This junior high school text provides a chronological presentation emphasizing ideas, issues, and confrontations that have shaped the United States. The treatment of ethnic groups and women is balanced throughout the narrative, which is written in a question-and-answer format designed to help students focus on significant points of history.

Brown, Richard C., and Herbert J. Bass. **One Flag, One Land.**
Morristown, NJ: Silver Burdett and Ginn, 1988.

818 pp. Hardbound. $22.95. (An annotated teacher's edition and teacher's resource files including a planning guide, masters for worksheets and tests, outline maps, wall maps, and a workbook are available to supplement the text.) ISBN 0-382-08414-4.

One Flag, One Land is designed for use in eighth-grade survey courses. It presents a chronological narrative of U.S. history, emphasizing political and economic history. Because the text is essentially the final book in the publisher's elementary series, a vast array of support material is provided the teacher.

Buggey, L. Joanne and others. **America! America!** Glenview, IL: Scott, Foresman, 1987.
768 pp. Hardbound. $22.65. (A teacher's annotated edition, teacher's resource book, workbook, and testing program are available to supplement the text.) ISBN 0-673-03501-9.

This junior high school text presents a chronological treatment of U.S. history, emphasizing the people who contributed to the history of our country. Primary source materials and a variety of illustrations enliven the text, which is written at the fifth- to seventh-grade reading level.

Conlin, Joseph R. **Our Land, Our Time: A History of the United States.** Austin, TX: Holt, Rinehart and Winston, 1986.
850 pp. Hardbound. $22.54. (A teacher's annotated edition, teacher's resource book, workbook, test book, and test generator are available to supplement the text.) ISBN 0-15-772000-4.

This senior high text is weighted heavily toward political, economic, and diplomatic history; it deemphasizes social and cultural history, but contains more law-related content than most history texts. The use of maps, graphics, and other kinds of artwork is particularly strong.

Davidson, James West, and John E. Batchelor. **The American Nation.** Englewood Cliffs, NJ: Prentice Hall, 1986.
816 pp. Hardbound. $24.48. (An annotated teacher's edition, teacher's resource manual, computer test bank, and critical thinking skill transparencies are available to supplement the text.) ISBN 0-13-027599-9.

This junior high school text provides a chronological treatment of U.S. history, with emphasis on the following themes: forging a national identity from a diverse population, strengthening our democratic institutions, and improving our economic and technological capacity. The text is easy to read, with such special features as "Americans in History," "Where History Happened," and "Arts in America" provided to stimulate interest.

Davidson, James West, and Mark H. Lytle. **A History of the Republic, Volume 2: The United States From 1865.**
Englewood Cliffs, NJ: Prentice Hall, 1986.
712 pp. Hardbound. $24.36. (An annotated teacher's edition, teacher's resource manual, and computer test bank are available to supplement the text.) ISBN 0-13-392002-X.

This text essentially repeats the last five units of *The United States: A History of the Republic,* providing chronological coverage of events from 1865. A lengthy section of primary source documents has been added to the end of the book. It should be noted that the first volume of this two-volume set is taken from *The American Nation,* so that the two volumes have somewhat different features and a different reading level.

Davidson, James West, and Mark H. Lytle. **The United States: A History of the Republic.**
Englewood Cliffs, NJ: Prentice Hall, 1986 (rev. ed.).
832 pp. Hardbound. $24.48. (An annotated teacher's edition, teacher's resource book, student study guide, computer test bank, and critical thinking skills transparencies are available to supplement the text.) ISBN 0-13-937301-2.

This high school text contains a chronological narrative that the authors believe will acquaint students with our nation's past experiences and prepare them to face the future. Special coverage is given to geography in history, primary sources, connections between past and present, and ties between U.S. and world events.

Drewry, Henry N., and Thomas H. O'Connor. **America Is.**
Columbus, OH: Merrill, 1987 (rev. ed.).
798 pp. Hardbound. $21.90. (A teacher's annotated edition, teacher's resource book, activity book, transparency package, and set of classroom posters are available to supplement the text.) ISBN 0-675-1013-6.

While *America Is* presents a chronological treatment of U.S. history, like other U.S. history texts for junior high students, the text also develops such themes as opportunity, independence, democracy, and power. An unusual feature of this readable text are the "City Sketches," which provide insight into urban life at various periods in U.S. history.

Drewry, Henry N. and others. **United States History, Volume 2: Reconstruction to the Present.**
Columbus, OH: Merrill, 1986.

672 pp. Hardbound. $19.80. (A teacher's annotated edition, teacher's resource book, citizenship activities, and testing program are available to supplement the text.) ISBN 0-675-02045-X.

This volume, designed for high school students, is comprised of the last six units of *American Tradition*, supplemented with a section of primary sources at the end of the text. Teachers should note that the first volume of this two-volume set is a junior high text comprised of the first five units of the 1984 edition of *America Is*, supplemented with a section of primary sources at the end of the text.

Garraty, John A. **American History.**
Orlando, FL: Harcourt Brace Jovanovich, 1986 (rev. ed.).
960 pp. Hardbound. $23.25. (A teacher's edition, teacher's resource book, workbook, and tests are available to supplement the text.) ISBN 0-15-370680-0.

Written by an eminent historian, this junior high text provides approximately equal coverage to the various periods of U.S. history, not stressing early history at the expense of more recent events. Special features of the text include numerous skill development activities and an emphasis on the use of "historical imagination." The narrative is written in an engaging style that would also appeal to high school students.

Graff, Henry F. **America: The Glorious Republic, Volume 2: 1877 to the Present.**
Boston, MA: Houghton Mifflin, 1986.
672 pp. Hardbound. $21.60. (A teacher's manual, teacher's resource book, workbook, and test generator are available to supplement the text.) ISBN 0-395-38175-4.

This text uses the traditional chronological approach to U.S. history, beginning with the end of the Civil War and ending with the election of Ronald Reagan. Special features of note are primary source readings, "How to Study American History" lessons, and geography lessons. This text is also available as a single-volume history of the full span of U.S. history.

Green, Robert P., Jr., Laura L. Becker, and Robert E. Coviello. **The American Tradition: A History of the United States.**
Columbus, OH: Merrill, 1986 (rev. ed.).
816 pp. Hardbound. $21.90. (A teacher's annotated edition, teacher's resource book, activity book, transparency package, and set of classroom posters are available to supplement the text.) ISBN 0-675-00960-X.

The major portion of the chronological narrative in this text stresses the development of America's government, economy, society, and role in world affairs. Basic values of the U.S. political system are also stressed. The text emphasizes the work of historians more than do most other texts, a feature that is appropriate for the high school audience.

Hart, Diane, and David Baker. **Spirit of Liberty: An American History.**
Menlo Park, CA: Addison-Wesley, 1987.
548 pp. Hardbound. $23.70. (A teacher's edition, teacher's resource manual, and test generator are available to supplement the text.) ISBN 0-201-20921-4.

This junior high school text provides coverage of political, economic, and social events from the first Americans through predictions about the twenty-first century. Special features stress reading skills, the importance of geography, and the influence of values in history.

Jordan, Winthrop D., Miriam Greenblatt, and John S. Bowes. **The Americans: The History of a People and a Nation.**
Evanston, IL: McDougal, Littell, 1985.
864 pp. Hardbound. $21.60. (A teacher's edition, teacher's manual, reinforcement activities, enrichment activities, and tests are available to supplement the text.) ISBN 0-86609-291-9.

This high school text presents a traditional chronological narrative. Emphasis is placed on the global aspects of various events, as well as relevant themes from U.S. literature. The history of women and ethnic groups is well integrated into the text.

King, David, and others. **United States History.**
Menlo Park, CA: Addison-Wesley, 1986.
848 pp. Hardbound. $24.30. (A teacher's edition, teacher's resource manual, book of readings, and test generating program are available to supplement the text.) ISBN 0-201-20916-0.

This 10-unit high school text focuses on politics, geography, and economics within a chronological framework. Emphasis is placed on recurring issues in U.S. history, contemporary observers in each period, and skill development in social studies. The second half of this book is available as a text titled *United States History From 1865*; a book with a similar title—*United States History to 1877*—is based on the first half of Hart and Baker's *Spirit of Liberty*, a fact teachers should be aware of.

Linden, Glenn M., Dean C. Brink, and Richard H. Huntington. **Legacy of Freedom, Volume 2: United States History From Reconstruction to the Present.**
Mission Hills, CA: Glencoe, 1986 (rev. ed.).
768 pp. Hardbound. $23.55. (A teacher's edition, teacher's resource binder, and study guide are available to supplement the text.) ISBN 0-8445-6926-7.

This high school text provides a traditional chronological narrative of events in U.S. history, supplemented with special features on the historian's skills, conflicting opinions on historical events, and the future. A lengthy section of primary source documents concludes the text. The text is also available as a one-volume comprehensive survey of U.S. history to the present.

Maier, Pauline. **The American People: A History.**
Lexington, MA: D. C. Heath, 1986.
800 pp. Hardbound. $22.95. (A teacher's edition, teacher's resource binder, workbook, testing program, posters, and transparencies are available to supplement the text.) ISBN 0-669-04883-6.

This chronological treatment of U.S. history for junior high school students emphasizes the Constitution, government, and citizenship. Special features focus on biographies, skills, and global connections throughout U.S. history.

May, Ernest R., and others. **The American People: A History From 1877.**
Evanston, IL: McDougall, Littell, 1986.
720 pp. Hardbound. $21.60. (A teacher's edition, teacher's manual, reinforcement activities, enrichment activities, and mastery tests are available to supplement the text.) ISBN 0-86609-645-0.

This high school text is based on the last several units of Jordan, Greenblatt, and Bowes' *The Americans,* with the addition of several brief excerpts from primary sources in each unit. Teachers should note that the first volume under this title is based on May's *A Proud Nation,* and is thus intended for junior high students.

May, Ernest R. **A Proud Nation.**
Evanston, IL: McDougall, Littell, 1984 (rev. ed.).
784 pp. Hardbound. $21.96. (A teacher's edition, teacher's manual, enrichment activities, reinforcement activities, and mastery tests are available to supplement the text.) ISBN 0-86609-285-4.

This chronological presentation covers historical periods from before Columbus through Ronald Reagan, encouraging historical analysis and comparison through the use of social studies skills. U.S. families—both famous and not-so-famous—are featured in each unit. The text is suitable for middle school and junior high students.

O'Connor, John R., Sidney Schwartz, and Leslie A. Wheeler. **Exploring United States History.**
New York: Globe Book Co., 1986 (rev. ed.).
824 pp. Hardbound. $23.98. (A teacher's resource manual, workbook, and testing program are available to supplement the text.) ISBN 0-87065-558-2.

This high school history text is aimed at average students with below-average reading skills. Emphasis is placed on domestic politics and social history from pre-Columbian days through the 1984 presidential election. The text is structured with short reading segments, organizing questions, and frequent reviews.

Patrick, John, and Carol Berkin. **History of the American Nation.**
New York: Macmillan, 1987 (rev. ed.).
802 pp. Hardbound. $21.96. (A teacher's manual, skills workbook, overhead transparencies, and tests are available to supplement the text.) ISBN 0-02-151200-0.

This chronological presentation incorporates both political and social history, with an emphasis on citizenship analysis and the role of the individual's values in history. The text is well-illustrated, with timelines that are particularly noteworthy.

Peck, Ira, Steven Jantzen, and Daniel Rosen. **American Adventures.**
Jefferson City, MO: Scholastic, 1987 (rev. ed.).
759 pp. Hardbound. $22.50. (A teacher's edition, print masters, and teacher's resource binder are available to supplement the text.) ISBN 0-8114-1638-0.

American Adventures is a basal U.S. history text for junior high students of average or mixed abilities or for high school students who are below-average readers. The materials emphasize short, easy-to-read chapters of high interest to the intended audience. Each chapter focuses on an important personality, event, or idea in U.S. history from the arrival of the first Native Americans to the Reagan years. Although the overall content coverage is not as extensive as in most typical texts, the coverage of social history is quite good.

Rawls, James J., and Philip Weeks. **Land of Liberty: A United States History.**
Austin, TX: Holt, Rinehart and Winston, 1985.
768 pp. Hardbound. $23.52. (A teacher's annotated edition, teacher's resource book, and study disk are available to supplement the text.) ISBN 0-03-064226-4.

This chronological survey of U.S. history is designed for junior high school courses. Focus is on economic and political history, with comprehensive coverage of events, dates, and facts. Skills, particularly those related to geography, chronology, critical thinking, and reading, are emphasized. Special features focus on U.S. contributions to technology.

Reich, Jerome R., and Edward L. Biller. **United States History.**
Austin, TX: Holt, Rinehart and Winston, 1988.

878 pp. Hardbound. $23.13. (A teacher's edition and teacher's resource book are available to supplement the text.) ISBN 0-03-14808-1.

This new text provides a traditional chronological survey of U.S. history. It is exceptionally well-illustrated and includes questions with every illustration to ensure that students attend to and think about the visual material. Skills, especially map skills, are emphasized. Advance organizers are used for every text section, which should help students understand the material presented.

Ritchie, Donald A. **Heritage of Freedom: History of the United States From 1877.**
Riverside, NJ: Scribner-Laidlaw, 1986.
702 pp. Hardbound. $24.57. (A teacher's resource book, workbook, and testing program are available to supplement the text.) ISBN 0-02-115510-0.

This high school text presents a chronological treatment of U.S. history that aims to cover both political and social history, as well as examining democratic values and their role in shaping our heritage. A lengthy section of primary source readings concludes the text. The one-volume survey by the same title covers U.S. history from the earliest times to the present.

Roden, Philip and others. **Life and Liberty: An American History.**
Glenview, IL: Scott, Foresman, 1987 (rev. ed.).
752 pp. Hardbound. $23.95. (A teacher's handbook, workbook, and testing program are available to supplement the text.) ISBN 0-673-22240-3.

This text provides secondary students who have difficulty using standard texts with a chronological introduction to U.S. history and the opportunity to strengthen communication, social studies, and critical thinking skills. Information about the culture and people of an era supplements the basic account of political and military events. Tables and graphs are particuarly well employed.

Schwartz, Melvin, and John R. O'Connor. **Exploring American History.**
New York: Globe Books, 1986 (rev. ed.).
570 pp. Hardbound. $19.47. (A teacher's resource manual, workbook, and testing program are available to supplement the text.) ISBN 0-87065-4497-7.

This text is aimed at junior high school students with reading and work-study difficulties. Arranged chronologically, the text contains 80 units based on the following themes: discovery and settlement, the growth of freedom, the law of the land, the Civil War, expansion, technology, the United States and the world, and the United States today. Each chapter begins with a question to be considered while reading, a feature that should aid less-able readers.

Smith, Lew. **The American Dream: A United States History.**
Glenview, IL: Scott, Foresman, 1983 (rev. ed.).
729 pp. Hardbound. $24.45. (A teacher's handbook, worksheets, and tests are available to supplement the text.) ISBN 0-673-13347-8.

The American Dream offers a survey of U.S. history that emphasizes the values and ideals to which Americans have paid homage. Political and economic history is not overlooked, but social and cultural history is the principal focus. This emphasis is borne out in such special features as "Who's Who," sections of primary source readings, and a section titled "Americanistic."

Sobel, Robert, and others. **The Challenge of Freedom.**
Mission Hills, CA: Glencoe, 1986.
768 pp. Hardbound. $23.55. (A teacher's edition, teacher's resource binder, study guide, workbook, tests, and enrichment activities are available to supplement the text.) ISBN 0-8445-6560-1.

This junior high school text presents a traditional chronological treatment of U.S. history. Two interesting content features are a case study in each chapter, which helps students look at one event in an era in depth, and an "investigation" of the social sciences at the end of each unit. Skills are also emphasized.

Todd, Lewis Paul, and Merle Curti. **Triumph of the American Nation.**
Orlando, FL: Harcourt Brace Jovanovich, 1986 (rev. ed.).
1,060 pp. Hardbound. $24.30. (An annotated teacher's edition, teacher's manual, test booklet, workbook, and posters are available to supplement the text.) ISBN 0-15-375950-X.

This best-selling—and longest—of U.S. history texts provides comprehensive, chronological coverage of the entire span of U.S. history. The new edition contains features that help students understand the importance of the individual, the humanities, and geography. History study skills are emphasized in skill-development sections.

Weisberger, Bernard A. **From Sea to Shining Sea: A History of the United States.**
New York: McGraw-Hill, 1982.
800 pp. Hardbound. $21.99. (A teacher's resource guide is available to supplement the text.) ISBN 0-07-069099-5.

This junior high school text is designed to teach average students about social, cultural, political, and economic history. Skills in reading, using maps, researching and writing, and critical thinking are developed.

Wilder, Howard B., Robert P. Ludlum, and Harriet McCune Brown. **This Is America's Story.**
Boston, MA: Houghton Mifflin, 1983 (rev. ed.).
792 pp. Hardbound. $23.76. (A teacher's edition, workbook, and tests are available to supplement the text.) ISBN 0-395-31145-4.

This Is America's Story is designed for use with average junior high students. The authors present a blend of political and social history in their chronological treatment. While adequate material is presented for a year-long course, this text does allow for incorporation of current events or special topics.

Wood, Leonard C., Ralph H. Gabriel, and Edward L. Biller. **America: Its People and Values.**
Orlando, FL: Harcourt Brace Jovanovich, 1985 (rev. ed.).
864 pp. Hardbound. $23.25. (An annotated teacher's edition, teacher's resource book, workbook, and tests are available to supplement the text.) ISBN 0-15-377785-0.

Like other texts annotated in this section, *America: Its People and Values* provides chronological coverage of events in U.S. history. Special features focus on people and the humanities. Emphasis is also given to development of map and chart skills.

Videocassettes and Films

The following listing does not include movies produced for theatrical release, although many such films could be used in secondary U.S. history classes as motivational tools. Teachers are cautioned, however, to preview all such films before showing them to students, making note of any historical inaccuracies for later discussion with the class.

America at War: World Wars I and II
Type: Color videocassette: VHS or ¾″ U-Matic, plus teacher's guide and 12 worksheets
Grades: 7–12
Length: 40 min.
Buy/Rent: VHS: $99/no rental; ¾″ U-Matic: $134/no rental (includes teacher's guide and 12 worksheets)
Source: Society for Visual Education
             1345 Diversey Parkway
             Chicago, IL 60614
Date: 1986

This program helps students look at the causes and the consequences of the two world wars. Changes in technology and how they affected the conduct of the wars are also covered. The program is divided into two 20-minute segments that can be used separately.

American City Series

Type: 3 color videocassettes: VHS, Beta, or ¾″ U-Matic, with teacher's manual
Grades: 10–adult
Length: 30 min. each
Buy/Rent: VHS and Beta: $129/$55; ¾″ U-Matic: $198/$55
Source: Films Incorporated
            5547 North Ravenswood Avenue
            Chicago, IL 60640
            (produced by WBET)
Date: 1981

This three-part series looks at issues related to urbanization in U.S. history. The first program looks at the causes of urban riots, comparing the New York draft riot of 1863 with race riots in Detroit in 1967. The second program looks at women in the city, focusing on New York and Indianapolis from 1880–1920. The final program compares the development of Harlem in the early 1900s to the emergence of a black community in Atlanta.

American Documents Series

Type: 10 color and black-and-white videocassettes: VHS or Beta
Grades: 7–12
Length: 52 min. each
Buy/Rent: $33.95 each/no rental
Source: Zenger Video
            P.O. Box 802
            Culver City, CA 90232
Date: not available

This series of programs uses newsreels, motion picture footage, radio recordings, and clippings from magazines and newspapers to convey information about the social and cultural history of various periods or movements. For example, programs cover immigration, the 1920s, the Great Depression, the women's suffrage movement, the development of U.S. technology, and the work of rocket scientist Robert H. Goddard.

American Heritage Media Collection

Type: 5 color videocassettes: VHS, each with teacher's guide
Grades: 7–12

Length: 35 min. each
Buy/Rent: $180 each/no rental
Source: Zenger Video
             P.O. Box 802
             Culver City, CA 90232
             (produced by Westport Media)
Date: 1985–1986

Each program presents the reenactment of a major event in U.S. history; the reenactments were supervised by *American Heritage* to ensure historical accuracy. Topics covered are the West, growth of the nation in the five decades following the Civil War, World War I, the 1920s and 1930s, and World War II.

American Treasure: A Smithsonian Journey

Type: Closed captioned, color videocassette: VHS
Grades: 7–12
Length: 90 min.
Buy/Rent: $26.95/no rental
Source: Zenger Video
             P.O. Box 802
             Culver City, CA 90232
Date: 1985

This tour of the Smithsonian Museum complex celebrates U.S. technology, art, politics, sports, and entertainment. Newsreel footage and photographs provide background on some of the objects pictured in the video.

American West: Myth and Reality

Type: Color videocassette: VHS or Beta, with teacher's guide
Grades: 7–12
Length: 52 min.
Buy/Rent: $149/no rental
Source: Educational Audio Visual
             Pleasantville, NY 10570
Date: 1986

This program looks at the myths of the West from James Fenimore Cooper to John Wayne, contrasting these with the reality of westward expansion. The difficulty of distinguishing between fantasy and reality is examined. The three-segment program includes daguerrotypes, tintypes, photographs, paintings, and movie stills.

America's Railroads: How the Iron Horse Shaped Our Nation

Type: Color videocassette: VHS, Beta, or ¾″ U-Matic; or 16mm film,
             with teacher's guide

Grades: 4–12
Length: 22 min.
Buy/Rent: Videocassette: $310/$40; 16mm film: $440/$40
Source: Churchill Films
            662 North Robertson Boulevard
            Los Angeles, CA 90069
            (produced by Cypress Films)
Date: 1985

This film traces the history of railroads in the United States, looking at their impact on growth, settlement, and the economy.

Andrew Carnegie: The Gospel of Wealth
Type: Color videocassette: VHS, Beta, or ¾″ U-Matic; or 16mm film
            (also available in Spanish)
Grades: 7–adult
Length: 26 min.
Buy/Rent: Videocassette: $300/$40; 16mm film: $445/$40
Source: Learning Corporation of America
            108 Wilmot Road
            Deerfield, IL 60015
Date: 1974

This program presents a dramatic portrait of industrialist Andrew Carnegie, which also illuminates the practices of big business.

Artists at Work
Type: Color videocassette: VHS, Beta, or ¾″ U-Matic; or 16mm film
Grades: 9–adult
Length: 35 min.
Buy/Rent: Videocassette: $275/no rental; 16mm film: $495/$60
Source: New Day Film Co-op
            22 Riverview Drive
            Wayne, NJ 07470
Date: 1981

This film focuses on federal programs of the 1930s designed to support visual artists during the Great Depression. Recollections by such artists as Alice Neel and Jacob Lawrence provide a close-up view of this period.

The Background of the Reconstruction Period
Type: Color videocassette: VHS, Beta, or ¾″ U-Matic; or 16mm film
Grades: 5–12
Length: 20 min.
Buy/Rent: Videocassette: $320/$50; 16mm film: $495/$50

Source: BFA Educational Media
         468 Park Avenue South
         New York, NY 10016
         (produced by Paul Burnford)
Date: 1986

This program describes how the South was rebuilt after the Civil War. The positions of the Lincoln, Johnson, and Grant administrations are covered, as are economic issues, reestablishment of state and local governments, and the relationships between blacks and whites.

The Ballad of the Iron Horse
Type: Color videocassette: VHS, Beta, or ¾" U-Matic; or 16mm film
         (captioned version available)
Grades: 5–adult
Length: 29 min.
Buy/Rent: Videocassette: $300/$40; 16mm film: $425/$40
Source: Learning Corporation of America
         108 Wilmot Road
         Deerfield, IL 60015
Date: 1970

This film recreates the flamboyant railroad era, emphasizing how the development of railroads transformed the United States. The building of the first transcontinental railroad is a special focus of the film.

Black Paths of Leadership
Type: Color videocassette: VHS, Beta, or ¾" U-Matic; or 16mm film
Grades: 10–12
Length: 27 min.
Buy/Rent: Videocassette: $295/$50; 16mm film: $425/$50
Source: Churchill Films
         662 North Robertson Boulevard
         Los Angeles, CA 90069
         (produced by the California Afro-American Museum)
Date: 1985

This rather scholarly film looks at the paths three black leaders took in their fight for black rights. The three are Booker T. Washington, W. E. B. DuBois, and Marcus Garvey.

Booker T. Washington: The Life and Legacy
Type: Videocassette: VHS, with paperback book
Grades: 7–12
Length: 32 min.
Buy/Rent: $75/no rental

Source: Zenger Video
             P.O. Box 802
             Culver City, CA 90232
             (produced by the National Park Service)
Date: not available

This film focuses on the work of Booker T. Washington, including the
founding of Tuskegee Institute and his political career. The opposing views
on his role are presented. Historical reenactments, location filming, and use
of historical photographs are features of the film.

Boom and Bust: The Dakota Experience
Type: Color videocassette: VHS, Beta, or ¾″ U-Matic; or 16mm film
Grades: 10–adult
Length: 20 min.
Buy/Rent: VHS or Beta videocassette: $259/$40; ¾″ U-Matic videocassette:
            $289/$40; 16mm film: $400/$40
Source: Centre Productions
            1800 30th Street, Suite 207
            Boulder, CO 80301
Date: 1986

The history of South Dakota is the subject of this film, which
chronicles how two cycles of booms and busts—one in the late 1800s
and one in the 1930s—changed the nature of the Great Plains. Paintings
and historical photographs, interviews with farmers who lived through
the Depression, and footage of the harsh landscape add to the film's
power.

Brother, Can You Spare a Dime?
Type: Color videocassette: VHS
Grades: 9–12
Length: 20 min.
Buy/Rent: $139/no rental
Source: Zenger Video
            P.O. Box 802
            Culver City, CA 90232
            (produced by Films for the Humanities)
Date: 1984

This film uses archival film and still photographs to convey what life
was like during the Great Depression. The film is produced as though
it were actually 1932, a technique that should interest students.
The fact that the Depression affected other parts of the world is
presented.

Civil Rights: Yesterday, Today, Tomorrow
Type: Color videocassette: VHS, Beta, or ¾″ U-Matic
Grades: 7–12
Length: 60 min.
Buy/Rent: VHS or Beta: $179/no rental; ¾″ U-Matic: $199/no rental
Source: The Associated Press
             P.O. Box 1000
             Mount Kisco, NY 10549
Date: 1987

This film, which is presented in four segments that can be used separately, focuses on the advances and setbacks since the events of the 1950s and 1960s. Government programs to promote equal opportunity and the political and economic efforts of minorities and women are emphasized.

Coal Mining Women
Type: Color videocassette: VHS or Beta; or 16mm film
Grades: 10–adult
Length: 40 min.
Buy/Rent: Videocassette: $300/$70; 16mm film: $650/$70
Source: Appalshop Films
             P.O. Box 743
             Whitesburg, KY 41858
Date: 1982

This documentary examines women's controversial entrance into the field of coal mining. Interviews with women working in the mines illuminate male prejudice and harassment, health and safety issues, and the pride they have in their accomplishments.

Different Drummer: Blacks in the Military
Type: 3 color videocassettes: VHS, Beta, or ¾″ U-Matic
Grades: 10–adult
Length: 58 min. each
Buy/Rent: $495 each or $1340 for series/$90 each
Source: Films Incorporated
             5547 North Ravenswood Avenue
             Chicago, IL 60640
             (produced by WNET)
Date: 1984

This comprehensive series looks at black Americans in the military. The first program, "Unknown Soldiers," starts with the Civil War and continues through the Indian Wars and Spanish-American War and World War I. "The Troops" focuses on black participation from World War II through Vietnam. The final segment, "From Gold Bars to Silver Stars," profiles today's highest ranking black officers.

Dwellings of the West
Type: Color videocassette: VHS
Grades: 4–12
Length: 12 min.
Buy/Rent: $49/no rental
Source: ·Centre Productions
            1800 30th Street, Suite 207
            Boulder, CO 80301
Date: 1981

This brief video focuses on the dwellings people have built throughout history on the Great Plains and in the Rocky Mountains. Dwellings covered include tents, cliff dwellings, tipis, adobe, log cabins, and others.

Eyes on the Prize: America's Civil Rights Years
Type: 6 color videocassettes: VHS, Beta, or ¾″ U-Matic
Grades: 8–adult
Length: 1 hour each
Buy/Rent: $59.95 each or $295 for series/no rental
Source: PBS Video
            1320 Braddock Place
            Alexandria, VA 22314
Date: 1987

This series focuses on the civil rights movement from 1954–1965 (a series covering the later years is now under development). Titles of the individual videos are *Awakenings (1954–1956), Fighting Back (1957–1962), Ain't Scared of Your Jails (1960–1961), No Easy Walk (1961–1963), Mississippi: Is This America? (1962–1964),* and *Bridge to Freedom (1965).* Several print resources are available to supplement the program.

The Fabulous 60s
Type: 10 color videocassettes: VHS
Grades: 8–adult
Length: approx. 1 hour each
Buy/Rent: $19.95 each or $189.50 for series/no rental
Source: Zenger Video
            P.O. Box 802
            Culver City, CA 90232
Date: 1978

This series includes one video for each year of the 1960s. The focus is on U.S. domestic controversies—the Bay of Pigs, the death of Marilyn Monroe, the civil rights movement, riots in Watts and Detroit, and the space program. Many other topics are also covered.

45/85: America and the World Since World War II

Type:	4 color videocassettes: VHS
Grades:	8–adult
Length:	52 min. each
Buy/Rent:	$35.50 each or $114.95 for set/no rental
Source:	Zenger Video
	P.O. Box 802
	Culver City, CA 90232
	(produced by ABC News)
Date:	1986

This series uses newsreel and newscast footage, still photographs, and interviews to create a "montage of world history between 1945 and 1985." A particular focus is U.S.-U.S.S.R. relations, but such other topics as entertainment, improvements in health care, and civil rights are covered.

F. D. R.—The Man Who Changed America

Type:	Black-and-white videocassette: VHS, Beta, or ¾″ U-Matic; or 16mm film
Grades:	7–adult
Length:	30 min.
Buy/Rent:	Videocassette: $250/$62; 16mm film: $455/$62
Source:	BFA Educational Media
	468 Park Avenue South
	New York, NY 10016
	(produced by CBS News)
Date:	1976

This program examines how Franklin D. Roosevelt was able to present the United States with the sense of leadership it craved in the midst of the economic crisis of the 1930s. The program also looks at expansion of the federal bureaucracy under Roosevelt.

The Frontier Experience

Type:	Color videocassette: VHS, Beta, or ¾″ U-Matic; or 16mm film (Spanish version available)
Grades:	7–adult
Length:	25 min.
Buy/Rent:	Videocassette: $300/$40; 16mm film: $445/$40
Source:	Learning Corporation of America
	108 Wilmot Road
	Deerfield, IL 60015
Date:	1976

This film presents a woman's perspective on the westward movement. The film focuses on Delilah Fowler's first year—1869—on the Kansas frontier. The film is based on diaries written by real settlers.

The Golden Age of the Automobile
Type: Color videocassette: VHS, Beta, or ¾″ U-Matic; or 16mm film
Grades: 7–adult
Length: 30 min.
Buy/Rent: Videocassette: $300/$40; 16mm film: $425/$40
Source: Learning Corporation of America
               108 Wilmot Road
               Deerfield, IL 60015
Date: 1970

The history of the automobile is traced, from its early years as a "toy" of the wealthy to the 1970s, when it had become transportation for the masses. The ways in which the automobile has changed U.S. society are covered.

Golden Spike
Type: Color videocassette: VHS
Grades: 7–12
Length: 21 min.
Buy/Rent: $65/no rental
Source: Zenger Video
               P.O. Box 802
               Culver City, CA 90232
Date: 1969

This video examines the completion of the transcontinental railroad, depicting the difficulties encountered in building the line and examining the long-term effects of the railroad.

Goodbye Billy: America Goes to War, 1917–1918
Type: Black-and-white videocassette: VHS, Beta, or ¾″ U-Matic; or
               16mm film
Grades: 7–adult
Length: 25 min.
Buy/Rent: Videocassette: $230/$40; 16mm film: $325/$40
Source: Churchill Films
               662 North Robertson Boulevard
               Los Angeles, CA 90069
Date: 1972

This film uses archival footage, period voices, and songs to examine the psychological preparation for going to war, the actual experience of fighting, and the tragic consequences.

The Great American Student
Type: Black-and-white videocassette: VHS, Beta, or ¾″ U-Matic; or
            16mm film
Grades: 7–adult
Length: 18 min.
Buy/Rent: Videocassette: $250/$75; 16mm film: $425/$75
Source: Coronet Film and Video
            108 Wilmot Road
            Deerfield, IL 60015
Date: 1985 (re-release)

Students will enjoy this film, compiled of scenes from educational guidance
films made in the 1950s. While students will laugh at such pieces as "Dating
Dos and Don'ts," they will also get a glimpse into social changes in the past
generation.

The Great Depression
Type: Color videocassette: VHS, Beta, or ¾″ U-Matic; or 16mm film
Grades: 7–adult
Length: 33 min.
Buy/Rent: Videocassette: $250/$53; 16mm film: $425/$53
Source: BFA Educational Media
            468 Park Avenue South
            New York, NY 10016
            (produced by CBS News)
Date: 1976

This film looks not only at the events of the Great Depression but also at the
values and psychology behind it—trust in businessmen, the importance of
economic success, and so on. Documentary footage gives the film an air of
authenticity.

The Growth of America's West Series
Type: 4 color videocassettes: VHS, Beta, or ¾″ U-Matic; or 16mm films
Grades: 5–12
Length: 14–22 min. each
Buy/Rent: Videocassettes: $180–$275/$43–$62 each; 16mm films:
            $295–$450/$43–$62 each
Source: BFA Educational Media
            468 Park Avenue South
            New York, NY 10016
            (produced by Capricorn Films and Allied Film Artists)
Date: 1978–1979

This four-part series looks at the American cowboy, contrasting the reality
of that life in the nineteenth century with our romanticized version today; the

mountain men and their role in westward expansion; the settlers who ventured west after the Louisiana Purchase; and the Spanish in the Southwest, from the earliest times to the present.

History Recovered: The Custer Battlefield Archaeological Survey of 1984
Type:	Color videocassette: VHS
Grades:	8–12
Length:	58 min.
Buy/Rent:	$99/no rental
Source:	Zenger Video
	P.O. Box 802
	Culver City, CA 90232
Date:	1985

This film presents archaeologists explaining how artifacts and rock carvings have been used to unravel the mystery of Custer's last stand. The program, filmed on location in Montana, employs paintings, maps, and portraits to present information.

The Homefront
Type:	Black and white videocassette: VHS, Beta, or ¾" U-Matic; or 16mm film (with book of interviews)
Grades:	10–adult
Length:	90 min.
Buy/Rent:	Videocassette: $495/$150; 16mm film: $895/$150
Source:	Churchill Films
	662 North Robertson Boulevard
	Los Angeles, CA 90069
Date:	1985

This three-part program looks at the "social stresses and changes on the homefront during World War II." The experiences of women, blacks, and Japanese-Americans are emphasized. Many interviews were conducted in preparing the program, and those not used in the program are published in a book that is free with purchase of the film or video.

Homeland
Type:	Color videocassette: VHS or ¾" U-Matic; or 16mm film
Grades:	10–adult
Length:	25 min.
Buy/Rent:	VHS videocassette: $279/$50; ¾" U-Matic videocassette: $299/$50; 16mm film: $470/$50
Source:	Centre Productions
	1800 30th Street, Suite 207
	Boulder, CO 80301
Date:	1986

This film provides a history of U.S. farming on the Great Plains, looking at the technology of farming, its successes and problems, and the people who farm.

Hopi: Songs of the Fourth World
Type: Color videocassette: VHS, Beta, or ¾″ U-Matic; or 16mm film
Grades: 9–12
Length: 58 min.
Buy/Rent: Videocassette: $600/no rental; 16mm film: $850/$100
Source: New Day Films
            22 Riverview Drive
            Wayne, NJ 07470
Date: 1984

This award-winning film focuses on how the Hopi have preserved the ways of life that have been handed down from generation to generation. Of special interest is the integration of art and daily life, both now and in the past.

Houses Have History
Type: Color videocassette: VHS, Beta, or ¾″ U-Matic; or 16mm film
Grades: 5–9
Length: 15 min.
Buy/Rent: Videocassette: $79/$40; 16mm film: $315/$40
Source: Churchill Films
            662 North Robertson Boulevard
            Los Angeles, CA 90069
Date: 1980

In this brief film, a group of young people learns about the history of their own community by studying buildings in their community and talking to long-time residents. A focus is the value of preservation and restoration.

How We Got the Vote
Type: Color videocassette: VHS or Beta
Grades: 8–adult
Length: 25 min.
Buy/Rent: $30/no rental
Source: National Women's History Project
            P.O. Box 3716
            Santa Rosa, CA 95402
            (produced by Lucerne Films)
Date: 1987

The subject of this video is the struggle for women's suffrage. Historical footage, cartoons, songs, and interviews are used to focus attention on the "last great push" for the Nineteenth Amendment.

"I Have a Dream . . .": The Life of Martin Luther King, Jr.
Type: Black-and-white videocassette: VHS, Beta, or ¾″ U-Matic; or
             16mm film
Grades: 7–adult
Length: 35 min.
Buy/Rent: Videocassette: $250/$49; 16mm film: $460/$49
Source: BFA Educational Media
             468 Park Avenue South
             New York, NY 10016
             (produced by CBS News)
Date: 1968

This film, released shortly after King's death, is both an autobiography of
Dr. King and a brief overview of the civil rights movement of the 1950s and
1960s. Excerpts from King's speeches and news footage lend authenticity.

The Immigrant Experience: The Long, Long Journey
Type: Color videocassette: VHS, Beta, or ¾″ U-Matic; or 16mm film
             (Spanish version available)
Grades: 7–adult
Length: 28 min.
Buy/Rent: Videocassette: $300/$40; 16mm film: $445/$40
Source: Learning Corporation of America
             108 Wilmot Road
             Deerfield, IL 60015
Date: 1973

This film tells the story of a Polish family who arrived in the United States in
1907. The story is told through the eyes of a young boy; at the end of the
film, the boy—now an adult—reflects on how his dreams were realized
through his grandchildren.

The Indomitable Teddy Roosevelt
Type: Color videocassette: VHS, Beta, or ¾″ U-Matic; or 16mm film
Grades: 7–adult
Length: 93 min.
Buy/Rent: Videocassette: $295/$150; 16mm film: $894/$150
Source: Churchill Films
             662 North Robertson Boulevard
             Los Angeles, CA 90069
Date: 1983

This three-part film looks at the public and private lives of Theodore
Roosevelt. Using archival footage and reenactments, the film gives a
broad view both of major events between 1858 and 1919 and of changes
in everyday life.

Isabella

Type:	Color videocassette: VHS or Beta
Grades:	7–12
Length:	16 min.
Buy/Rent:	$59/no rental
Source:	Centre Productions
	1800 30th Street, Suite 207
	Boulder, CO 80301
Date:	1980

This brief program looks at the experiences of Isabella Bird, a woman who traveled alone from Scotland to Colorado in 1873. The program, which is based on her collected letters, presents a realistic picture of the American West.

Japanese Relocation

Type:	Black-and-white videocassette: VHS, with book
Grades:	10–12
Length:	10 min.
Buy/Rent:	$60/no rental
Source:	Zenger Video
	P.O. Box 802
	Culver City, CA 90232
Date:	1943

This film presents the U.S. government's wartime justification for the internment program that moved more than 100,000 Japanese-Americans from their homes to internment camps in the interior. The film provides a useful lesson in the tactics of persuasion. A copy of a 1982 government report, *Personal Justice Denied,* comes with the video to provide balance.

John F. Kennedy: Great Figures in History

Type:	Color videocassette: VHS
Grades:	9–12
Length:	104 min.
Buy/Rent:	$60.95/no rental
Source:	Zenger Video
	P.O. Box 802
	Culver City, CA 90232
	(produced by CBS News)
Date:	1981

This three-part program looks at "The Childhood Years" through an informal interview with the president's mother; "The Presidential Years," with excerpts from televised speeches, interviews, and news programs; and "Four Dark Days," focusing on the assassination, funeral, and slaying of Oswald.

Kitty Hawk to Paris: The Heroic Years
Type: Color videocassette: VHS, Beta, or ¾″ U-Matic; or 16mm film
Grades: 7–adult
Length   51 min. (a 29-minute version is also available)
Buy/Rent: Videocassette: $450/$50; 16mm film: $595/$50
Source: Learning Corporation of America
             108 Wilmot Road
             Deerfield, IL 60015
Date: 1970

The history of early aviation is chronicled in this film, which looks at the Wright brothers, World War I fighter planes, and Lindbergh's transatlantic flight.

Letter from an Apache
Type: Color videocassette: VHS, Beta, or ¾″ U-Matic; or 16mm film
Grades: 4–9
Length: 11 min.
Buy/Rent: Videocassette: VHS or Beta: $139; ¾″ U-Matic: $199; 16mm
             film: $240; all formats rental: $30
Source: Centre Productions
             1800 30th Street, Suite 207
             Boulder, CO 80301
Date: 1985

This film was adapted from a letter written in 1905 by an Apache man taken by Pima Indians when he was a boy of five and later sold to a white man. The letter describes the life of this unusual man, who became the nation's first Native American doctor.

Lowell Thomas Remembers
Type: 8 color and black-and-white videocassettes: VHS or Beta
Grades: 10–12
Length: 142 min. each
Buy/Rent: $42.50 each or $325 for series/no rental
Source: Zenger Video
             P.O. Box 802
             Culver City, CA 90232
Date: 1986

This eight-part program presents clips from the newsreels shown at movie theaters. Narrated by Lowell Thomas, who explains the importance of the events covered and analyzes how the newsreels affected public opinion, the programs each cover approximately five years between 1919 and 1959. Major world events, events in the United States, and "feature" items (fashion, movies, etc.) are presented.

The Lure of Empire: America Debates Imperialism
Type: Color videocassette: VHS, Beta, or ¾" U-Matic; or 16mm film
             (Spanish version available)
Grades: 7–adult
Length: 27 min.
Buy/Rent: Videocassette: $300/$40; 16mm film: $445/$40
Source: Learning Corporation of America
             108 Wilmot Road
             Deerfield, IL 60015
Date: 1974

This program explores the decision to annex the Philippines. Newsreel clips are combined with reenactments to lend reality to this difficult decision.

The Masses and the Millionaires: The Homestead Strike
Type: Color videocassette: VHS, Beta, or ¾" U-Matic; or 16mm film
             (Spanish version available)
Grades: 7–adult
Length: 26 min.
Buy/Rent: Videocassette: $300/$40; 16mm film: $445/$40
Source: Learning Corporation of America
             108 Wilmot Road
             Deerfield, IL 60015
Date: 1974

This film recreates the bloody strike at the Carnegie Steel Company in 1892. The film portrays the workers' living and working conditions and their defiant stand against overwhelming odds. An Irish labor organizer and a Slavic laborer are followed through this important chapter in labor history.

Mastervision History of America Series
Type: 10 color videocassettes: VHS
Grades: 7–12
Length: 60 min. each
Buy/Rent: $64.95 each/no rental; $649.95 for series/no rental
Source: Perfection Form Company
             1000 North Second Avenue
             Logan, IA 51546
             (produced by McGraw-Hill)
Date: 1982

This comprehensive series covers U.S. history through World War II. Topics related to the later years are immigration, westward expansion, industrialization, the Great Depression, and the world wars.

Modern U.S. History: From Cold War to Hostage Crisis
Type: 3 color videocassettes: VHS, Beta, or ¾″ U-Matic
Grades: 7–12
Length: approx. 40 min. each
Buy/Rent: VHS or Beta: $179 each or $429 for series/no rental;
             ¾″ U-Matic: $199 each or $469 for series
Source: Guidance Associates
             Communications Park
             P.O. Box 3000
             Mount Kisco, NY 10549
Date: 1988

This three-part series covers turning points in our nation's history since World War II. The first program, which covers 1945–1960, focuses on the cold war, McCarthyism, the Korean War, and the U.S. response to *Sputnik*. Covering 1961–1968, the second program focuses on the Kennedy-Johnson years and the struggle for civil rights; reaction to escalating U.S. involvement in Vietnam is also examined. The final program covers 1969–1981, looking at the Nixon, Ford, and Carter years; confrontations with OPEC and Iran are discussed.

Moonwalk
Type: Color videocassette: VHS, Beta, or ¾″ U-Matic; or 16mm film
             (Spanish, Danish, and captioned versions are available)
Grades: 5–adult
Length: 95 min. (an edited 40-minute version is also available)
Buy/Rent: Videocassette: $500/$90; 16mm film: $995/$90
Source: Learning Corporation of America
             108 Wilmot Road
             Deerfield, IL 60015
Date: 1976

This film chronicles the voyage of *Apollo 11* in great detail. It would be suitable for use not only in U.S. history courses, but could also be used in an interdisciplinary science/technology/society unit presented in conjunction with science faculty.

North American Indians and Edward S. Curtis
Type: Color videocassette: VHS, Beta, or ¾″ U-Matic; or 16mm film
Grades: 7–12
Length: 29 min.
Buy/Rent: Videocassette: $315/$65; 16mm film: $525/$65
Source: BFA Educational Media
             468 Park Avenue South
             New York, NY 10016
Date: 1985

This unique film presents film footage and still photographs of Native Americans at the turn of the century taken by Edward S. Curtis. The focus of the film is traditional culture of various Indian nations.

Nothing to Fear: The Legacy of FDR

Type: Color videocassette: VHS, Beta, or ¾" U-Matic; or 16mm film
Grades: 10–adult
Length: 52 min.
Buy/Rent: VHS or Beta videocassette: $198/$75; ¾" U-Matic videocassette: $298/$75; 16mm film: $750/$75
Source: Films Incorporated
             5547 North Ravenswood Avenue
             Chicago, IL 60640
             (produced by NBC News)
Date: 1982

This film combines present-day interviews with extensive historical material to analyze Roosevelt's response to the Depression. Such radical changes in the role of the federal government as social security, unemployment compensation, and control of financial institutions are analyzed.

Of Black America Series

Type: 5 color videocassettes: VHS, Beta, or ¾" U-Matic; or 16mm films
Grades: 7–12
Length: 24–54 min. each
Buy/Rent: Videocassettes: $190–$475 each/$38–$90 each; 16mm films: $325–$850 each/$38–$90 each
Source: BFA Educational Media
             468 Park Avenue South
             New York, NY 10016
Date: 1968

This series covers a range of topics related to black history. *Black History: Lost, Stolen or Strayed* reviews black contributions to the United States. *The Black Soldier* focuses on the history of blacks in the military. *Body and Soul, Part 1* and *Body and Soul, Part 2* look at black athletes and black entertainers. *The Heritage of Slavery* includes interviews with the descendants of plantation owners and black activists of the 1960s to illustrate the long-lasting impact of slavery on attitudes.

One-Third of a Nation

Type: Color and black-and-white videocassette: VHS, with guide and script
Grades: 10–12
Length: 54 min.

Buy/Rent: $149/no rental; script: $6
Source: Zenger Video
             P.O. Box 802
             Culver City, CA 90232
             (produced by Brooklyn College, CUNY)
Date: 1984

This unusual film is a dramatization of a 1930s Federal Theater Project "living newspaper." The film focuses on how free-market capitalism affected housing in New York City from colonial days to the 1930s.

Paul Robeson: Tribute to an Artist
Type: Color videocassette: VHS or Beta; or 16mm film
Grades: 10–adult
Length: 29 min.
Buy/Rent: Videocassette: $129/$50; 16mm film: $490/$50
Source: Films Incorporated
             5547 North Ravenswood Avenue
             Chicago, IL 60640
Date: 1980

This film focuses not only on the artistry of Paul Robeson but also on his political activism and the reaction of white society to his views. Footage of Robeson throughout his career is presented.

The Plow That Broke the Plains
Type: Black-and-white videocassette: VHS
Grades: 9–12
Length: 25 min.
Buy/Rent: $65/no rental
Source: Zenger Video
             P.O. Box 802
             Culver City, CA 90232
             (produced by U.S. Resettlement Administration)
Date: 1936

This classic documentary features music, poetry, and haunting black-and-white images of the people and land of the Dust Bowl. The natural and human dimensions of the problem are presented.

Profiles in Courage
Type: 26 color videocassettes: VHS, Beta, or ¾″ U-Matic
Grades: 7–adult
Length: 50 min. each
Buy/Rent: VHS or Beta: $49.95 each, $1,250 for series/no rental; ¾″
             U-Matic: $59.95 each, $1,495 for series/no rental

Source: Zenger Video
P.O. Box 802
Culver City, CA 90232
Date: 1964

This series, inspired by John F. Kennedy's book, covers the lives of the following Americans from the period covered in this volume: Andrew Johnson, Hamilton Fish, Edmund Ross, Grover Cleveland, John Peter Altgeld, Richard T. Ely, Benjamin Barr Lindsey, John M. Slaton, Woodrow Wilson, George Norris, Mary S. McDowell, Charles Evans Hughes, Robert A. Taft, and Oscar W. Underwood.

The Quiet One
Type: Black-and-white videocassette: VHS, Beta, or ¾″ U-Matic; or 16mm film
Grades: 9–12
Length: 68 min.
Buy/Rent: Videocassette: VHS or Beta: $224/$70; ¾″ U-Matic: $399/$70; 16mm film: $600/$70
Source: Films Incorporated
5547 North Ravenswood Avenue
Chicago, IL 60640
Date: 1948

This classic documentary presents life on the streets of Harlem in the late 1940s. The film focuses on the effect of the environment on a ten-year-old boy named Donald.

Sitting Bull
Type: Color videocassette: VHS, Beta, or ¾″ U-Matic; or 16mm film (Spanish version available)
Grades: 10–adult
Length: 26 min.
Buy/Rent: Videocassette: $250/$30; 16mm film: $325/$30
Source: Learning Corporation of America
108 Wilmot Road
Deerfield, IL 60015
Date: 1977

This film provides an imaginary dialogue between the Sioux leader, Sitting Bull, and a present-day interviewer. The focus is the story of U.S.-Indian relations in the nineteenth century. Many of the eloquent leader's own words are used.

Some Call It Greed
Type: Color videocassettes: VHS, Beta, or ¾″ U-Matic; or 16mm film, with guide

Grades: 10–adult
Length: 52 min.
Buy/Rent: Videocassette: $500/$60; 16mm film: $750/$60
Source: Learning Corporation of America
             108 Wilmot Road
             Deerfield, IL 60015
Date: 1980

This film presents an economic history of the United States in the twentieth century. The work of such capitalists as J. P. Morgan, Andrew Carnegie, Henry Ford, and Ray Kroc is examined, using archival footage, historical photos, and contemporary film.

Stop Thief
Type: Color videocassette: VHS, Beta, or ¾" U-Matic; or 16mm film
Grades: 7–adult
Length: 31 min.
Buy/Rent: Videocassette: $315/$74; 16mm film: $565/$74
Source: BFA Educational Media
             468 Park Avenue South
             New York, NY 10016
Date: 1976

This film chronicles the life of Boss Tweed, covering the ways in which he manipulated the public to keep his "puppets" in control in New York. Although the presentation is both colorful and humorous, it does look at the serious effects of Tweed's corruption.

Teddy Roosevelt: The Right Man at the Right Time
Type: Color videocassette: VHS, Beta, or ¾" U-Matic; or 16mm film
             (Spanish version available)
Grades: 7–adult
Length: 28 min.
Buy/Rent: Videocassette: $300/$40; 16mm film: $445/$40
Source: Learning Corporation of America
             108 Wilmot Road
             Deerfield, IL 60015
Date: 1974

This biography traces the key events of Roosevelt's administration, highlighting the connection between Roosevelt's ebullient personality and the aggressive leadership needed to instigate social and economic reforms and force arbitration between management and labor.

Too Much, Too Little
Type: Color videocassette: VHS, Beta, or ¾" U-Matic, with teacher's
             guide

Grades: 10–college
Length: 25 min.
Buy/Rent: $105/$35
Source: Agency for Instructional Technology
             P.O. Box A
             Bloomington, IN 47402
             (produced by the Federal Reserve Bank of New York)
Date: 1985

This program traces the development of the nation's monetary system from the colonial era to the present. Highlights from the later years of U.S. history include the issue of currency backing, the Panic of 1907, and the establishment of the Federal Reserve System.

Transportation in America . . . A History
Type: Color videocassette: VHS or ¾″ U-Matic; or 16mm film
Grades: 5–9
Length: 17 min.
Buy/Rent: Videocassette: $230/$40; 16mm film: $325/$40
Source: Churchill Films
             662 North Robertson Boulevard
             Los Angeles, CA 90069
Date: 1983

This film provides a history of U.S. transportation, focusing on economic and social pressures and the changes brought about by steam and internal combustion engines. Animation enlivens the film.

The Transportation Revolution: Story of America's Growth
Type: Color videocassette: VHS, Beta, or ¾″ U-Matic; or 16mm film
             (Spanish version available)
Grades: 4–9
Length: 19 min.
Buy/Rent: Videocassette: $220/$25; 16mm film: $295/$25
Source: Learning Corporation of America
             108 Wilmot Road
             Deerfield, IL 60015
Date: 1970

This film traces important developments in the history of road, rail, and air transportation. Students will find the footage of early trains, airplanes, and cars interesting.

The Truman Years
Type: 4 black-and-white videocassettes: VHS, Beta, or ¾″ U-Matic; or
             16mm film
Grades: 7–adult

Length: 15-18 min. each
Buy/Rent: Videocassettes: $125/$25 each; 16mm films: $225/$25 each
Source: Learning Corporation of America
108 Wilmot Road
Deerfield, IL 60015
Date: 1969

These four films provide an in-depth look at the Truman administration. Topics covered include *Truman and the Atomic Bomb, Truman and the Cold War, Truman and the Korean War,* and *Truman and the Uses of Power.*

Union Maids

Type: Black-and-white videocassette: VHS or ¾″ U-Matic; or 16mm film
Grades: 10-adult
Length: 48 min.
Buy/Rent: Videocassette: $550/$70; 16mm film: $600/$70
Source: New Day Films
22 Riverview Drive
Wayne, NJ 07470
Date: 1977

Presenting an oral history of the activities of women labor unionists in the 1930s, this film covers such topics as sit-downs, scabs, unemployment, hunger marches, and red baiting. The film focuses on the activities of three women who participated in the birth of the CIO.

The United States as a World Leader

Type: Color videocassette: VHS, Beta, or ¾″ U-Matic, with activity masters and guide
Grades: 7-12
Length: 30 min.
Buy/Rent: $69/no rental
Source: Educational Activities
P.O. Box 392
Freeport, NY 11520
Date: 1986

This program looks at the position of the United States in the twentieth century, from Wilson's failure to gain support for the League of Nations, through the United States' role in World War II, to the cold war and beyond. The costs and benefits of assuming a leadership role in the world are examined.

Vietnam: A Case Study for Critical Thinking
Type: Color videocassette: VHS or Beta, with worksheets and guide
Grades: 9–12
Length: 40 min.
Buy/Rent: $104/no rental
Source: Educational Audio Visual
             Pleasantville, NY 10570
Date: 1987

Developed by "an authority on critical thinking," this program is designed to help students use their thinking skills to analyze varying viewpoints on the Vietnam War. The persuasion techniques used by historians on both sides of the issue are a particular focus of attention.

Vietnam: Lessons of a Lost War
Type: Color videocassette: VHS, Beta, or ¾″ U-Matic
Grades: 10–12
Length: 50 min.
Buy/Rent: VHS or Beta videocassette: $198/$90; ¾″ U-Matic: $298/$90
Source: Films Incorporated
             5547 North Ravenswood Avenue
             Chicago, IL 60640
             (produced by NBC News)
Date: 1985

This film aims to shed light on enduring controversies about the Vietnam War. Facts and myths about the events of the war and the decisions made are examined in light of the research of a new generation of scholars.

Vietnam: A Television History
Type: 7 color videocassettes: VHS, Beta, or ¾″ U-Matic
Grades: 10–adult
Length: 90–120 min. each
Buy/Rent: $189 for series/no rental
Source: Society for Visual Education
             1345 Diversey Parkway
             Chicago, IL 60614
Date: 1987

Thirteen hours of film relate the history of the Vietnam War, using interviews with soldiers, civilians, and policymakers as well as footage of the war itself. The program begins with the roots of the war in the 1940s, tracing its development throughout the 1950s and 1960s to its end in the 1970s. Protests at home are also covered.

Watergate
Type: Color videocassette: VHS, Beta, or ¾″ U-Matic, with guide
Grades: 7–12
Length: 40 min.
Buy/Rent: $97/no rental
Source: Associated Press
             P.O. Box 1000
             Mount Kisco, NY 10549
Date: 1986

This program focuses on Watergate as a significant turning point in history. Interviews are used to examine the event and its effects. A day-by-day analysis of the events that led to Nixon's historic resignation is presented, along with a look at the role of such individuals as Ehrlichman, Haldeman, and Dean.

Why Vietnam?
Type: 2 color videocassettes: VHS, Beta, or ¾″ U-Matic
Grades: 10–adult
Length: 40–55 min. each
Buy/Rent: $295 each or $495 for both/$75 each
Source: Churchill Films
             662 North Robertson Boulevard
             Los Angeles, CA 90069
Date: 1986

This two-part film is based on a conference held to examine the lessons that could be learned from the Vietnam War. The first film, "The Roots of U.S. Involvement and the Role of the Press," traces the history of the war and presents a debate among journalists about the influence of press coverage on the war's outcome. The second film, "The Vets, the Vietnamese, and Lessons from the War," presents veterans discussing how the war affected them, examines the effects of the war on Vietnam and the Vietnamese people, and concludes with a discussion of the lessons learned.

Will Rogers' 1920s
Type: Black-and-white videocassette: VHS, Beta, or ¾″ U-Matic; or
             16mm film
Grades: 10–adult
Length: 41 min.
Buy/Rent: Videocassette: $375/$50; 16mm film: $535/$50
Source: Churchill Films
             662 North Robertson Boulevard
             Los Angeles, CA 90069
Date: 1976

This film uses excerpts from Rogers' comments on politics and life to illustrate archival materials portraying the period from World War I to the start of the Depression. Students will enjoy Rogers' humor while gaining a deeper understanding of the era.

With All Deliberate Speed

Type: Color videocassette: VHS, Beta, or ¾″ U-Matic; or 16mm film
Grades: 7–adult
Length: 32 min.
Buy/Rent: Videocassette: $340/$81; 16mm film: $595/$81
Source: BFA Educational Media
            468 Park Avenue South
            New York, NY 10016
            (produced by CBS News)
Date: 1976

This film dramatizes the struggle of those who fought to end the doctrine of "separate but equal" before the landmark *Brown* decision in 1954. The effects of school segregation are also documented.

With Babies and Banners

Type: Color videocassette: ¾″ U-Matic; or 16mm film, with study guide
            and booklet
Grades: 9–adult
Length: 45 min.
Buy/Rent: Videocassette: $600/$75; 16mm film: $650/$75
Source: New Day Films
            22 Riverview Drive
            Wayne, NJ 07470
Date: 1977

The role of women in the General Motors sit-down strike of 1937—a key strike in the success of the CIO—is examined in this film, which presents the reunion of nine of the women who participated in the event, 40 years later. The relevance of their experiences to working women today is a special focus of the film.

Witness to History Series

Type: 4 color videocassettes: VHS, Beta, or ¾″ U-Matic
Grades: 7–12
Length: approx. 20 min. each
Buy/Rent: VHS or Beta: $39 each or $139 for series/no rental; ¾″ U-Matic:
            $59 each or $212 for series
Source: Associated Press
            P.O. Box 1000
            Mount Kisco, NY 10549
Date: 1987

Designed to give students a taste of what events in the early twentieth century were like, these programs look at *Turn of the Century America, World War I, The Depression,* and *World War II.* Newsreels and newsphotos are an integral part of the program.

A Woman's Place

Type: Black-and-white videocassette: VHS
Grades: 7–12
Length: 25 min.
Buy/Rent: $41.95/no rental
Source: Zenger Video
             P.O. Box 802
             Culver City, CA 90232
             (produced by *Time*)
Date: not available

This film focuses on women who were "first" to accomplish particular feats in government, sports, the arts, science, and other disciplines. Such women as Barbara Jordan, Elizabeth Blackwell, Frances Perkins, and Dorothea Lange are profiled.

World War II Series

Type: 5 color videocassettes: VHS, Beta, or ¾″ U-Matic; or 16mm films
Grades: 7–adult
Length: 11–16 min. each
Buy/Rent: Videocassettes: $185–$245/$75 each; 16mm films:
             $275–$350/$75 each
Source: Coronet Film and Video
             108 Wilmot Road
             Deerfield, IL 60015
Date: 1985

Featuring documentary footage, this series provides detailed coverage of the causes and events of World War II. Titles of individual programs are *A Fragile Peace (1918–1929), The Roots of Aggression (1929–1939), The Inevitable War (1939–1940), The Expanding Conflict (1940–1941),* and *A World at War (1942–1945).*

Years of Change Series

Type: 3 color videocassettes: VHS, Beta, or ¾″ U-Matic; or 16mm films
Grades: 8–12
Length: 20–22 min. each
Buy/Rent: Videocassettes: $225/$54 each; 16mm films: $385/$54 each or
             $1,021.50 for series

Source: BFA Educational Media
            468 Park Avenue South
            New York, NY 10016
Date: 1979

This three-part series looks at the United States in the turbulent year of 1968. Topics covered include race riots and war protests at home, the Vietnam War itself, and the Paris peace talks. The three programs look at *Government and Politics, People and Culture,* and *World Affairs.*

You Are There Series
Type: 15 color videocassettes: VHS, Beta, or ¾" U-Matic; or 16mm films
Grades: 5–9
Length: 22 min. each
Buy/Rent: Videocassettes: $285/$72 each; 16mm films: $480/$72 each
Source: BFA Educational Media
            468 Park Avenue South
            New York, NY 10016
            (produced by CBS)
Date: 1972

Narrated by Walter Cronkite, this series presents a series of "eyewitness enactments." Events in later U.S. history covered in the series include the trial of Susan B. Anthony, President Wilson's dilemma in the face of publication of the Zimmermann telegram, and the disappearance of Amelia Earhart.

Glossary

adobe   Clay-like material characteristic of building construction in the southwest United States.

affirmative action   Policy that sets goals for admission, hiring, or promotion of women and minorities.

allies   Countries with which a nation has mutual defense agreements; when capitalized, refers to the coalitions of nations with which the nation fought in World War I and World War II.

amend   To change or add to a legal document, a law, or a constitution.

American system of manufacturing   Refers to the method of producing manufactured goods through mass production and interchangeable parts.

anarchist   A person who does not believe in the idea of government.

annex   To attach new territory to an already existing area, usually a political entity such as a nation or a city.

appeasement   Policy of pacifying an opposing force by giving in to or satisfying it.

apportion   Literally to distribute among; usually refers to distributing taxes or representatives among election districts.

archives   Places where documents and other historical sources are deposited and preserved.

arms race   Competition between the United States and the Soviet Union to build the most numerous and most powerful nuclear weapons.

assembly line   Workers and machines that create a product by each performing a particular task and then passing the work on to the next worker and/or machine.

Axis powers   During World War II, the alliance of Italy, Germany, and Japan.

balance of power   A condition of relatively equal power (military and economic) between or among two countries or two alliances in which neither side is dominant.

balance of trade   The relationship of the amount of a country's imported goods to the amount of its exported goods. If imports are greater than exports, a negative balance occurs and vice versa.

barrio   A neighborhood of Spanish-speaking people, particularly in the cities of the Southwest.

Bill of Rights   The first ten amendments to the United States Constitution; promise of their inclusion was important to the ratification of the Constitution.

blacklist   A list of workers whom employers agree not to hire because they are union organizers or "troublemakers."

black power   Used in the 1960s to refer to the mobilization of the economic and political power of black Americans.

Blitzkrieg   In World War II, a sudden, massive offensive used by Germany against Great Britain in hopes of winning a swift victory.

bonds   Notes or promises to repay debts issued by governments.

boss   A person who controls a political organization, often at a citywide level.

boycott   An organized refusal to buy or use a product as a means of forcing some person or party to take certain action.

bracero   A Mexican worker in the 1950s and 1960s who was temporarily admitted to the United States to meet demands for labor.

cabinet   A group of advisers who often head executive departments and who counsel the president.

canal   An artificial body of water usually designed to link other (natural) bodies of water for improved transportation.

capital   Wealth used to produce more wealth; e.g., capital goods usually refers to machinery.

carpetbaggers   Northerners who went into the South during Reconstruction; so-called because of the valises made of carpet in which they carried their belongings.

cartel   A group of individuals, corporations, or nations that join together to gain a monopoly of a particular resource or product.

cash crops   Crops raised to give growers money with which they can buy other goods they themselves cannot produce. In U.S. history, cotton and tobacco are the best-known examples, but other crops have also generated surpluses that produced cash.

caucus   Meeting of party members (or like-minded persons) to plan political strategy.

cede   The act of giving another party (usually country) some portion of one's territory.

census   An official enumeration of a population.

charter   An official document given by a government that grants special rights or privileges to a person or company.

checks and balances   System of government in which the various branches are given some power to check or oversee the workings of the other branches.

Chicano   A U.S. citizen of Mexican descent.

civil disobedience   Act of breaking the law to protest a government policy or action.

civil rights   Rights due all U.S. citizens by virtue of their citizenship.

civil war   War between two factions within one country.

cold war   Political and economic conflict between the United States and the Soviet Union after World War II.

collective bargaining   Process by which workers are represented by a union in negotiations with management.

collective biography   Refers to extracting the common elements from the biographies of persons of the same period in order to make generalizations about the group.

colony   A land area settled by emigrants from a country who continue their allegiance to their home country; a territory that is ruled by another country.

Communist   Person who opposes private ownership of the means of producing and distributing goods.

compromise   Reaching a general agreement among all sides in a dispute or controversy, usually by each side giving up something it wants.

consensus school of U.S. historians   Refers to many of those historians who wrote in the period after World War II; they tended to emphasize continuity and agreement on basic "American values" in U.S. history.

constitution   A plan of government; the fundamental and supreme law of a country.

containment   Post–World War II policy of keeping Soviet influence from expanding to new areas of the world.

craft union   Labor organization in which all members practice the same skill or craft.

Creole   A person of European descent (usually refers to French or Spanish) born in the West Indies or Spanish America; sometimes refers to settlers on the Gulf coast.

customs duties   Taxes levied on imported goods.

de facto   Means "in fact" or "in actuality"; compare to the term *de jure,* which means "as a matter of law."

deficit spending   A government practice of spending more than is generated through taxes.

democracy   A form of government in which power is vested in the people (the electorate) and is usually exercised by them through a system of representation based on free elections.

demography   The study of population, including, among many other things, birth and death rates, sickness, age, distribution.

depression   A long, usually severe, decline in economic activity.

détente   Lessening of tensions between the United States and Soviet Union in the 1970s.

discrimination   The act of prejudging people based on such arbitrary characteristics as race, religion, or ethnic group.

disenfranchise   Take away the right to vote.

dollar diplomacy   Early twentieth-century policy of encouraging financial investment in other nations as a means of increasing U.S. influence/power in those nations.

domino theory   Notion that if one nation became Communistic, its neighbors would quickly follow; used to justify U.S. involvement in Southeast Asia.

due process   Fair judicial procedures in civil and criminal cases.

Dust Bowl   Area of the Great Plains where weather conditions and farming practices combined to create conditions in which topsoil blew away in huge dust storms in the 1920s and 1930s.

economic history   A specialized subfield that deals with economic activity, growth, and technological change over time.

elastic clause   The portion of the Constitution that says Congress can make all laws "necessary and proper" to put its stated powers into effect.

embargo   A law or government order that prohibits trade with another nation.

excise tax   A tax on goods, usually paid by the manufacturer but passed on to the consumer.

fascism   Belief in rule by a dictator, with great restrictions on individual liberties and intense nationalism and militarism.

federal system of government   A system of government in which some powers are given to a central government, some to local governments, and others shared between the two.

feminism   Belief in equal rights and opportunities for women.

franchise   Usually refers to the right to vote in elections.

free enterprise   An economic system in which there is little if any public regulation or control of business practices.

frontier   The sparsely settled area on the edge of more densely settled regions; defined by the Census Bureau as an area that contains two or fewer persons per square mile.

General Assembly   Body of United Nations in which all member-nations are represented.

general strike   Work stoppage by all unions in a particular area.

ghetto   Section of a city in which a particular ethnic or racial group is concentrated, for political or economic reasons.

gold standard   System in which the value of a nation's money is based on the value of gold.

graduated personal income tax   Tax levied on individual earnings, in which the percentage of income paid as tax rises with income.

grandfather clause   Portion of a law used to keep blacks from voting in the South after Reconstruction; required that in order for a man to vote, his father or grandfather had to have been eligible to vote in 1867.

grange   Farm organization founded in 1867; it served both social and political purposes and actively sought railroad regulation.

Great Depression   Severe worldwide economic depression of the 1930s.

gross national product   GNP is a measure of the total value of goods and services produced by a nation's economy in a given year.

Harlem Renaissance   In the 1920s, a flowering of literary and artistic works by blacks living in Harlem, a section of New York City with a large black population.

hippies   In the 1960s and early 1970s, people who rejected conventional behavior and standards.

historiography   Usually refers to the history of historical writing; philosophy of history is a synonym.

House of Representatives   The lower house of the federal legislature established by the Constitution.

illegal aliens   People who enter the United States illegally (i.e., without the proper papers); also called "undocumented workers."

immigrant   A person who enters one country from another, usually with the intention of staying.

impeachment   A formal charge of wrongdoing brought against a high government official.

imperialism   Policy of expanding the role of a nation to other areas, usually for economic or military reasons.

industrial revolution   The change in the United States in the nineteenth century from home and artisan production to machine-based factory production of goods.

industrial union   Labor organization whose members, while practicing various skills or jobs, work in the same industry, such as steel manufacturing.

inflation   Rapidly increasing prices.

initiative   Procedure by which citizens can propose legislation by gathering signatures on a petition.

injunction   Court order to do or to stop doing something; often used against workers in nineteenth-century labor disputes.

intellectual history   A subfield of history devoted to the study of ideas and the people who produce those ideas.

interchangeable parts   The process by which parts of a certain product are manufactured to the exact same size, shape, and weight; each part so produced may be substituted for any other.

internment   Confinement to a restricted area; often refers to forced relocation of Japanese-Americans from the west coast to the interior during World War II.

isolationism   Belief, popular in the 1920s and 1930s, that the United States should stay out of international affairs.

Jim Crow laws   Segregation laws passed in the South in the 1880s.

jingoism   Excessive national pride; often associated with the period around the Spanish-American War.

judicial review   The right of the courts to review laws and test their legality under the Constitution.

Ku Klux Klan   Group of white supremacists formed after the Civil War and active in various periods since then.

laissez-faire   The doctrine that government should not meddle in the affairs of business; "that government is best which governs least."

League of Nations   In the 1920s, an international organization devoted to protecting the political independence of nations; the United States failed to join the League because of isolationist feelings.

loose constructionist   Person who believes that the powers of the federal government may be expanded beyond the powers explicitly stated in the Constitution.

lynch   Put to death by hanging without a legal trial; many black Americans were lynched by whites in the first half of the twentieth century.

machine   A political group that controls a political party or even a city government.

manifest destiny   The idea, prevalent in the 1840s and 1850s, that it was the destiny of the United States to occupy the entire North American continent, without regard for the rights of other inhabitants of the area.

Marshall Plan   Program to help Europe rebuild after World War II.

Mason-Dixon line   The boundary between Pennsylvania and Maryland, also the traditional dividing line between the North and the South.

McCarthyism   Use of unsubstantiated charges of communism to discredit individuals; named for U.S. Senator Joseph McCarthy, who practiced such tactics in the 1950s.

monograph   A term used for historical writing, especially as it relates to books and articles about richly researched but somewhat limited questions.

monopoly   Control of a product or service by one organization or a coalition of several organizations.

muckrakers   Journalists of the early twentieth century whose writings exposed social problems and political corruption.

nationalism   Patriotic feelings for one's own country.

nativists   People who feel so fervently for their own country that they believe that everyone else is unworthy of being a part of it.

NATO   North Atlantic Treaty Organization; formed in 1949, NATO is a military alliance among ten western European nations, Canada, and the United States.

naturalization   Granting full U.S. citizenship to a person born in a foreign country.

nazism   Philosophy of militarism, racism, anti-Semitism, and world conquest perpetrated by Adolf Hitler.

neutrality   A policy of not taking sides in a dispute between two other nations.

New Deal   Franklin Roosevelt's programs to provide relief from the Great Depression.

new immigrants   Immigrants who came to the United States in the late 1800s and early 1900s from central and eastern Europe; called "new" because they were different from the previous dominant groups of immigrants, who were from northern and western Europe.

Oval Office   The president's White House office; often used to refer to the presidency itself.

patronage   The distribution of government jobs to political supporters; also known as the "spoils system."

poll tax   Fee charged to vote; used to prevent black Southerners from voting after Reconstruction.

pooling   In the 1870s and 1880s, practice of railroad companies that involved dividing the total volume of freight among their companies.

Populist party   A new political party established in 1892; represented farmers and other groups seeking reform.

primary election   An election to choose the candidates for an office; this system was considered more democratic than selection of candidates by party bosses.

primary source   Document written or otherwise created by someone who was directly involved in or directly observed an event.

progressive historians   People who saw the past as the conflict between the good guys and the bad guys; writing during a period of reform, they were optimistic that the good guys would win in the end.

progressivism   Reform movement in the early twentieth century; sought to address social, political, and environmental problems.

protective tariffs   High taxes (or customs duties) on imported goods levied with the express intent to protect some product from foreign competition.

recall election   Special election initiated by voters through petition and allowing voters to remove an officeholder before his/her term expires.

recession   A mild and temporary economic decline; less serious than a depression.

Reconstruction   Period after the Civil War (1865–1877) during which the U.S. government sought to secure rights for former slaves and readmit Confederate states to the Union.

referendum   Special election in which citizens vote directly on a proposed law.

reparations   Payments made by defeated nations for damage caused during a war.

representative government   A form of government in which the people are represented by persons elected in free elections.

republic   A form of government in which power is exercised by representatives elected by the people.

reservations   Geographical areas set aside by the U.S. government for Native American tribes.

revolution   Although the term has changed significantly over time, the word now usually refers to the sudden, often violent, overthrow of an existing government.

scalawags   White Southerners who cooperated with the U.S. government's efforts during Reconstruction.

secondary source   In contrast to a primary source, a secondary source is one written by a historian who usually used primary sources—those contemporary to the events described.

sectionalism   Loyalty (similar to patriotism) to a region of the country such as the South, the North, or the West.

Security Council   Part of the United Nations consisting of 15 member-nations who resolve disputes brought before it; each member has a veto.

segregation   The separation of people according to some arbitrary criterion—usually race—in housing, schools, and public accommodations.

self-determination   A nation's right to decide how to govern itself.

Senate   The upper body of the U.S. Congress, to which each state elects two members for terms of six years each.

separation of powers   The constitutional principle that gives the powers of making (legislative), enforcing (executive), and interpreting (judicial) the laws to different branches of government.

sharecropper   Farm worker who, in exchange for land and supplies, returns part of the crop to the landowner.

sit-down strike   Job action in which workers refuse to leave the workplace, sitting down on the job to prevent management from bringing in nonunion workers.

sit-ins   Demonstrations in which protesters sit at segregated facilities (such as lunch counters) until blacks are served; popular form of protest in the civil rights movement of the 1950s and 1960s.

social history   A subfield of history concerned with the history of the family, of women and children, of racial and ethnic groups, among other topics.

Social Security   Government program introduced under Franklin Roosevelt to provide pensions for the elderly and disabled.

sovereignty   Refers to the locus of ultimate authority in a governmental system; the U.S. Constitution located that authority with "the people," rather than with the states.

staple crop   The primary agricultural crop grown in a specific region.

status quo   The way things are at any particular time.

stock   Shares of ownership in a joint-stock company or other corporation.

strict constructionist   Person who believes that only those powers explicitly given the government by the Constitution are legitimate powers.

strike   Work stoppage by employees to force management to negotiate better pay or working conditions.

subsidies   Government payments to underwrite various kinds of businesses seen as keys to the economy but not succeeding on their own.

subsistence farmers   Farmers who produce almost entirely for their own consumption.

suburbs   Towns around a larger core city; once almost exclusively residential, suburbs now are home to many businesses and industries as well.

suffrage   The right to vote.

tariff   A duty or tax placed on imported goods, the intent of which is either to produce revenue or to protect domestic businesses.

Temperance movement   The movement to prohibit the consumption of alcoholic beverages.

trust   Business organization, common in the 1880s and 1890s, in which rival companies operated as one large firm to control the market.

union   Labor organization devoted to improving working conditions and pay of working people.

United Nations   International organization formed in 1945 to promote world peace and economic and social well-being of the world's peoples.

urbanization   Trend toward increasing the percentage of people living in metropolitan areas rather than rural areas.

vaqueros   Spanish cattle herders who invented virtually all the tools of the cowhand's trade.

veto   The power given the president to reject bills enacted by Congress.

women's liberation   Name given to movement to achieve freedom of choice in such areas as family and the workplace and full economic and political participation for women.

Index